A VENETIAN AFFAIR

Come ho io vivuto jeri dopo pranzo? Dove ero io a due ore
di notte, cosa facevo alle tre? Cosa sarà di noi oggi dopo pranzo,
questa sera? Questa mattina io vado a buon conto dalla
Contessa Sanbonini; poi dal Smith. Oggi facilmente non
passerò per casa tua per poter essere a tempo di trovar-
mi t·pk·pn:: a t:a:+·v:q:t: e::·uvv: o z·pp: o p:·o t·t·tem:u
s::pp: a °z: ob·nn:t·+ u :: a s::nq: a :·:p:t:l:q: u s:q°b: u::·a
°q::: a °z:·t·:·::·q·:q:·:q·:: e:·o o p::w:th::· Mi dispiace
solamente che in jeri non ho potuto vedere Harietine
che l'avrei avvisate perché oggi si trovasse da Sauitino.
Questo sarà per un altra volta: non vorrei che sospet-
tassi anche questo mio desiderio per uno dei miei soliti
progetti dei quali tu sempre m'incolpi.

Cosa vuoi che ti dica adesso? Avrei assai cose, ma voglio
salvarle per altro tempo. Io son molto contento di te, e
per dir il vero anche di me medesimo che sans aucune
sorte de gêne je peux te sacrifier tous les momens de ma
vie .... Que dis-je sacrifier! oh que ce mot est detestable
a ce propos bien que en bonne langue Françoise, il ne signifie
que simplement dedier.... Io t'amo assai. Ciò che vedrai
adesso non n'è che l'ultimo contrassegno. Mon esprit est toujour
hors de soi même, il est chatouillé de cette aimable coquine ......

A Venetian Affair

A True Story of Impossible Love
in the Eighteenth Century

ANDREA DI ROBILANT

FOURTH ESTATE • *London* and *New York*

First published in Great Britain in 2004 by
Fourth Estate
A Division of HarperCollins*Publishers*
77–85 Fulham Palace Road
London W6 8JB
www.4thestate.com

A catalogue record for this book is available
from the British Library

ISBN 1-84115-541-1

Printed in Great Britain by
Clays Ltd, St Ives plc

In memory of my father,
Alvise di Robilant

A VENETIAN AFFAIR

Prologue

Some years ago, my father came home with a carton of old letters that time and humidity had compacted into wads of barely legible paper. He announced that he had found them in the attic of the old family *palazzo* on the Grand Canal, where he had lived as a boy in the twenties. Many times, my father had enthralled my brothers and me with stories from his enchanted childhood—there had been gondola rides and children's tea parties and picnics at the Lido, and in the background the grown-ups always seemed to be drinking champagne and giving fancy-dress balls. Equally romantic to us, though much more melancholy, was his account of how my grandparents' lavish and extravagant lifestyle had begun fraying at the edges. By the early thirties, art dealers were dropping by more and more frequently. Large empty patches appeared on the walls. Pieces of antique furniture were carried out of the house. Even the worn banners and rusty swords our fierce ancestors had wrested from the hated Turks were sold at auction. Eventually, my spendthrift grandfather sold off the palace floor by floor, severing the family ties to Venice and leaving my father so bereft that he yearned for his Venetian heritage for the rest of his life. He never lived in Venice again, but even as an older man he continued to make nostalgic pilgrimages to the places of his childhood and especially to that grand old house, which had long ceased to belong to us, but where the family still kept a few old boxes and crates.

The di Robilant family is actually of Piedmontese origin. The Venetian connection was established at the end of the nineteenth century when Edmondo di Robilant, my very tall and rather austere great-grandfather from Turin, married my great-grandmother Valentina Mocenigo, a formidable Venetian *grande dame* with beautiful black eyes and a very sharp tongue. The Mocenigos were one of the old ruling families of Venice—"they gave seven doges to the Republic" my father never tired of repeating to us children. Of course, the glorious days of the Venetian Republic were long gone when my great-grandparents married, but the last Mocenigos still had palaces and money and beautiful paintings. So the impecunious di Robilants moved to Venice after World War I and fairly quickly ran through what remained of the Mocenigo fortune.

My father, having grown up in the fading grandeur of Palazzo Mocenigo, came to revere his Venetian ancestry more than the Piedmontese. To him the box of letters was a small treasure he had miraculously retrieved from his Venetian past. And I remember well the look of cheerful anticipation he had on his face when he arrived at our house in Tuscany and placed it on the dining room table for all the family to see.

The letters were badly frayed and had wax marks and purplish traces of wine on them. They looked intriguing. They were not the usual household inventories that occasionally surfaced, like timeworn family flotsam, in some forgotten recess of the *palazzo* in Venice. We pried them open one by one and soon realized they were intimate love letters that dated back to the 1750s. Some pages were covered with mysterious hieroglyphs that added mystery to my father's discovery. We spent a rainy weekend cracking the strange cipher and trying to make some sense of the first fragments we were able to read. I remember we were wary of delving into secrets buried so long ago. Yet we labored on because the spell was irresistible.

At the end of that long weekend I went back to Rome, where I was then working as a journalist, while my father took on the task of deciphering and transcribing the cache of one hundred or so letters in his possession. What eventually emerged from his painstaking labor was the remarkable love story between our ancestor Andrea Memmo, scion of one of the oldest Venetian families, and Giustiniana Wynne, a bright and beautiful Anglo-Venetian of illegitimate birth. The letters revealed a deep romantic passion that was at odds with the gallant, lighthearted lovemaking one often thinks of as typical of the eighteenth century. It was also, very clearly, a clandestine relationship: the curious-looking dots and circles and tiny geometric figures scribbled across the pages were a graphic testimony to the fear the two lovers must have felt lest their letters fall into the wrong hands.

When my father began to dig around Andrea and Giustiniana's story, he soon found traces of their romance in the public archives in Venice, Padua, and even Paris and London. It turned out that students of eighteenth-century Venice had first become acquainted with the relationship through the writings of Giacomo Casanova, who had been a close friend of both Andrea and Giustiniana. In the first years of the last century Gustav Gugitz, the great Casanova scholar, identified the Mademoiselle XCV who figures prominently in Casanova's memoirs as Giustiniana.[1] Then, in the twenties, Bruno Brunelli, a Venetian historian, found two small volumes of handwritten copies of letters from Giustiniana to Andrea in the archives in Padua. He wrote a book based on those letters and lamented the fact that he had not found Andrea's letters as well. He consoled himself with the notion that they could not possibly have been "as absorbing as Giustiniana's." Judging from her correspondence, he said, it did not appear that Andrea "had the temperament of a great lover."[2]

Other Casanova specialists were drawn to Andrea and Giustiniana. Many combed old bookshops and antique stores hoping to find Andrea's letters, but in vain. The stash my father had stumbled upon as he rummaged in the attic of Palazzo Mocenigo proved to be the missing part of the story—the other voice. Clearly these letters had at some point been returned to Andrea by Giustiniana and preserved by the family; but they were by no means all of Andrea's letters. Many had been burnt, and many more had probably been left to rot and then thrown away. But those we had were rich enough to provide a far more complete picture of the love story—and to disprove Brunelli's contention about Andrea's temperament as a lover.

Once my father finished transcribing the letters, he tried to publish them. Time went by, and I wondered whether he would ever complete his project. My father did not have the natural inclination to put together a book: his real talent was in *telling* a good story. Over the years I heard him talk about Andrea and Giustiniana again and again as he polished their romance into a perfect conversation piece. How vividly he comes back to me now, glass of red wine in hand, charming dinner guests with yet another elegant account of *his* Venetian love story. He revered Andrea, who went on to become one of the last in a long line of Venetian statesmen. And, lady's man that he was, he adored Giustiniana—for her looks, her spirit, and her lively intelligence. My father rooted for them with genuine affection even as he explained to his listeners, who were perhaps not sufficiently well versed in Venetian laws and customs, that it had been *"un amore impossibile"*—an impossible love. It was unthinkable in those days for a prominent member of the ruling elite such as Andrea to marry a girl with Giustiniana's murky lineage. She had been born out of wedlock, her mother's background was checkered at best, and her father was an obscure English baronet and a Protestant to boot. For this reason, my father would explain, they saw each other in secret and often wrote to each other using their strange alphabet. Whereupon he would bring his audience to a peak of excitement by scribbling a few words in the private code of Andrea and Giustiniana.

In the end the treasured letters became, above all else, an excuse for my father to ramble on about his heroes and the city he loved so much. And they probably would have remained just that if events had not taken a sad and completely unexpected turn. In January 1997 an intruder entered my father's apartment in Florence and bludgeoned him to death. It was a senseless, incomprehensible act—a violent end for a gentle, life-loving man. After the funeral my brothers and I stayed in Florence for a week in the hope of being of some assistance to the investigation. During those difficult days the story of Andrea and Giustiniana could not have been further from my mind—until it suddenly appeared in the local newspapers. The carabinieri had found my father's laptop computer open on his worktable, so they had seized it as evidence, together with the floppy disks on which he had transcribed the letters. They went on to leak information about Andrea and Giustiniana to the press.[3] In an even more bizarre twist, the carabinieri sent a few agents up to Venice to check into possible leads.

The murder investigation led nowhere, and two years later it was abandoned. My father's belongings, including Andrea's original letters, the discs with the transcriptions, and the notes on the cipher, were returned to us. By that time I had moved to Washington as the new correspondent for the Italian daily *La Stampa*. But I made a promise to myself that I would do my best to carry out my father's original plan to publish the letters in one form or another once my assignment in the United States was over. My resolve was further strengthened when I found another trove of letters in a library just a short distance away from my new posting as foreign correspondent.

James Rives Childs was an American diplomat and scholar who developed a minor passion for Giustiniana as a result of his studies on Casanova. In the early fifties he was in Venice looking for the unexpected nugget that might enrich his collection of Casanoviana. He came upon a small volume of letters from Giustiniana to Andrea, which added another fascinating chapter to their love story. He never got around to publishing them, although a few excerpts appeared in his newsletter, *Casanova Gleanings*. Ambassador Childs died in 1988, having bequeathed his collection—including Giustiniana's letters—to his alma mater, Randolph Macon College, in Ashland, Virginia, a mere two hours away from Washington, D.C. That part of Virginia was already very familiar to me. Childs—the coincidence would have delighted my father—came from Lynchburg, where my mother had grown up (she attended Randolph Macon Women's College). So for me the quest that had begun several years earlier with the letters my father had found in the attic of his childhood home in Venice ended, rather eerily, a few miles up the road from my mother's birthplace in America.

The early 1750s—the period when Andrea and Giustiniana first met—was a particularly poignant moment in Venice's long twilight. The thousand-year-old Republic was less than five decades away from its swift collapse before Napoleon Bonaparte's invading army. Signs of decline had been evident for a long time, and no reasonable Venetian believed the Serenissima, as the Republic had been known for centuries, could reclaim the place it had once occupied among the powerful nations of the world. Yet Venice did not seem like a civilization that was drawing its last breath. On the contrary, it was living a vibrant, even self-confident old age. The economy was growing. The streets were busy, and the stores were filled with spices, jewelry, luxurious fabrics, and household goods. On the mainland, agriculture and stock farming underwent revolutionary changes, and wealthy Venetians built grand villas on their country estates. The population was rising, and Venice, with its 140,000 inhabitants, was still one of the most populous cities in Europe. An experienced and generally conservative government composed of a maze of interlocking councils and commissions (whose members derived from the most powerful families) ran the city in a manner that had altered little for centuries. Venice's ruling class remained an exclusive caste, whose symbol was the Golden Book—the official record of the Venetian patriciate. Its obstinate refusal to let new blood into its ranks, coupled with a deep-seated resistance to change after such a long and glorious history, was weakening its hand. But, as one historian has observed, "the future of this state founded on an intelligent form of paternalism still seemed assured."[4]

The middle years of the eighteenth century also saw an extraordinary flowering of the arts that hardly fits the image of a dying civilization. In fact, it turned out to be the last, glorious burst of Venice's creative genius, and what a feast it was—Tiepolo at work on his celestial frescoes at Ca' Rezzonico, Goldoni writing his greatest comedies, Galuppi filling the air with his joyful music. There had never been more amusements and distractions in Venice. One pictures the endless Carnival, the extravagant balls, and the theaters fairly bursting with boisterous spectators. The stage was flourishing: there were seven major theaters operating in the 1750s and they were filled with rowdy crowds every night. The most popular meeting place of all, however, was the Ridotto, the public gambling house that was famous across Europe. Venetians were in the grip of a massive gambling addiction, and they were especially hooked on faro, a card game similar to baccarat ("faro" stood for "pharaoh," and was the king card). There were several gambling rooms at the Ridotto, with as many as eighty playing tables in all. They opened up on a long, candlelit hall—the *sala lunga*—where an eclectic crowd of masked men and women mingled and gossiped about who was piling up sequins that night and who was piling up debt.

The mask, perhaps more than anything else, was the symbol of those carefree days. It had become, by then, an integral part of the Venetian attire, like wigs and fans and beauty spots. Masks came in two kinds: the more casual black or white *moreta*, that covered only the eyes, and the "cloaked" mask, or *bautta*, which hid the entire head down to the shoulders. Venetians were allowed to wear masks in public from October until Lent, with the exception of the novena—the nine-day period before Christmas—and everyone wore one, from the doge down to the women selling vegetables at the market. The custom added a little mystery and intrigue to everyday life.

The Seven Years' War (1756–1763) between the major European powers would soon come to darken spirits and change the atmosphere in the city. The Venetian Republic, neutral throughout this long conflict, which put an end to French expansionism and marked the rise of Great Britain as the dominant power, was going to feel adrift and ultimately lost after the war. But until then there prevailed a sense that things would go on unchanged as they had for centuries and that life should therefore be enjoyed to the fullest.

In those happier years the house of Consul Joseph Smith, a rich English merchant turned art collector, was one of the busiest and most interesting places on the Venetian scene—a meeting point of fashionable artists, intellectuals, and foreign travelers. It was in Smith's art-filled drawing room at Palazzo Balbi, on the Grand Canal, that Andrea met Giustiniana sometime in late 1753. He was twenty-four; she was not yet seventeen. Andrea was tall and vigorous—handsome in a Venetian sort of way, with the long, aquiline nose that was typical of many patrician profiles. His sharp mind was tuned to the new ideas of the Enlightenment, and he was possessed of the natural self-confidence that came with his class—assured as he was of his place in the Venetian oligarchy. His elders already looked upon him as one of the brightest prospects of his generation. And indeed he must have seemed quite the dashing young man to a girl eight years his junior—wise beyond his age and so much at ease in Consul Smith's rather intimidating *salon*. But Giustiniana too stood out in those assemblies. Behind that innocent, awestruck gaze was a lovely girl brimming with life. She was bright, alert, and possessed of a quick sense of humor. Andrea was instantly taken with her. She was so different from the other young women of his set—familiar, in a way, for after all she was a Venetian born and raised, yet at the same time very distinctive, even a little exotic, not only on account of her English blood but also because of her unique character.

Andrea and Giustiniana met again and again at Consul Smith's. The physical attraction between them was plain to see: soon they could not bear to be apart. But something deeper was going on, too, more magical and mysterious: it was the blending of two souls that were very different and nevertheless yearned for each other. "My passion for him swallowed everything else in my life,"[5] Giustiniana recalled many years later. Andrea too was overwhelmed by his feelings in a way he had never been before.

Alas, the earliest part of their love story has remained blurred. If they wrote letters to each other during that time—as is probable—those letters have never surfaced. But in the later correspondence there are echoes of their first enchanted days together, as they chased each other in the rooms of Palazzo Balbi searching for a darkened corner where they could hold each other and kiss in the full rapture of new love.

From the very beginning the love story of Andrea and Giustiniana bore a note of defiance toward the outside world. Carried along by the sheer power of their feelings, they pursued a relationship in the face of social conventions that were clearly stacked against them. It is true that by the mid–eighteenth century, as pre-Romantic stirrings spread through Venetian society, young men and women who loved each other were beginning to challenge the rigid customs of the aging Republic. The number of clandestine marriages, secretly sanctioned by the Church, saw a considerable increase in those years. But the costs of breaking the rules were still very high. As one historian has put it, "Any patrician who attempted a secret marriage put himself quite inevitably in direct conflict with his family and institutions. By bringing dishonor on himself he renounced any political career and lost the privilege of seeing his own children recognized as members of the patriciate. He might lose all economic assistance from the family and be disinherited."[6]

The clandestine marriages that did take place mostly involved impoverished patricians or members of the lesser nobility, who did not have much to lose by defying their elders. To Andrea, with his family history, his education, his strong sense of duty toward the Republic, the idea of secretly marrying Giustiniana seemed completely irrational. Apart from the shame it would have brought on his family, it was hard to see how the marriage would have survived from a practical point of view. Where would they have lived? What would they have lived on? Despite her youth and her intense emotions, even Giustiniana was realistic enough to see that if they fought the time-honored customs of the Republic they would be crushed.

A few months into their affair, Giustiniana's mother stepped in. Mrs. Anna had one pressing task, which was to find a suitable husband for her eldest daughter. This meant she had to keep Giustiniana at a safe distance from hot-blooded young Venetian patricians—who might try to seduce her for the sake of intrigue and entertainment but would never marry her—while she looked out for a sensible if less glamorous match. She could not allow Giustiniana to wreck her plans with a relationship that in her eyes had no future and would only bring dishonor upon the family. So in the winter of 1754 she told Andrea never to call on Giustiniana at their house again and forbade the two lovers from seeing each other.

Mrs. Anna's ban seemed to spell the end of their forbidden love. But their timeworn letters have continued to surface over the years—in the archives in Padua, in the attic at Palazzo Mocenigo, at Randolph Macon College—to reveal that in fact this was only the beginning of a remarkable love story.

CHAPTER *One*

E arly in the evening Andrea caught up with Giustiniana at the theater. She was radiant in her brocaded evening cape, and the anxious way she was looking around for him made her seem lovelier than ever. She smiled as she saw him, and they exchanged a few signals from a safe distance, apparently without raising Mrs. Anna's suspicions. After the play, Andrea followed mother and daughter to the Ridotto, keeping close to the walls of the narrow streets and casting nervous glances ahead. In the gambling halls, among the late-night crowd of masked men and women hovering around the faro tables, he had a much harder time avoiding Mrs. Anna as she flitted in and out of the shadows in the candlelit rooms. He was terrified she might suddenly come upon him and make a horrible scene. Unnerved by all the difficulties, he finally gave up and went home without having had his cherished moment alone with Giustiniana.

That night he hardly slept, shifting restlessly in his bed, wondering if he had abandoned the Ridotto too abruptly and not made it sufficiently clear to Giustiniana why he was leaving the scene. The next morning he rose early and wrote to her at once:

My beloved,
I am very anxious to know whether your mother noticed any-
thing last night—any act of imprudence on my part—and if you
yourself were satisfied or had reason to be cross. Everything is so
uncertain. At the theater things didn't go badly, but at the
Ridotto—I don't know how it all ended at the Ridotto. As long as
I was in your mother's range I tried to conceal myself—as you
probably saw. And rest assured that when I did not show myself to
you it was because Mrs. Anna was looking in my direction. Once

*you left the rooms I no longer saw our tyrant and imagined we
had lost her for good—your own gestures seemed to suggest as
much. . . . But I asked around and was told she was still there. . . .
I waited a while to see for myself, and sure enough there she was
again. So I resolved to put myself out of her sight.**

Mrs. Anna clearly hoped that, thanks to her intervention, the
passion so perilously ignited in the house of Consul Smith would
subside before any irreparable damage was done to her daughter.
But she had wrenched them apart just as they were falling deeply
in love. Their need to be together was stronger than any obstacle
she could put in their way; the thrill of their forbidden relationship
only drew them closer. As Andrea pointed out to Giustiniana, her
mother's relentless watch and the atmosphere of general disapproval she helped to foster around them made their desire to be
together "even more obstinate." In fact, there had been no separation to speak of in the wake of Mrs. Anna's pronouncement. The
two lovers continued to look for each other ever more frantically,
playing a highly charged game of hide-and-seek in the streets of
Venice, at the theater, among the crowd at the Ridotto.

It is easy to see Mrs. Anna in the role of the insensitive and
overly censorious mother—a tyrant, as the two lovers called her.
But she had good reason to be firm. She was a woman of experience
who had worked hard to gain respectability, and she well understood the intricate workings of Venetian society, in which the interests of the ruling families were supreme. She was also very much
aware of Andrea's special place in that society—and what a formidable opponent he was in her struggle to protect her daughter.

. . .

*In order to avoid burdening the general reader with repetitive notes I have not
sourced each quotation drawn from the correspondence between Andrea and Giustiniana (unless otherwise specified), hoping that a short note on the various sets of
letters, to be found after the text on page 293, will make it easy enough for readers
with a bibliographical interest to know where the quotation comes from. The reader
may also wish to know that in translating the letters from Italian into English I did
my best to preserve their original eighteenth-century flavor, though I eliminated
excessive capitalization and made changes in the punctuation in order to facilitate
the reader's ease and comprehension.

The Memmos were among the founding fathers of Venice in the eighth century—historians have even traced the lineage of Andrea's family as far back as the *gens Memmia* of Roman times. There was a Memmo doge as early as the year 979, and over the next eight centuries the family contributed a steady flow of statesmen and high-ranking public servants to the Republic. By Andrea's day they were still very influential in Venetian politics—an elite within the elite, at a time when many other patrician families living in the city had become politically irrelevant.* But they were not among the richest families; by the 1750s, their income had dwindled to about 6,000 ducats a year, and they would have needed at least double that amount to face comfortably the expenditures required of a family of such elevated rank (the wealthiest families had incomes ten times as large). They earned barely enough from their estates on the mainland to live with the necessary decorum at Ca' Memmo, the large family *palazzo* at the western end of the Grand Canal.[1]

Andrea's father, Pietro Memmo, was a gentle, virtuous man long weakened by ill health. His mother, Lucia Pisani, came from a wealthy family that had given the Republic its greatest and most popular admiral—the fierce Vettor Pisani, who had saved Venice from the Genoese in the fourteenth century. Pietro was always a rather remote figure—he and Andrea could find little to say to each other—and Lucia was not especially warm with her children either; her stiff manner was fairly common among the more old-fashioned patrician ladies of that time. Nevertheless, she was by far the more forceful of the two parents, and Andrea felt closer to her than he did to his father. The one person in the family he truly adored was Marina, his older sister by six years: a sensitive, kind-hearted young woman whom he could always confide in. Andrea had two brothers: Bernardo, who was one year younger than him, and Lorenzo, who was four years younger. The three boys, being fairly close in age, spent much of their time together when they were growing up. There was also a younger sister, Contarina.

The family patriarch was Andrea Memmo, Andrea's venerable uncle, known for his courage and strength of character; he had

*Regardless of political influence, twenty-four families were considered founding families of Venice, and of these, twelve traced their roots to early Christianity and called themselves "apostolic." The Memmos were among these twelve.

been imprisoned and tortured by the Turks while he was ambassador to Constantinople in 1713. The senior Andrea served the Republic with great distinction and ended his political career as procuratore di San Marco, the second most prestigious position in government after the supreme office of doge. He went on to become a respected elder statesman whom his peers considered "possibly the greatest expert in Venetian matters."[2] He died at the age of eighty-six in 1754—the same year Andrea and Giustiniana's secret love affair began.

Andrea's uncle ruled over the family with a steady hand for decades, overseeing everything from political alliances to business decisions, from household expenses to the education of the younger Memmos. During his long stewardship, Ca' Memmo was known for its strong attachment to tradition. But it was also considered a progressive house where writers, artists, and composers were always welcome. The new ideas from Paris, especially the political writings of Montesquieu (Venetians had a predilection for anything involved with the machinery of government), were discussed spiritedly at the dinner table.* Their friend Goldoni, the great playwright, was a frequent lunch guest. So was the German composer Johann Adolph Hasse, the "divine Saxon" who had married the diva Faustina Bordoni and ran the music conservatory at the Incurabili, one of the hospices where young orphans were trained as musicians and singers.

Very early on, Andrea senior had chosen his favorite nephew and namesake as his successor. Over the years he instilled in him a sense of duty toward family and nation that would remain with him all his life. And he prepared him for a career in the service of "our wise Venetian Republic, which has seen the largest and wealthiest kingdoms fall over the past ten centuries and more, and yet has managed to stand firm amid everyone else's misfortune."[3]

Andrea received his first formal education from Eugenio Mecenati, a Carmelite monk who worked as preceptor in several patri-

---

*Montesquieu's *Esprit des lois* was published in Venice in 1749. Montesquieu himself had come to Venice to study its laws and system of government. He was run out of town by the inquisitors and legend has it that he threw all his notes into the lagoon as he made his escape toward the mainland. Jean-Jacques Rousseau was also a familiar figure, having been secretary to the French ambassador in Venice in 1743–1744.

cian families. But his mind wasn't really turned on until he met Carlo Lodoli, a fiery and charismatic Franciscan monk. During the 1740s Lodoli established himself as Venice's controversial resident philosopher. He was a brilliant scholar and teacher, equally at ease talking to his students about astronomy, philosophy, or economics. Lodoli's great passion was architecture, a field in which he applied the principles of utilitarianism to develop his own visionary theories about function and form. Wrapped in his coarse habit, the monk had a rugged, unkempt look about him that could be quite intimidating: "The red spots on his face, his wild hair, his unshorn beard, and those eyes like burning coals—he very nearly scared off the weaker spirits,"4 Andrea wrote many years later. Lodoli's disciples came from the more enlightened families in Venice. He never wrote books but kept students under his spell through the force of his personality and the probing power of his Socratic "conversations." His mission, as he saw it, was to open the mind of young patricians. The Venetian authorities were wary of the strong influence the monk had on his disciples. But Lodoli was not interested in subverting the established political order, as his conservative critics suggested: he wanted to improve it—by improving the men who would soon be called upon to serve the Republic.

Andrea remained devoted to Lodoli all his life, but the moral rigor of the Franciscan, his ascetic lifestyle, could be a little hard going. It is easy to see why Andrea's sensual side was somewhat starved in his company, and why he spent more and more of his time in the splendid house-museum of Consul Smith on the Grand Canal, just a short walk down the street from Ca' Memmo. He spent hours studying the vast collection of paintings and sculptures the consul had assembled over the previous thirty years and happily buried himself in the library—an exceptional treasure trove of classics and moderns in beautifully bound volumes.

Smith had arrived in Venice in the early years of the century, when the city still attracted a good number of foreign merchants and businessmen. He had gone to work for the firm of his fellow Englishman Thomas Williams and had been successful enough to take over the company when Williams retired a few years later and returned to England. Smith went on to build a considerable fortune trading in the East, buying goods from Venetian merchants and selling them on the British market. In 1717 he married Catherine Tofts, a popular singer who had made a name for herself in the London theaters before coming to Venice. Wealthy and well connected, Catherine was certainly the major drawing card of the Smith ménage in the early years of their marriage. But over time she gradually withdrew from society, perhaps never recovering from the loss of their son, John, who died in 1727 at the age of six.

As his business flourished, Smith purchased Palazzo Balbi, which he had rented ever since his arrival in Venice, and commissioned the architect Antonio Visentini, a friend and protégé, to renovate the façade. After some plotting within the English community in Venice and a great deal of pleading with the government in London, he eventually obtained the consular title in 1740. Much to his chagrin, he never became the British Resident (ambassador).

Consul Smith would probably have long faded into history had he not branched out into art and become one of the greatest dealers of his time. He made a habit of visiting artists, many of whom had studios a short walk away from his home. Smith had a good eye, and he delighted in friendly haggling. His collection included beautiful allegorical paintings from Sebastiano Ricci and Giovan Battista Tiepolo, grand vistas by Francesco Guardi, intimate scenes of Venetian life by Pietro Longhi, and several exquisite portraits by Rosalba Carriera. But his special admiration was reserved for Canaletto's clean and detailed views of the city, and over the years he developed a close professional relationship with the great Venetian *vedutista*.

Smith combined the eye of an art lover with the mind of a merchant. He realized he was living at the heart of an extraordinary artistic flowering and was in a unique position to turn his patronage into a profitable business. He commissioned works from his favorite artists and sold them to wealthy English aristocrats just as the fashion of collecting art was spreading. (He was so successful in marketing his beloved Canaletto that the artist eventually moved to London to paint views of the Thames for his growing clientèle.) In the process, Smith built up his own collection, enriching it with important paintings by old masters. Works by Bellini, Vermeer, Rembrandt, Van Dyck, and Rubens adorned the walls of his *palazzo*. Books, perhaps even more than paintings, were his true passion. He purchased valuable editions of the great classics as well as original manuscripts and drawings, and he participated directly in the publishing boom that was taking place in Venice. Smith invested in Giovan Battista Pasquali's printing shop and bookstore, and together they published the works of Locke, Montesquieu, Helvetius, Voltaire, Rousseau, and Diderot and his fellow Encyclopédistes (the first volumes of the revolutionary *Encyclopédie* appeared in 1751). Pasquali's shop soon became a favorite gathering place for the growing Venetian book crowd. "After having enjoyed the fresh air and shared the pleasures of Saint Mark's Square," wrote the French traveler Pierre Jean Grosley, "we would go to Pasquali's shop or to some other bookseller. These shops serve as the usual meeting point for foreigners and noblemen. Conversations are often seasoned with that Venetian salt which borrows a great deal from Greek atticism and French gaiety without being either."[5]

Smith's drawing room was, in a way, an extension of Pasquali's shop in more elegant surroundings. It was the center of the small English community (and it somehow never lost its touch of English quaintness). But more important, it was a place where artists, intellectuals, and Venetian patricians could congregate in an atmosphere of enlightened conviviality. Carlo Goldoni dedicated one of his plays—*Il filosofo inglese*—to Smith. In his flattering introduction, he wrote: "All those who enter your house find the most perfect union of all the sciences and all the arts. You are not a lover who merely gazes with admiration but a true connoisseur who is keen to share the meaning and beauty of the art around him. Your good taste, your perfect knowledge have inspired you to choose the most beautiful things, and the courage of your generous spirit has moved you to purchase them."[6] Andrea spent many happy days at Palazzo Balbi. It was in the consul's library that he learned his Vitruvius, studied Palladian drawings, and pored over the latest volume of the *Encyclopédie* (he got into the habit of copying out long passages to better absorb the spirit of French Enlightenment). Smith, his only child having died so many years earlier, developed a genuine affection for Andrea and as he grew older came to depend on him as a confidant and assistant. By 1750 he was already in his seventies. He had lost his sure touch in business transactions, and his weakened finances would only get worse. Having no heir and less and less money, he conjured up the deal of his lifetime—an ambitious plan to sell his huge art collection and his library to the British Crown.[7] He enlisted Andrea to help him catalogue all his paintings and books.

Under the influence of Goldoni, Andrea also developed a strong interest in the theater. During the season, which ran from October through May, he went to the theater practically every night. He threw himself with enthusiasm into the raucous debate that was raging between conservative and progressive critics. Though Goldoni was twenty years older than Andrea, he enjoyed the young man's company, regarding him not just as a promising member of the ruling class but also as a possible ally in his crusade in favor of plays that were closer to the everyday life of Venetians. In 1750 he dedicated his *Momolo cortesan* to Andrea, telling him he hoped that together they would "rid the stage of the obscene and ill-conceived plays"[8] produced by his conservative rivals. With Goldoni's encouragement, Andrea started to work in earnest on the idea of opening a new theater entirely dedicated to French plays, from Molière's classics to the light comedies of Marivaux. The goal, he said, was "to improve our own theater . . . and lift the common spirit in an honest way."[9]

While Andrea waited patiently for his turn to serve as a junior official in the Venetian government, his days were filled with his work for Smith, his new theater project, and the increasing load of family responsibilities being thrust upon his shoulders by his aging uncle. There was still plenty of time for evening strolls and gallantries in Campo Santo Stefano and Piazza San Marco, late-night discussions in the coffeehouses and *malvasìe* (wine shops that specialized in the sale of malmsey) and even the occasional trip to the Ridotto—though Andrea was never much of a gambler and went there mostly to meet friends and survey the scene.

Among his new friends was Giacomo Casanova, who returned to Venice in 1752 after his first trip to Paris. He and the three Memmo brothers were often seen together at one of the popular *malvasìe,* where they drank until late, played cards, and boisterously panned the latest play by the Abbé Pietro Chiari, Goldoni's chief conservative rival. Andrea's mother was not happy about her sons' friendship with Casanova. She saw him as a dangerous atheist with low morals who was bound to corrupt her children, and she alerted the authorities through her political connections. It turned out that the Inquisitori di Stato—the secretive three-member committee that oversaw internal security—viewed Casanova much in the same light and were already compiling a hefty dossier on him. Indeed, the band of merry revelers was being watched by the few shopworn informers still on the government payroll, one of whom confidently explained in his report that what bound Casanova and his friends was the fact that "they are philosophers of the same ilk . . . Epicureans all."[10]

In spite of his busy life and his many distractions, Andrea's sense of duty to the Republic was so ingrained in his mind that he saw his passion for architecture, his love of the theater, and his knowledge of painting and drawing not as ends unto themselves but as additional endowments that he would put to practical use during his public service. It did not occur to him to seek a different road from the one his uncle Andrea had set for him. He clearly considered marriage from the same perspective. Before meeting Giustiniana, Andrea had enjoyed a number of affairs. He loved the company of women and from a young age was much in demand among his female friends—he was also quite a dancer, which helped. But he had had no great romance or lasting relationship. He knew and accepted the fact that he was bound to marry a young woman from his own social class and that the families would seal the marriage after long negotiations that would have little to do with the feelings of the bride and the groom. Everything young men like Andrea had been taught at home "underscored the irrationality of choices made solely on the basis of sentimental feelings."[11]

Andrea's world—rich and varied and challenging but also largely predictable—was suddenly shaken up when Giustiniana stepped into it in late 1753. She came from another sphere entirely, having just returned with her mother and siblings from London, where they had traveled to collect the family inheritance after the death of Sir Richard, her beloved father. During her yearlong absence, she had blossomed into a lively and very attractive young woman. The Wynnes had a two-year, renewable residency permit; they were not Venetian citizens and therefore, like all other foreigners, had to obtain a special authorization to stay in the city. They settled in a rented house in the neighborhood of Sant'Aponal and at first led a quiet life, mostly within the small English community.

Sir Richard Wynne had left his native Lincolnshire distraught after the death of his first wife, Susanna. He journeyed across Europe and arrived in Venice in 1735 "to dissipate his affliction for the loss of his lady,"[12] as Lady Mary Wortley Montagu, famed and restless English traveler disapprovingly put it during one of her many stays in Venice. He was soon introduced "by his gondolier" to Anna Gazzini, a striking twenty-two-year-old Venetian with a less-than-immaculate past. Anna had actually been born on Lefkos, a Greek island in the Ionian Sea, where her father, Filippo Gazzini, had once settled to trade, but the family returned to Venice when she was still a little girl.

Anna became Sir Richard's lover soon after they met. Two years later, she gave birth to a baby girl who was baptized Giustiniana Francesca Antonia Wynne on January 26, 1737, in the Church of San Marcuola. Sir Richard doted on his daughter. He did not return to England, married Anna in 1739, and legalized Giustiniana's status six years later. (The legalization papers refer to Anna's father as "Ser Filippo Gazzini, nobleman from Lefkos,"[13] but this belated claim to nobility had a dubious ring to it even back then.) Anna gave birth to two more daughters: Mary Elizabeth in 1741 and Teresa Susanna in 1742, known as Bettina and Tonnina. Their first son, Richard, was born in 1744, followed by William in 1745. A fourth daughter, Anna Amelia, was born in 1748 and died two years later.

Mrs. Anna must not have been much fun to be around. Perhaps to atone for sins of her youth, she became a fierce Catholic who dragged her children to church and pestered her Anglican husband endlessly to convert. She was a strict disciplinarian, bent on giving

as traditional an education as possible to Giustiniana and her
younger brothers and sisters: music, dance, French, and little else.
Sir Richard was quite content to leave the upbringing of the children to his wife and retreat to his well-stocked library. As his gout
worsened, he withdrew from family life even more. Many years
later, Giustiniana remembered him sitting with a book in his
favorite armchair "the six months of the year he didn't spend
in bed."[14]

Despite his poor physical condition, Sir Richard developed a
close bond with Giustiniana. They shared a love of literature, and
he gave her the keys to his library. From a young age she read
eagerly but with no guidance or method, moving randomly from
travel books to La Fontaine's fables to heavy-going tomes such as
Paolo Sarpi's history of the Council of Trent—a book the Inquisi-
tion had banned for its sympathetic view of the Reformation.
Giustiniana was caught reading it secretly. From the little we know
of Sir Richard, he must have chuckled at his daughter's temerity.
Anna, on the other hand, had a fit and threatened to lock Giustiniana up in a convent.

Sir Richard died in 1751, and the following year Mrs. Anna
dragged her five children to London to claim their inheritance. It
was a long, tedious journey. Many years later, Giustiniana would
remember only the dirty hotels, the bad food, and "all those
churches [in Germany] so heavy with ornaments." But she loved
London—"the parks, the noise in the streets, the pretty hats . . .
and the general air of opulence"—and she would have gladly
stayed on. "I had learned English well enough, was rather good at
handling a fork, and was expecting to put my new skills to good
use."[15] Mrs. Anna, however, was there for the money. When she
finally got her hands on some of it, thanks to the intercession of
the children's guardian, Robert d'Arcy, Earl of Holderness, a former British Resident in Venice, the family packed up once more
and headed home—this time taking the more pleasant route, via
Paris.

Giustiniana was not yet sixteen when she arrived in Paris with
her mother and her brothers and sisters. But she did not go unnoticed during her brief stay. Casanova met her in the house of

Alvise Mocenigo, the Venetian ambassador. Forty years later, he still had a vivid memory of that first encounter. "Her character," he wrote in his memoirs, "was already delineated to perfection in her beautiful face."[16] Giustiniana loved Parisian life—"the theater, the elegance of men, the rouge on women's cheeks"[17]—but Mrs. Anna was anxious to get back to Venice, so they made their way home, taking with them a French governess, Toinon, who was much loved for her skill in combing the girls' hair.

The return of the Wynne sisters— *"le inglesine di Sant'Aponal, "*[18] as they quickly became known—generated a certain amount of excitement among the young men in town. Sure enough, Casanova—who had also returned to Venice in the meantime— came knocking at their door shortly after they had settled in, claiming that he had fallen in love with Giustiniana. Mrs. Anna, aware of his reputation and keen to keep her daughter out of trouble, turned him firmly away. (In his *History of My Life,* Casanova claimed that Giustiniana then wrote him a charming letter "which made it possible for me to bear the affront calmly."[19]) Mrs. Anna had every intention of keeping her daughters on a very short leash, and Giustiniana, who was just beginning to enjoy the pleasures of society, discovered, to her dismay, that their life in Venice "had been reduced to a small circle indeed." Much of their time was spent at home, "where we went on about Paris and London."[20] It was all rather glum.

The house of Consul Smith, one of the few Mrs. Anna allowed her daughters to frequent, was their link to the world. The consul, who had known Sir Richard well, was one of the most prominent foreign residents in town. He had seen the Wynne children grow up and had promised his old friend he would watch over his family and help Mrs. Anna sort out her finances. Palazzo Balbi became a second home to the young Wynnes, a place removed from their dreary house at Sant'Aponal, filled with beautiful objects, where the conversation had a cosmopolitan quality that reminded them of Paris and London. The consul, for his part, looked upon the Wynne children with avuncular affection. He was especially pleased with Giustiniana, who always brought a breath of fresh air to his house. "Mister Smith shared with me his love for his paintings, his antiquities, his library in order to enrich my passion for learning,"[21] she later reminisced. One suspects he also rather enjoyed parading through his magnificent rooms with such a lovely young girl on his arm.

During one of her visits to Palazzo Balbi the consul introduced Giustiniana to his dashing young assistant. As soon as Mrs. Anna heard about her daughter's infatuation, she became very anxious. Since the death of Sir Richard, she had lived in the fear that the respectability she had so stubbornly built up over the years might abate, leaving her and her family exposed to insidious and materially damaging forms of social discrimination. Her fear was well founded. Even in the relatively tolerant atmosphere of eighteenth-century Venice, many people still made a point of remembering that Lady Wynne was in fact the daughter of a "Greek" merchant. And there were lingering rumors about the amorous adventures of her youth: some even murmured that she had given birth to a child before taking up with *il vedovo inglese*—the English widower. Now she was a widow herself, living in a rented house with five children and with past sins to hide, and it is easy to see why she felt her position in society was so precarious—all the more so since she was in Venice at the pleasure of the authorities. Her residency permit might not be renewed or might even be revoked. So she had to act judiciously to maintain the standing Sir Richard had bequeathed to her.

However detestable her unyielding attitude must have seemed to the two lovers, it was certainly justified in the eyes of the English community. Consul Smith was fond of both Andrea and Giustiniana, but he was a practical man. When Andrea confided in him he sympathized with the lovers to a point. Nonetheless, he was very much on Mrs. Anna's side. The few Venetian families with whom the Wynnes socialized also supported her—especially the powerful Morosinis, with whom the Memmos had a long-running political feud and whom Andrea detested. But her chief ally, as opposed as they were in character and inclination, was Andrea's mother. Lucia saw, perhaps more clearly than the rest of the Memmos, the material disadvantages that a union with Giustiniana would bring to an old house which needed to reinvigorate its weak finances. And she feared the political damage the Memmos would suffer if her eldest and most promising son ever betrayed the family and crossed the inquisitors by marrying a woman beneath his rank.

The difference between the two mothers was that Lucia simply wanted to make sure Andrea did not get it into his head to marry Giustiniana. If in the meantime he dallied with her, as young men often did before settling down, it was no great worry to her and would not damage his future prospects. Mrs. Anna, on the other hand, was fighting a daily battle to prevent any contact between the lovers that might taint the family's reputation and jeopardize her daughter's chances of a respectable marriage.

Mrs. Anna was losing the battle. Andrea's courtship was assiduous, visible to everyone, and highly compromising. He saw Giustiniana every day at the Listone in Piazza San Marco, where Venetians gathered for their evening stroll, and often later on as well, at one of the theaters. He frequently moored his gondola to the narrow dock below the Wynnes' house and called on Giustiniana in full view of the family. In the winter of 1754 Mrs. Anna finally confronted him. She caused a terrible scene, declaring Andrea persona non grata in their house and making it clear she never wanted to see them together again. All communication was forbidden: letters, messages, the merest glance. It had to finish, she yelled—and sent him on his way.

News of Mrs. Anna's dramatic stand traveled quickly around town. Andrea referred to the scene as his *cacciata funesta*[22]—his fateful banishment, and the starting point of all their misery.

Mrs. Anna was a fierce watchdog, always on the alert and obsessively suspicious. She kept a close eye on her eldest daughter and did not let her go out without a chaperon—usually herself. Her spies were planted wherever the lovers might seek to escape her gaze, both within the English set and among Venetian families, and she kept her ears constantly pricked for gossip about the lovers. Venice was a small world. Everyone knew who was losing his fortune at the Ridotto on a particular night and who was having an affair with whom. Andrea and Giustiniana were aware of the risk they were taking in defying Mrs. Anna's ban; they had to be extremely careful about whom they spoke to and what they said. At a deeper level, they knew the future offered little promise of an end to their difficulties. But it was too soon, and they were too young, to worry about the future. For all the trouble their love had already caused, only one thing mattered to them in the winter and spring of that year: exploiting every opportunity to be together.

Just as Mrs. Anna resorted to the Venetian arts of intelligence, Andrea set up a small network of informers to obtain daily information about Giustiniana's movements. His chief spy was Alvisetto, a young servant in the Wynne household, who was not always dependable because his fear of Mrs. Anna was sometimes stronger than his loyalty to his secret paymaster. He had the unfortunate habit of disappearing during his missions, leaving Andrea flustered and clueless on a street corner or at the side of a bridge. "Alvisetto did not make it to our appointment and I went looking for him all morning in vain," he complained. "Poor us, Giustiniana. Sometimes I lose all hope when I think in whose hands we have put ourselves."

Alvisetto was also the chief messenger, and he shuttled back and forth between Andrea and Giustiniana with letters and love notes. Occasionally, the gondoliers of Ca' Memmo would moor at a dock near the Wynnes' to drop off or pick up an envelope. If Mrs. Anna was at home, the two lovers would fall back on "the usual *bottega* for deliveries," a general store around the corner from Giustiniana's home, run by a friendly shopkeeper. When Andrea's message could not wait—or if the urge to see her was irrepressible—he would appear at the window of Ca' Tiepolo, the imposing *palazzo* across a narrow waterway from the Wynnes' more modest house.

Ca' Tiepolo belonged to one of the oldest and grandest Venetian families. Its wide neoclassical façade stood majestically on the Grand Canal. From the side window of the mezzanine it was possible to look directly across to the Wynnes' balcony. The ties between the Tiepolos and the Memmos went back many centuries. Andrea was a good friend of the young Tiepolos and especially close to Domenico, better known by his nickname Meneghetto, who was among the few to know from the start that Andrea's love affair with Giustiniana was continuing in secret. Meneghetto was happy to help, and Andrea often dropped by after sending Giustiniana precise instructions. "After lunch," he advised her in one note, "find an excuse to come out on the balcony. But for heaven's sake be careful about your mother. And don't force me to edge out as far as the windowsill because she will certainly see me."

Andrea's portable telescope was very useful. He would point it in the direction of Giustiniana's balcony from a *campiello,* a little square, across the Grand Canal, to check whether she was at home or to find out whether she might be getting ready to go out or, best of all, to watch her as she leaned lazily over the balcony, her hair wrapped in a bonnet, watching the boats go by. When he observed her from such a distance—about a hundred yards—Giustiniana was not always aware Andrea was spying on her. "Today I admired you with my *canocchiale* [telescope]," he announced to her mischievously. "I don't really care if your mother saw me. . . . After all, the rules merely state that I cannot come into your house and that I cannot write to you."

From a purely technical point of view he was also within bounds when, thanks again to the benevolence—and the sweat— of his gondoliers, he came down the Grand Canal and signaled to Giustiniana from the water. On days when she was confined to the house and they had no other way of seeing each other, Andrea's sudden appearance at her neighbor's window or the familiar plashing of the Memmo gondola down below was a welcome consolation. "Come by the canal as my mother doesn't want me to go out," she would plead. "And make an appearance at Ca' Tiepolo as well, if you can."

They developed their own sign language so they could communicate from a distance during the evening walk at the Listone or at the theater or, later in the night, at the gambling house. "Touch your hair if you're going to the Ridotto," he instructed her. "Nod or shake your head to tell me whether you plan to go to the piazza." These little signals sometimes caused confusion if they were not worked out in advance. They also had to be given very discreetly, lest they set off Mrs. Anna's alarm bells. "When you left the theater," Andrea wrote anxiously, "you signaled something to me just as your mother turned around, and I think she might have noticed that. If this were the case it could damage us, since she might also have noticed all the other gestures we had made to each other from our boxes." Despite his occasional burst of bravado, Andrea remained deeply worried not just by what Mrs. Anna might have seen but also by what she *thought* she might have seen. He went to such extremes to avoid creating false impressions that he sometimes sounded like an obstinate stage manager. "You must realize that if your mother catches you laughing with someone she can't see, she will assume that you are laughing with me," he once said to her in a huff. "So try to be careful next time."

Andrea fretted constantly about how dangerous it was to write to each other. If their correspondence ever fell into the wrong hands, there would be an explosion "that would reduce everything to a pile of rubble." Still he deluged Giustiniana with letters and notes, often filling them with practical advice and detailed descriptions of his frantic chases around town. "We are completely mad. . . . If only you knew how afraid I am that your mother might find out we are seeing each other again."

It was a glorious adventure. There were times when they managed to get close enough to steal a quick embrace in an alcove at the Ridotto or in the dark streets near the theaters at San Moisè, and the thrill was always powerful. "Last night, I swear," Andrea wrote to his beloved the morning after one of these rare encounters, "you were so heated up, oh so heated up, such a beautiful girl, and I was on fire." But in the beginning they tended to hold back. They made their moves with deliberation. They kept each other at a safe distance: lovemaking was mostly limited to what their eyes could see and what their eyes could say.

It is easy to imagine how, in a city where both men and women wore masks during a good portion of the year, the language of the eyes would become all-important. And what was true in general was especially true for Andrea and Giustiniana on account of the rigid restrictions that had been imposed on them. Andrea was being very literal when he asked anxiously, "Today my lips will not be able to tell you how much I love you. . . . But there will be other ways. . . . Will you understand what my eyes will be saying to you?" What their eyes said was not always sweet and not always clear. With such strong emotions at play, it could take days to clear up a misunderstanding precipitated by a wrong look or an averted gaze. One night, Andrea returned to Ca' Memmo after a particularly frustrating attempt to make contact with Giustiniana. It had taken him all evening and a great deal of effort and ingenuity to find her at one of the theaters. Yet in the end she had displayed none of the usual complicity that made even the briefest encounter a moment of joy. In fact, she had been so annoying as to make him wish he had not seen her at all:

> *Yesterday I tried desperately to see you. Before lunch the gondoliers could not serve me. After lunch I went looking for you in Campo Santo Stefano. Nothing. So I walked toward Piazza San Marco, and when I arrived at the bridge of San Moisè I ran into Lucrezia Pisani!* I gave her my hand on the bridge, and then I saw you. I left her immediately and went looking for you everywhere. Finally I found you in the piazza. I sent Alvisetto ahead to find out whether you were on your way to the opera or to the new play at the Teatro Sant'Angelo, so that I could rush over to get a box in time. Then I forged ahead and waited for you, filled with desire. Finally you arrived and I went up to my box so that I could contemplate you—not only for the sheer pleasure I take in admiring you but also in the hope of receiving a sign of acknowledgment as a form of consolation. But you did nothing of the sort. Instead you laughed continuously, made loud noises until the end of the show, for which I was both sorry and angry— as you can well imagine.*

A few days later Andrea tracked her down after yet another chase along crowded streets and across canals. This time the reward was well worth the pursuit:

> *I caught sight of your mother and hoped you would be with her. I looked for you left and right. Nothing. Your mother left, I followed. She went to San Moisè, I went to San Moisè. In fact, I got so close to her that we would have bumped into each other at the entrance of a* bottega *if I had not been so quick. . . . [Later] I waited in vain for Alvisetto, whom I had instructed to follow your mother. . . . Then I got your letter telling me that you would be going to San Benetto, so I rushed over only to realize with regret*

---

*Andrea's cousin by marriage and a close friend.

that you had already arrived and that the opera had begun. . . .
Oh Lord, what will Giustiniana say. . . . Let's see how she will
treat me. . . . Goodness, there she is, that naughty girl [who
wouldn't look at me] the other evening. . . . Will she look at me
this time or won't she. . . . Come, look this way my girl! . . . And
little by little I began to feel better. And then much better when I
moved into that other box because I could see you and you could
see me so well and with no great danger that your mother might
notice every little gesture between us.

As an overall strategy, Andrea felt it was important to convince
Mrs. Anna that the love between him and Giustiniana had indeed
subsided and that she could finally let her guard down. It would be
easier for them to find ways to see each other. So whenever Mrs.
Anna took her daughter to a place where there was a good chance
they might see him, Giustiniana was to feign complete disinterest:

Sometimes, in taking risks, one must be willing to be la dupe
de soi-même. *So arrange things in such a way that she will feel*
she is forcing you to go to all the places where she knows you
might run into me, such as San Benetto or the Ridotto. . . . And
when the weather is nice, show little interest, even some resis-
tance, to taking a walk to the square. . . . Believe me, our good
fortune depends on the success of our deception. . . . To avoid
coming to San Benetto, all you have to do is tell her you don't feel
well. As for the Ridotto, you can say, "In truth, Mother, it bores
me too much. Besides, we have no one to speak to and I don't feel
like playing [cards]. And we don't make a good impression any-
way, walking around with no other company. So let me go to
bed." And if she refuses and takes you out with her, you will see
me and she will say, "Giustiniana doesn't fret about Memmo
anymore."

In public Andrea and Giustiniana behaved like two strangers.
Yet if their relationship was ever to develop, if they were to make
arrangements in order to meet somewhere safely and actually
spend time together, they were going to need more reliable allies

than Alvisetto—friends willing to take the risk of giving them cover and providing them with rooms where they could see each other in private. Andrea worked hard to identify those who might be most useful to them. He gave precise instructions to Giustiniana as to how she should behave to bring this or that friend over to their side. But his instructions were not always clear. When Giustiniana innocently told a potential ally that she no longer loved Andrea when in fact Andrea had asked her to say the opposite, he gave her a sharp rebuke: "As soon as I do a good piece of work, you ruin it for me. The truth is . . . and I am very sorry to have to say this, you have not been up to my expectations."

Andrea could be equally hard when he thought Giustiniana was not keeping enough distance from possible enemies. He was wary of the young Venetian nobles who hung around the Ridotto and who delighted in gossip and intrigue. It was important not to give them a reason to unleash their malicious tongues. As a rule, he explained to Giustiniana, "it is good for us to have the greatest number of friends and the least number of enemies." But there was no need to be closer to that crowd than was strictly necessary. And he criticized her when he saw her displaying too much friendliness to acquaintances he did not consider trustworthy.

He was especially suspicious of the Morosinis, who had always sided with Mrs. Anna in her battle against the two lovers—merely to spite him, Andrea thought. The Wynnes were often lunch guests at Ca' Morosini on Campo Santo Stefano, and Giustiniana's persistent socializing with the enemy infuriated Andrea. She had to choose, he finally said to her, between him and "those Morosini asses":

> *I know it is a lot to ask, but I can ask no less. . . . I must put you through this test, and I shall measure your love for me by it. . . . Giustiniana, I shall be very disappointed if you disregard my wish. I have never met anyone so impertinent and so false toward both of us. . . . They like you merely because you amuse them. . . . By God, you will not be worthy of me if you lower yourself to the point of flattering these . . . stupid enemies of mine . . . these rigid custodians of Giustiniana who spy for your mother. . . . They are evil people with no human qualities and no respect for friend-*

*ship. . . . Forgive me for speaking this way to you, but I am so
angry that I cannot stand it anymore.*

In the early stages, Andrea had a patronizing tone toward Giustiniana and a tendency to take control of every aspect of their relationship. He was, of course, several years older than she, and it
was fairly natural that he should take the lead while she deferred to
his judgment. But over the months she grew more confident in her
ability to conceal and deceive. And in spite of Andrea's occasional
hectoring, she began to enjoy plotting behind her mother's back.
She took a more active role in planning their meetings and often
marveled at her own audacity: "Truly, Memmo, I do not recognize
myself. I do things I never would have done. I think in ways so different that I do not seem to be myself anymore."

It was Giustiniana who eagerly informed Andrea that N., a
friend on whom they had worked hard to bring over to their side,
had finally agreed to let them meet at his *casino*, one of the little
pleasure houses that were all the rage in those years and were
Venice's very practical answer to a diffuse desire for comfort and
pleasure. (There were as many as 150 such *casini* in the city, which
were used as boudoirs, as seditious salons, and—quite often—as
discreet love nests.) "I've made arrangements for Friday," she
wrote self-confidently. "We can't see each other before. I didn't
feel I could press him and so I let him choose the date. He has
become my friend entirely and confides his worries to me and even
vents his domestic frustrations."

Their excitement grew every day in anticipation of the
moments they would spend together. It was not enough anymore
to exchange loving glances and signals from afar. If Giustiniana
had become much bolder in just a few weeks, it was because her
yearning was now so powerful. She longed to be kissed by Andrea,
to be held in his arms. And their scheming was finally producing
results. Here is Giustiniana, three days before their secret appointment at N.'s *casino:*

*Friday we shall meet—at least we know as much. But my
God, how the time in between will seem interminable! And afterward what? Afterward I shall think about our next meeting so*

*that I shall always be having sweet thoughts about you. . . . Tell
me, Memmo, are you entirely happy with me? Is there any way I
can give you more? Is there something in my behavior, in my way
of life that I might change to suit you better? Speak, for I shall do
anything you want. I cannot think of anything more precious than
to see you happy and ever closer to me. I never thought it was possible to love with such violence.*

The following evening Alvisetto appeared in Giustiniana's
room bearing a reply from her lover. "My soul," Andrea wrote,
"what a complete delight it will be. Love me, adore me. . . . I
deserve it because I know your heart so well. Oh Lord, I am so
dying to see you that I am jumping out of my skin." Alvisetto
also handed to Giustiniana a small, delicately embroidered fan—
a gift to make the waiting more bearable. In order to avoid raising Mrs. Anna's suspicions, Andrea suggested that Giustiniana ask
her aunt Fiorina to pretend the fan was for her. In the past Mrs.
Anna's sister had shown a certain amount of sympathy for her
niece's predicament. Andrea, always in search of reliable allies,
felt this subterfuge would not only allay whatever doubts Mrs.
Anna might have about his gift but also give them a sense of how
much Aunt Fiorina was prepared to help them in the future.

On Thursday, the day before their meeting, Alvisetto delivered
a long, tender letter to Andrea:

*And so, my dear Memmo, tomorrow we shall be together. And
what, in the whole world, could be more natural between two people who love each other than to be together? I could go on forever,
my sweet. I am in heaven. I love you. I love you, Memmo, more
than I can say. Do you love me as much? Do you know I have this
constant urge to do well, to look beautiful, to cultivate the greatest possible number of qualities for the mere sake of pleasing you,
of earning your respect, of holding on to my Memmo. . . . Be
warned, however, that your love for me has made me extremely
proud and vain. . . . Where does one find a man so pleasant, so at
ease in society, yet at the same time so firm, so deeply understanding of the important things in life? Where does one find a*

young man with such a rich imagination who is also precise and clearheaded in his thinking, so graceful and convincing in expressing his ideas? My Memmo, so knowledgeable in the humanities, so intelligent about the arts, is also a man who knows how to dress and always cuts quite a figure and knows how to carry himself with grace . . . he is a man who possesses the gift of being at once considerate and bold. And even if at times he goes out of bounds, he does it to satisfy the natural urges of his youth and his character. And therein lies the path to happiness. You are wild as a matter of principle, as a result of hard reasoning. Aren't you the rarest of philosophers? . . . And what have you done, what do you do to women? Just the other day N. said to me: How did you manage to catch that fickle young man? And I was so proud, Memmo.

As for the fan, she added, "I will ask Fiorina to accept it in my place. I don't know whether she is on our side or not, but at least she seems willing to fake it."

The morning after their meeting at N.'s, Giustiniana, enthralled by the sweetest memories of the previous evening, wrote to Andrea entirely in French—not the language she knew best but the one she evidently felt was most appropriate in the lingering afterglow of their reunion:

Ah, Memmo, so much happiness! I was with you for close to two hours; I listened to your voice; you held my hand, and our friends, touched by our love, seem willing to help us more often. After you had left, N. told me how much you love me. Yes, you do love me, Memmo, you love me so deeply. Tell me once more; I never tire of hearing you say it. And the more direct you are, the more charmed I shall be. The heart doesn't really care much for detours. Simplicity is worth so much more than the most ornate embellishments. You are the most charming philosopher I have ever listened to. . . . If only I could be free . . . and tell the world about my love! Ah, let us not even speak of such a happy state. Farewell, I take leave of you now. When shall I see you? Tell me, are you as impatient as I am?

She added teasingly:

> *Oh, by the way, I have news. My mother received a marriage proposal for me from a very rich Roman gentleman. . . . Isn't it terrible, Memmo? Aren't you at least a little bit jealous? And what if he is as nice as they say . . . and what if my mother wanted him. . . . I can't go on. Not even in jest. . . . I am all yours, my love. Farewell.*

CHAPTER *Two*

$\overline{\qquad\qquad}$

Andrea and Giustiniana were so secretive during the first months of their clandestine relationship that only a handful of trusted friends knew what they were up to. As Andrea had predicted, Mrs. Anna eventually began to lower her guard and focus on possible new suitors for her eldest daughter. By the fall of 1754 the two lovers were seeing each other with great frequency and daring. They now had several locations at their disposal. N.'s *casino* was often available. Meneghetto Tiepolo had given them access to an apartment on the mezzanine of his *palazzo*. They also went to a woman named Rosa, who lived in a small and very simple house near the Wynnes and often let them have a room. Setting up a secret encounter was often the work of several days. It took reliable intelligence and good planning. Alvisetto shuttled furtively between the Wynnes' house and Ca' Memmo, delivering letters with the latest arrangements or news of an unexpected change of plan. Much was written about the dropping off and picking up of keys.

The feverish preparatory work, coupled with the constant fear of being caught, made their encounters all the more passionate. "How could they be so stupid," Giustiniana noted with delight, "not to realize what refinement they bring to our pleasure by imposing all these prohibitions? [At the beginning of our relationship] I was always very happy to see you, of course, but the emotions I feel now, the sheer agitation, the overwhelming feeling of sweetness, were certainly not as intense."

As their love deepened and their relationship became more sexual, jealousy too began to creep into their little world. Despite Mrs. Anna's more relaxed attitude, Giustiniana was still not as free to move around town as Andrea was. This put her at a psychological disadvantage. Who was Andrea seeing when he wasn't with her? She had his letters, of course, filled with detailed accounts of his daily activities. But how reliable were they? In her relative confinement in the house at Sant'Aponal she had plenty of time to work herself into a state of anxiety. A hint of unpleasant gossip was enough to send her into a rage.

One of Andrea's best friends was his cousin Lucrezia Pisani, the young lady he had bumped into on the bridge as he was chasing Giustiniana. She was lively and attractive and popular among Andrea's set. She often had interesting company at her house, and Andrea liked to drop by. His breezy reports on his visits there, however, made Giustiniana feel excluded. When she heard he was seeing Lucrezia more and more frequently on the days when they could not be together, she protested angrily. Andrea was taken aback by her attitude. Lucrezia was an old friend, he argued, an ally; she was one of the few who knew about their love affair. He reacted to Giustiniana's indignation with even greater indignation:

> *What have I done to you? What sort of creature are you? What on earth are you thinking? And what doggedness! What cruelty! So now it would appear that I have been courting Lucrezia for the past ten days. . . . Well, first of all, the timing is wrong: she's been in the countryside for the past several days. I would have gone with her. I chose not to. Meanwhile, I've been at home most of the time, evenings included. I've had lunch with her once. True, every time I have met her at the theater I have sat in her box. . . . But could I have sat alone or even with a single friend throughout an entire show? . . . I am mad to even defend myself. Yes, I like her company and I admit it. First of all because she is one of the easiest women to be around. . . . She is also witty, knowledgeable, clever. You can talk to her freely, and she often has good company. . . . Besides, she is your friend, she often asks about you with interest. . . . You are crazy, crazy, crazy. You will drive me mad with your endless suspicions. Still, I guess I must try to appease you in any case. So rest assured: I won't be seen with her anymore. But where may I go? Anywhere I went there*

would be new gossip and new scenes. . . . By God, I will have to lock myself up in my room, under permanent surveillance, otherwise you still won't believe me. But of course when no one sees me around people will start thinking that I'm enjoying myself even more secretively. What a life.

Giustiniana's suspicions, however, were not entirely unjustified: there was talk around town that Lucrezia did indeed have a liking for Andrea that went beyond their old friendship. When Giustiniana's mood did not improve, Andrea realized he would have to do something more drastic to placate her. He went about it in a manner that revealed his own penchant for intrigue:

This is a difficult thing to ask, but you are so easy, so free from prejudice, you have such a good spirit and are always so obliging with me that it is possible you might grant me this favor. Lucrezia torments me by always asking if she can see some of your letters to me—which I have never permitted her to do. Therefore I would like for you to write me a letter in French in which you praise her. You might add in passing that, while not jealous of her, you do think she is too intelligent not to realize that it would be preferable if I were not seen so often with her. She already knows all the love I have for you and your commitment to me. I assure you that the only reason I am asking you to do this is so that she will convince herself that I am in love with a woman more special than her. . . . If you're not up to it, it doesn't really matter. It's enough that you love me.

Giustiniana was uncomfortable with this sort of game playing. A little deception to avoid Mrs. Anna's controls and to meet Andrea on the sly was one thing. But she found his recourse to artifice for the sake of artifice a little unsettling. The ease with which he could transform himself from the most tender and loving companion to the craftiest manipulator was a trait that seemed embedded in his character. And whereas Lucrezia, an experienced operator herself, would probably not have given Andrea's behavior great significance, Giustiniana found it much harder to understand. She too had a seductive side, a propensity to flirt with men both young and old. But excessive ambiguity made her ill at ease. She held fast to a rule of love that was not very common among other young Venetians: the exclusivity of romantic feelings. So she was stunned to hear, when she went over to the Morosinis' for lunch shortly after the Lucrezia episode, that Andrea was also flirting with Mariettina Corner, another well-known seductress. Mariettina's love life was complicated enough as it was: she was married to Lucrezia's brother, had an official lover and was having an affair with yet a third man, Piero Marcello—a gambler and philanderer who happened to be a neighbor of the Wynnes'. Giustiniana was told that though Mariettina was carrying on the relationship with Piero, it was really Andrea she had her eyes on.

Again she confronted him, and again he blamed her for believing every scrap of gossip floating around the Morosinis': "What are they telling you, these people with whom you seem to enjoy yourself so much? And why do you believe them if you know they hate me? You accuse me of making love to Mariettina. . . . But why is it you always fear I'm causing you offense with all the women I see?"

The story of Andrea's presumed affair with Mariettina had all the ingredients of a Goldoni farce. It turned out that Andrea, at Mariettina's request, had acted as a go-between in her secret romance with Piero. And Giustiniana—as Andrea was quick to remind her—had even encouraged him to take on that role because she felt that as long as Mariettina was busy with other men she would not present a threat to her. But Andrea's comings and goings between the two lovers had provided the gossipmongers with plenty to talk about. In the ensuing confusion Giustiniana didn't know whom to believe. Andrea acknowledged that "some people might well have thought Mariettina had developed an interest in me. . . . After all, I was constantly whispering in her ear and she was whispering in mine. . . . She talked to me, gestured to me, sat next to me while apparently not caring a hoot about [her lover], her husband—indeed the world." He insisted it was all a terrible misunderstanding: he was innocent and Giustiniana was "stupid" if she bothered "to spend a moment on all this talk the Morosinis fill your head with."

It wasn't easy for her to dismiss the things she heard about Andrea, because so much of his life was invisible to her, out of reach. The rumors were all the more hurtful because they reverberated in circles to which she was admitted but to which she did not truly belong. Giustiniana knew or was acquainted with most of Andrea's friends and was a welcome guest in the houses of many patrician families. But even though the veil of social discrimination was perhaps not as visible as elsewhere in Europe, it was very real; it governed Venetian society in subtle and less subtle ways—as in the case of marriage. When Giustiniana wrote to Andrea about his woman friends, there was often an undercurrent of anxiety that went quite beyond a natural romantic jealousy.

Still, she had her own little ways of getting back at him.

As Andrea and Giustiniana struggled to clear up the misunderstanding about his role in their friends' affair, Mariettina threw one of her celebrated balls on the Giudecca—an island separated from the southern side of Venice by a wide canal, where patricians had pleasure houses with gardens and vineyards. This was one of the major social events of the season. Preparations went on for days. Young Venetian ladies had a notorious taste for luxury. They liked to wear rich and elaborate but relatively comfortable outfits, so they could move with greater ease during the minuets and *furlane,* a popular dance that originated from the Friuli region. They spent hours having their hair coiffed into tall beehives, which they decorated with gems and golden pins. Their long fingernails were polished in bright colors. They drenched themselves with exotic perfume and chose their beauty spots with special care (the *appassionata* was worn in the corner of the eye, the *coquette* above the lip, the *galante* on the chin, and the *assassina*—the killer—in the corner of the mouth).[1] They carried large, exquisitely embroidered fans and wore strings of pearls and diamonds. High heels had long been out of fashion: Venetian ladies preferred more sensible low evening shoes, often decorated with a diamond buckle. These were fabulously expensive but very comfortable, especially for dancing. Men wore the traditional French costume: silk long jacket, knee-length culottes, and white stockings. Elaborate cuffs and jabots of lace from the island of Burano gave a Venetian touch to their attire. Their elegant evening wigs were combed and groomed for the occasion.

Mariettina's ball offered a chance for Andrea and Giustiniana to see each other and clarify things once and for all. But Giustiniana, still feeling vexed by the whole imbroglio, was not in the mood for such a demanding social event. She sent this note to Andrea just as he was dressing for the evening:

> *If the bad weather continues I will certainly not come to Marietta Corner's festa. You know my mother and how she fears the wind. She has warned that she will not cross the canal if there is the slightest bit of wind. In the end it is probably better that such a reasonable pretext should excuse me from coming as I believe you and I would both have a terrible time. . . . Still I will try to convince my mother to get over her fear—I hope you will acknowledge my goodwill. I have already opted for a new course: henceforth you will be able to do as you please; I will neither complain nor bother you with accusations. When you will cause me displeasure I will try to convince myself that you won't have done so out of ill will but because you do not believe I am sensitive to those things. . . . By the way, all those pleas for forgiveness and that habit you have of carrying on exactly in the same manner even though you know you offend me—I really cannot stand it. The truth is, I will continue to give you proof of my real affection while you will hurt me more and more. And who knows if all my suffering will change you one day. . . . Good-bye now, Memmo. I would not want to keep you from your toilette.*

In the end Giustiniana did not prevail over her mother—if she ever tried—and she did not go to Marietta's ball. The next day she sent Andrea this bittersweet note: "I did not write to you this morning because I felt you might be tired after last night and needed your sleep. The bad weather prevented me from coming, but as I told you I believe in the end it was for the better. Today I was half hoping I would see you at the window at Ca' Tiepolo, but I guess I fooled myself. This evening we are going to Smith's. I will write to you tomorrow. I have nothing else to ask you except to love me much—if you can. Farewell."

Andrea always reacted defensively, even impatiently, to Giustiniana's outbursts of jealousy. He was not immune to similar feelings, but in the abstract he espoused what he considered a "philosophical" approach. "It is practically impossible for me to be jealous," he explained:

Not because I have such high esteem for myself that I do not recognize others might be worthy [of your attentions]. No, the reason is that I don't want to believe you are flighty or coquettish or fickle or careless or mean. If ever there came a point in which I really did nurture doubts about you . . . then I would simply think of you as a different woman. The pain I would feel on account of your transformation would certainly be intense, but to me you would no longer be the lovable, the rarest Giustiniana. And by losing what ignited my deepest love and continues to nourish it, I would lose all feeling for you and return to the Memmo I was before meeting you.

This was the theory. In reality Andrea was fairly quick to lose his cool when other young men prowled around Giustiniana. He was particularly wary of Momolo Mocenigo, better known as Il Gobbo—the Hunchback—on account of a slight curvature of his spine, but in fact rather good-looking and quite the ladykiller. "He was the handsomest of all the patrician gamesters at the Ridotto," Casanova wrote in his memoirs.[2] When he was not taking bets at his faro table, Il Gobbo hung around the theaters, where he bothered the ladies and tried to make mischief. He especially enjoyed gallivanting with Giustiniana, and her willingness to indulge him annoyed Andrea to no end. Once, after catching her yet again in "a very long conversation" with him, he let her have it: "Everyone knows Il Gobbo for the first-class whoremonger that he is. You should know he once [told me] in front of other people that I should be thankful to him because he chose not to seduce you even though you showed a certain kindness to him. . . . I refused to give in to such abuse, and I dare say my reaction did not make him very happy. . . . But why did you have to go talk to him without your mother? Why speak to him practically in the ear? Why whisper to him that you were going to San

Moisè so he could then come and tell me with a tone that so displeased me?"

Another evening, Andrea was at home nursing a fever and a terrible sore throat when he suddenly learned that the "first-class whoremonger" was on his way to meet Giustiniana. He became so upset that he dashed out of the house, ran across town, and burst into the busy gambling rooms of the Ridotto. "I looked for you everywhere, and I finally found you in the same room where [Il Gobbo] had just been," he wrote to her angrily and with a good deal of self-pity. The incident, he assured Giustiniana, had "redoubled the flames that were already engulfing my throat."

Still, Il Gobbo was a lesser irritant than Piero Marcello, the handsome *coureur de femmes* who was courting Mariettina Corner but also had eyes for Giustiniana. Andrea considered Piero to be frivolous and vain, the sort of young man who would buy a new coat and then "make a ruckus just to attract attention to it." Piero's gondola was often moored at the same dock as the Wynnes'. "How appearances can trick one," Andrea noted, for he was worried people might wrongly assume that Piero was visiting Giustiniana and her sisters, when in fact Piero simply lived nearby. Indeed, some already referred to them as "Piero Marcello's girls." Piero not only flirted with Giustiniana, he also needled Andrea in public, wondering aloud whether he and Giustiniana were secretly still seeing each other. The two nearly came to blows over her, as Andrea reported to Giustiniana with more than a hint of braggadocio in this account of their confrontation:

> PIERO: *Are you jealous of me? Oh . . . but I have no designs on her. True, when women call me it is hard for me to resist. . . . But I am your friend, I would not betray you. I stay away from my friends' women. And if you have the slightest suspicion, I will never see her again.*
>
> ANDREA: *Who do you think you are, the Terror of the World? Do you really think I'm afraid of losing Giustiniana to you? If she were crazy, like all your previous lovers were, if she wanted your money, . . . if she had all the weaknesses, all the silliness, all the prejudices of the average woman, if she could not tell the true value of better men, if she were a coquette or worse, then, yes, I*

probably wouldn't trust her. But my dear Piero, who do you think you're dealing with?

Andrea concluded, "I told him these things with my usual straightforwardness, so that after affecting surprise he turned the whole thing into a joke."

Things did not end there. Days later Andrea saw Piero and Giustiniana talking to each other again. He gave her a stern warning: "Now I speak to you as a husband: I absolutely do not want you to show in public that you know Piero Marcello. I was very sorry that Mariettina, noticing that I was trying to see with whom you were laughing, came over and whispered into my ear: 'She's laughing with Piero down there.'"

Even after such a reprimand Andrea would not admit to being the slightest bit jealous:

> *I've told you a hundred times: I don't forbid you to see Piero out of jealousy. . . . But I absolutely do not want you to look at him in public or even say hello, all the more so because he affects an equivocal manner that I simply don't like and that I find insolent in the extreme. . . . Piero and Momolo are not for you. . . . Piero frets while Momolo affects his usual mannerisms, both with the same end: to make people believe that there has been at least a little bit of intimacy with all the women they are barely acquainted with. And for this reason the two of them are a real nuisance to young lovers.*

Despite the misunderstandings and squabbles that ensued, Andrea and Giustiniana's relationship deepened through the spring and summer of 1755 to the point that very little else seemed to matter to them anymore. All their energies were devoted to making time for themselves and finding places to meet. They had become experts at escaping the restrictions imposed on them and moved stealthily from alcove to alcove. Their love affair consumed their life, and it gradually transformed them.

Giustiniana had been known as a lively and gregarious young woman. The affectionate nickname *inglesina di Sant'Aponal* conjured up a refreshing image of youth and grace. Soon after returning to Venice, Giustiniana, being the eldest, had begun to share with her mother the duties of a good hostess while Bettina, Tonnina, Richard, and William were still under the care of Toinon. This role had come naturally to her. She had felt at ease in their drawing room or over at the consul's, delighting everyone with her charm. But by 1755 she was tired of all that, tired of performing onstage. She hardly recognized herself. "Coquetry was all I really cared for once," she told Andrea in a moment of introspection. "Now I can barely manage to be polite. Everything bores me. Everything annoys me. People say I have become stupid, silly; that I am hopeless at entertaining guests. I realize they're right, but I don't much care." She spent her days writing letters to Andrea, worrying about whom he was seeing, planning their next meeting—where, at what time, and, always, what to do with the keys. When she did go out with her mother—to lunch at the consul's, or to church, the theater, the Ridotto—the people she chose to talk to, what she said, how she said it: everything she did, in one way or another, related to Andrea.

The affair had become all-consuming for Andrea as well. "My love, you govern my every action," he confessed to her. "I do not think, I do not feel, I do not see anything but my Giustiniana. Everything else is meaningless to me. . . . I simply cannot hide my love for you from others anymore." He still made the usual rounds—a family errand, a trip to the printer Pasquali on behalf of the consul, a lunch at Ca' Tiepolo, and in the evening a visit to the theater. But his life outside the secret world he shared with Giustiniana no longer seemed very stimulating or even much fun. After the death of his uncle Andrea the year before, Ca' Memmo had received fewer visitors and had ceased to be the scintillating intellectual haven of years past. At this time, too, Andrea's mother, obsessed about Casanova's influence on her three boys, finally had her way and convinced the inquisitors to have him arrested.* The

---

*It is probable that a combination of factors determined Casanova's arrest on July 25, 1755—his openly proclaimed atheism, his dabbling with numerology, his reputation as an able swindler of a rather gullible trio of old patricians. Lucia Memmo's pressure on the inquisitors also played a role. Certainly Casanova was convinced of this. "His [Andrea's] mother had been a party to the plot that sent me to prison,"[3] he later wrote in his *History of My Life*. But he never bore a grudge toward the sons.

heated, late-night conversations at the crowded *malvasìe* on the latest book from Paris or the new play by Goldoni had lost their most entertaining participant.

Andrea's personal project for establishing a French theater in Venice was going nowhere, and Giustiniana worried that she might be the main cause of his lack of progress: "Are you not working on it because of me? Dear Memmo, please don't give up. If only you knew how much I care about your affairs when your honor is at stake. Especially this project, which, given its scale, the detailed manner in which you planned it, and the excellence with which you carried out every phase, was meant to establish your reputation. And to think that my feelings for you—true as they are—might have caused you so much damage. I am mortified." Andrea admitted that he had made little progress and "all the people involved" in the project were furious with him. "They say I have been taking them for a ride all along. The talk of the town is that the theater project has fallen through because of my excessive passion for you. By God, I couldn't care less. I only wish to tell you that I love you, my heart." Sweetly, he added that he would now start working on it again "because it will feel I will be doing something for you. [After I received your letter] I dashed off to the lawyers to get them started again. They weren't in the office, but I shall find them soon enough." In the end, despite fitful efforts, the project never got off the ground.

Andrea kept up with his mentor Carlo Lodoli, the Franciscan monk who continued to hold sway among the more open-minded members of the Venetian nobility. Now that he was no longer Lodoli's student, Andrea saw him less often, but he was anxious that Giustiniana should also benefit from the mind that had influenced him so profoundly. He encouraged his old teacher to visit her as much as possible and draw her into his circle of followers. Giustiniana always welcomed these visits, starved as she was of new books and new ideas in the restricted intellectual environment her mother fostered at home. Most of all she delighted in the chance to spend time with a person who knew the man she loved so well. When Lodoli came to visit, it was as if he brought Andrea with him—at least in spirit. "He just left," Giustiniana reported to her lover. "He kept me company for a long time, and we spoke very freely. I appreciated our conversation today immensely—more than usual. He is the most useful man to society. . . . But beyond that, he talked a lot about you and he praised you for the virtues men should want to be praised for—the goodness of your soul and the truthfulness of your spirit."

For several years Consul Smith's library had been a second home for Andrea. He continued to visit the consul regularly during his secret affair with Giustiniana, helping him catalogue his art and book collections. Nearly two years had gone by since the two lovers first met in that house. As Andrea worked, he luxuriated in tender memories of those earlier days, when they had been falling in love among the beautiful pictures and the rare books. "Everything there [reminds] me of you. . . . Oh God, Giustiniana, my idol, do you remember our happiness there?"

In reality, Andrea stopped at the consul's more out of a sense of duty and gratitude than for pleasure. The old man could be demanding. "When he starts talking after his evening tea, he never stops," Andrea reported with a sense of fatigue. "He generally asks me to stay on even while he has himself undressed." These man-to-man ramblings often touched on the Wynnes, and on several occasions Andrea could not help but notice with amusement the vaguely lustful tone Smith had begun to use when he talked about Giustiniana.

Inevitably, as Andrea and Giustiniana's lives became more entwined and inextricable, so the hopelessness of their situation gradually sank in, bringing with it more tension and crises. Andrea filled his letters with declarations of love and devotion, but he never offered much to look forward to—there was no long-term plan that, however vague, might allow Giustiniana to dream about a future together. Instead, he made offhand remarks about how much simpler it would be if she were married to someone else or, better still, if she were a young widow "so that we wouldn't have to take all these precautions and I could show the world how much I adore you."

Giustiniana was having a harder time than Andrea. Her letters, always more impulsive and emotional than his, grew wilder as she swung between bliss and despair. Venice could seem such a hostile place—a watery labyrinth of mirrors and shadows and whispers. She could not get a grip on Andrea's life or, as a consequence, on her own. The more time passed, the more she felt she was losing her way. Again and again she was overcome by waves of jealousy that brought her to breaking point.

Caterina (Cattina) Barbarigo was a great beauty and a notorious *femme fatale*. She held court in a *casino* that was much in vogue among progressive patricians and viewed with suspicion by the inquisitors. Though older than Andrea—she was married and the mother of two beautiful daughters—she liked surrounding herself with promising young men. He, in turn, was delighted to be drawn into her circle of friends—even at the cost of hurting Giustiniana's feelings. "All day you've been at Cattina Barbarigo's, haven't you?" she asked accusingly. "Enough, I shan't complain about it. But why have I not seen you? Why have I not received a line from you? Now that I think of it, it is perhaps better not to have received a note from you because you probably would have written late at night, in haste, and maybe only out of a sense of duty. Tomorrow, perhaps, you will write to me with greater ease." But there was no letter on the following day, or the next, or the one after that. On the fourth day of silence her anxiety turned into rage:

> You should be ashamed of yourself, Memmo. Could one possibly behave worse toward a lover one claims to be desperately in love with? I write to you on Saturday, and you don't answer because you are at Barbarigo's house. Sunday I never see you even though I spend the entire day at my window. And no letter—even though you know very well that on Mondays I go out and you should want to find out what the plan is in order to see me. Or perhaps you did write to me but your friend could not deliver? Do you suppose I will believe that you could not find another way of getting a letter to me, considering I had been two days without any news about you? . . . My mother has been ill for many days, and we could have been seeing each other with fewer precautions. But no—Memmo is having fun elsewhere. He does not even think about Giustiniana except when a compelling urge forces him to.

*What must I think? I hear from all sides about your new games
and your oh-so-beloved old friendships.*

Naturally, Andrea pleaded complete innocence: "For heaven's
sake, don't be so mean. What rendezvous are you talking about?
What have I done to merit such scorn? My dear sweet one, you
must quiet down. Trust me or else you'll kill me." He explained,
rather obliquely, that tactical considerations and nothing else occasionally forced him to be silent for a few days or to interrupt the
flow of letters. But she should never forget that if he sometimes
made himself scarce, it was for *her* sake and certainly not because
he was chasing young ladies around: "You know I love you, and
for that very reason, instead of complaining about your perpetual
diffidence, I only worry about your position. I would have written
to you every day to tell you what I was up to, but you know how
afraid I am about writing to you—your mother is capable of all
sorts of beastliness. All I care about is making sure the members of
your household and our enemies and the crowd of people that follow every step we take do not discover our relationship by some
act of imprudence on our part."

Giustiniana was not reassured by Andrea's words. In fact, his
shifty attitude was making her more upset and more defiant:

*How could you swear to me that all you cared about was my
position, when in fact you were merely trying to get away from
me using prudence as a pretext to rush over to see N.*? Don't be so
sure of the power you have over me, for I shall break this bond of
ours. I have opened my eyes at last. My God! Who is this man to
whom I have given my deepest love! Leave me, please leave me
alone. I'm just a nuisance to you. Before long you will hate me.
You villain! Why did you betray me? . . . Everyone now speaks
of your friendship with N. At first you explained yourself, and so
I was at peace again and I even allowed you to be seen with her in
public . . . and after our reconciliation you rushed off to see her
again. What greater proof of your infidelity? Damn you! I am*

---

*Clearly a different N. from the one who was lending them the *casino*.

*so angry I cannot even begin to say all I want. . . . Don't even
come near me, I don't want to see you. . . . Now I see why you told
me to pretend that our friendship was over; now I plainly see how
fake your sincerity was, your infamous caution. . . . Now I know
you. Did you think you could make fun of me forever? Enough. I
cease to be your plaything.*

Were the rumors true? Was Andrea pursuing N., or was Giustiniana working herself into a spiral of groundless jealousy? Whatever was going on, Andrea had clearly underestimated the depth
of Giustiniana's desperation. He suddenly found himself on the
defensive, struggling to contain her rage: "How can I describe to
you the state I am in, you cruel woman? My mind is busy with a
thousand thoughts. I'm agitated and worried about a thousand
questions. And you, for heaven's sake, find nothing better to do
than to treat me in the most inhuman way. Where does it all come
from? What have I done to deserve all this? . . . Can it be that you
still don't know my heart? . . . Come here, my sweet Giustiniana,
speak freely to your Memmo."

Andrea understood more plainly now that as long as Giustiniana
felt locked into a relationship with no future she would only become
more anguished and more intractable and their life would become
hell. But he remained ambivalent: "Tell me if you want to get yourself out of this situation you're in. Tell me the various possibilities,
and however much they might be harmful to me, if they will make
you happy. . . . Speak out, and you will see how I love you." Was he
conjuring up the idea of an elopement? Was he beginning to consider
a secret marriage, with all the negative consequences it would have
entailed? If so, he was going about it in a very circuitous and tentative
way, as if this were merely a short-term device to placate Giustiniana's wrath. In fact, already in his next letter he retreated to his older,
more traditional position: their happiness, as far as Andrea was concerned, hinged on finding Giustiniana a husband. "Alas, until you are
married and I am able to see you more freely, there won't be much to
gain. Meanwhile let us try to hurt each other as little as possible."

Giustiniana, however, had not exhausted her rage. Andrea's
letters suddenly seemed so petty and predictable. Where was

the strong, willful young man she had fallen so desperately in love with? In the increasingly frequent isolation of her room at Sant'Aponal, she decided to put an end to their love story. Better to make a clean break, as painful as it would be, than to endure the torture Andrea was inflicting upon her.

This is the last time I bother you, Memmo. Your conduct has been such that I now feel free to write you this letter. I do not blame you for your betrayal, your lack of gratitude, the scarcity of your love, your scorn. No, Memmo. I was very hurt by all this, but I've decided not to complain or to wallow in vindictive feelings. You know how much I have loved you; you know what a perfect friend I have been to you. God knows that I had staked my entire happiness on our love. You knew it. Yet you allowed me to believe that you loved me with the same intensity. . . . And now that I know you, that I see how you tricked me, I give you an even greater token of my passion by breaking this tenacious bond. After all your abuse, your disloyalty, I was already on the verge of abandoning you. But your scorn of the last few days, the lack of any effort on your part to explain yourself, your continuous indulgence in the things you know make me unhappy, your complete estrangement have finally made me see that you could not hope for a better development. I have opened my eyes, I have learned to know you and to know me, and I have become adamant in my resolution never to think again about a man capable of such cruelty, such contempt, such utter disloyalty to me.

So everything between us is over. I know I cannot give you a greater pleasure than this. . . . And I also know that my peace of mind, my well-being, maybe even my life will depend on this break. I shall never hate you (see how much I can promise), but I will feel both pleasure and displeasure in your happiness as well as in your misfortunes. I will say more: I will never again love anyone the way I have loved you, ungrateful Memmo. You will oblige me by handing over all my letters . . . as they serve no other purpose than to remind me of my weakness and your wickedness. So please give them back so that I may burn them and remove from my sight everything that might remind me of all I have done for such an undeserving man.

    Here is your portrait, once my delight and comfort, which I don't want anywhere near me. Ask the artist* to bring me the one you had commissioned of me—I will pay for it in installments and keep it. Your vanity has already been sufficiently satisfied as it is. Everyone knows how much I have loved you. Please don't let me see you for another few days. I know how good our several days' separation has been for me, and I have reason to believe that I will benefit by extending it. I forgive you everything. I have deserved this treatment because I was foolish enough to believe that you were capable of a sincere and enduring commitment; and I guess you are not really to blame if you can't get over your own fickleness, which is so much a part of your nature. I ask neither your friendship nor a place in your memory. I want nothing more from you. Since I can no longer be the most passionate lover, I don't want to be anything else to you. Adieu, Memmo, count me dead. Adieu forever.

Giustiniana's dramatic break cleared the air. Within days the poisonous atmosphere that had overwhelmed them dissolved and they were in each other's arms again, filled with love and desire. Giustiniana even laughed at her own foibles:

    Oh God, my Memmo, how can I express these overflowing emotions? How can I tell you that . . . you are my true happiness, my only treasure? Lord, I am crazy. Crazy in the extreme. And what about all that happened to me in the last few days? Do you feel for me? . . . With my suspicions, my jealousy, my love. . . . Only you can understand me because you know my heart and the power you have over it. . . . I don't know how my mood has changed so quickly, and why I even run the risk of telling you this! No, I really don't know what's happening to me. . . . Anyway, we'll see each other tomorrow. Meanwhile I think I'll just go

---

*Andrea had commissioned a portrait from "Nazari," possibly Bartolomeo Nazzari (1699–1758), a fashionable artist in Venice at the time and a protégé of Consul Smith. Alas, the portrait has never been found.

straight to bed. After having been wrapped up in sweet thoughts
about my Memmo and so full of him, I couldn't possibly spend
the rest of the evening with the silly company downstairs!

Andrea was so eager to hold Giustiniana in his arms again that
even the twenty-four-hour wait now seemed unendurable to him.
Alone in his room at Ca' Memmo he let himself drift into erotic
fantasies, which he promptly relayed to his lover:

> *Oh, my little one, my little one, may I entertain you with my*
> *follies? Do you have a heart to listen? I am so full of dreams*
> *about you that the slightest thing is enough to put me into a cos-*
> *mic mood. For example, I read one of your letters . . . and I focus*
> *on a few characters in your handwriting and I begin to stare at*
> *them and I tell myself: here my adorable Giustiniana wrote . . .*
> *and sure enough I see your hand, your very own hand, oh Lord, I*
> *kiss your letter not finding anything else to kiss, and I press it*
> *against me as if it were you, oh, and I hug you in my mind, and*
> *it's really too much; what to do? I cannot resist any longer. Oh my*
> *Lord, oh my Lord, now another hand of yours is relieving me, oh,*
> *but I can't go on. . . . I cannot say more, my love, but you can*
> *imagine the rest. . . . Oh Lord, oh Lord. . . . I speak no more, I*
> *speak no more.*

In such moments of playful abandon Andrea felt he was capable
of doing "even the most irresponsible thing . . . yes . . . I feel this
urge to take you away and marry you." And when he opened
up that way, Giustiniana always gave herself completely: "My
Memmo, I shall always be yours. You enchant me. You overwhelm
me. I will never find another Memmo with all the qualities and all
the defects that I love about you. We are made for each other so
absolutely. All that needs to happen is for me to become less suspicious and for you to moderate that slight flightiness, and then we'll
be happy."

After these moments of ecstasy, however, the gloominess of
their situation would steal over their hearts once more. Andrea
wondered how their relationship could possibly survive. "We will
never have a moment of peace and quiet. Meanwhile, you, believ-

ing as you do in everything you hear. Good Lord, I don't know what to do anymore! You will never change as long as I have to be away from you. I see that it is impossible for you to believe that I am all yours, as I am, and it is impossible to change your mother, or your situation, so what am I to do?" he asked Giustiniana with quiet desperation. "I don't know how to hold on to you."

CHAPTER *Three*

In early December 1755, news quickly spread that Catherine Tofts, the elusive wife of Consul Smith, had died after a long illness. She had once been an active and resourceful hostess, often giving private recitals in her drawing room. There is a lovely painting by Marco Ricci, one of Smith's favorite artists, of Catherine singing happily with a chamber orchestra. But the picture was painted shortly after her marriage to Smith and before the death of her son. As the years went by, she was seen less and less (Andrea never mentions her in his letters). Toward the end of her life it was rumored that she had lost her mind and her husband had locked her up in a madhouse.

Smith organized a grand funeral ceremony, which was attended by a large contingent of Venice's foreign community (the Italians were absent because the Catholic Church forbade the public mourning of Protestants). A Lutheran merchant from Germany, a friend of the consul, recorded the occasion in his diary: "Signor Smith received condolences and offered everyone sweets, coffee, chocolate, Cypriot wine and many other things; to each one he gave a pair of white calfskin gloves in the English manner." Twenty-five gondolas, each with four torches, formed the procession of mourners. The floating cortege went down the Grand Canal, past the Dogana di Mare, across Saint Mark's Basin, and out to the Lido, where Catherine's body was laid to rest in the Protestant cemetery: "The English ships moored at Saint Mark's saluted the procession with a storm of cannon shots."[1]

The consul was eighty years old but still remarkably fit and energetic. He had no desire to slow down. By early spring gossips were whispering that his period of mourning was already over and he was eager to find a new wife—a turn of events that caused quite a commotion in the English community.

John Murray, the British Resident, had had a prickly relationship with Smith ever since he had arrived in Venice in 1751. Smith had vied for the position himself, hoping to crown his career by becoming the king's ambassador in the city where he had spent the better part of his life. But his London connections had not been strong enough to secure it, and Murray, a bon vivant with a keener interest in women and a good table than in the art of diplomacy, had been chosen instead. "He is a scandalous fellow in every sense of the word," complained Lady Mary Wortley Montagu, who, rather snobbishly, preferred the company of local patricians to that of her less aristocratic compatriots. "He is not to be trusted to change a sequin, despised by this government for his smuggling, which was his original profession, and always surrounded with pimps and brokers, who are his privy councillors."[2] Casanova, predictably, had a different view of Murray: "A handsome man, full of wit, learned, and a prodigious lover of the fair sex, Bacchus and good eating. I was never unwelcome at his amorous encounters, at which, to tell the truth, he acquitted himself well."[3]

Smith did not hide his disappointment. In fact he went out of his way to make Murray feel unwelcome, and the new Resident was soon fussing about the consul with Lord Holderness, the secretary of state, himself an old Venice hand and a friend to the Wynnes: "As soon as I got here I tried to follow your advice to be nice to Consul Smith. But he has played so many unpleasant tricks on me that I finally had to confront him openly. He promised me to be nice in the future—then he started again, forcing me to break all relations."[4]

Catherine's death and, more important, Smith's intention to marry again brought a sudden thaw in the relations between the Resident and the consul. Murray conceived the notion that his former enemy would be the perfect husband for his aging sister Elizabeth, whom he had brought over from London (perhaps Murray also calculated that their marriage would eventually bring the consul's prized art collection into his hands). Smith was actually quite fond of Betty Murray. He enjoyed her frequent visits at Palazzo Balbi. She was kind to him, and on closer inspection he found she was not unattractive. Quite soon he began to think seriously about marrying "that beauteous virgin of forty," as Lady Montagu called her.[5]

Murray and his sister were not alone in seeing the consul in a new light after Catherine's death. Mrs. Anna too had her eye on him, because she felt he would be the perfect husband for Giustiniana: Smith could provide her daughter a respectable position in society as well as financial security. Furthermore, he had been a friend of the family for twenty years, and he would surely watch over the rest of the young Wynnes—at least for the short time that was left to him. After all, wasn't such a solution the best possible way to fulfill the promise he had made to look after Sir Richard's family? Mrs. Anna began to lure the consul very delicately, asking him over to their house more frequently, showing Giustiniana off, and dropping a hint here and there. She set out to quash the competition from Betty Murray while attempting to preserve the best possible relations with her and her brother. Inevitably, though, tensions in their little group rose, and Betty Murray reciprocated by drawing the consul's attention to the fact that, as far as she could tell, Giustiniana still seemed very much taken with Andrea.

At first Giustiniana was stunned by her mother's plan, but she knew that the matter was out of her hands. And although she was only eighteen, she did not express disgust at the idea of marrying an octogenarian. She was fond of Smith, and she also recognized the material advantages of such a marriage. But all she really cared about was how the scheme would affect her relationship with Andrea. Would it protect their love affair, or would it spell the end? Would it be easier for them to see each other or more difficult? The consul was so old that the marriage was bound to be short-lived. What would happen after he died?

Andrea had often said, sometimes laughing and sometimes not, that their life would be so much happier if only Giustiniana were married or, even better, widowed. It had been fanciful talk. Now, quite unexpectedly, they contemplated the very real possibility that Giustiniana might be married soon and widowed not long after. Andrea became quite serious. He set out his argument with care:

> *I want you to understand that I want such a marriage for love of you. As long as he lives, you will be in the happiest situation. . . .*

You will not have sisters-in-law and brothers-in-law and God knows who else with whom to argue. You will have only one man to deal with. He is not easy, but if you approach him the right way from the beginning, he will eagerly become your slave. He will love you and have the highest possible regard for you. . . . He is full of riches and luxuries. He likes to show off his fortune and his taste. He is vain, so vain, that he will want you to entertain many ladies. This will also open up the possibility for you to see gentlemen and be seen in their company. We will have to behave with great care so that he does not discover our feelings for each other ahead of time.

Andrea began to support Mrs. Anna's effort by dropping his own hints to Smith about what a sensible match it would be. Giustiniana stepped into line, though warily, for she continued to harbor misgivings. As for the consul, the mere prospect of marrying the lovely girl he had seen blossom in his drawing room put him into a state of excitement he was not always able to contain. Andrea immediately noticed the change in him. "[The other evening] he said to me, 'Last night I couldn't sleep. I usually fall asleep as soon as I go to bed. I guess I was all worked up. I couldn't close my eyes until seven, and at nine I got up, went to Mogliano,* ate three slices of bread and some good butter, and now I feel very well.' And to show me how good he felt he made a couple of jumps that revealed how energetic he really is."

Word about a possible wedding between the old consul and Giustiniana began to circulate outside the English community and became the subject of gossip in the highest Venetian circles. Smith did little to silence the talk. "He is constantly flattering my mother," Giustiniana wrote to Andrea. "And he lets rumors about our wedding run rampant." Andrea told Giustiniana he had just returned from Smith's, where a most allusive exchange had taken place in front of General Graeme,† the feisty new commander in chief of Venice's run-down army, and several other guests:

*The consul had a villa at Mogliano Veneto, on the mainland.
†General William Graeme, a Scotsman, had succeeded Marshal Johann Matthias Shulenburg that very same year (1756). Throughout its history the Republic hired non-Venetians to lead its land forces.

*[The consul] introduced the topic of married women and after
counting how many there were in the room he turned to me:*

"Another friend of yours will soon marry, " he said.

*"I wonder who this friend might be that he did not trust me
enough to tell me," I replied.*

*"Myself. . . . Isn't that the talk of the town? Why, the General
here told me that even at the doge's . . ."*

*". . . Absolutely, I was there too. And Graeme's main point
was that having mentioned the rumor to you, you did nothing to
deny it."*

*"Why should I deny something which at my old age can only
go to my credit?"*

Andrea had come away from the consul's rather flustered, not
quite knowing whether Smith had spoken to him "truthfully or in
jest." He asked Giustiniana to keep him informed about what she
was hearing on her side. "I am greatly curious to know whether
there are any new developments." No one really knew what the
consul's intentions were—whether he was going to propose to
Giustiniana or whether he had decided in Betty's favor. It was not
even clear whether he was really interested in marriage or whether
he was having fun at everyone's expense. Giustiniana too found it
hard to read Smith's mind. "He was here until after four," she
reported to her lover. "No news except that he renewed his invitation to visit him at his house in Mogliano and that he took my hand
as he left us."

Andrea feared Smith might be disturbed by the rumors, ably
fueled by the Murray clan, that his affair with Giustiniana was
secretly continuing, so he remained cautious in his encouragement: perhaps the consul felt he needed more time; his wife, after
all, had only recently been buried. Mrs. Anna, however, was determined not to lose the opportunity to further her daughter's suit,
and she eagerly stepped up the pressure.

In the summer months wealthy Venetians moved to their estates in
the countryside. As its maritime power had started to decline in the

sixteenth century, the Venetian Republic had gradually turned to the mainland, extending its territories and developing agriculture and manufacture to sustain its economy. The nobility had accumulated vast tracts of land and built elegant villas whose grandeur sometimes rivaled that of great English country houses or French châteaux. By the eighteenth century the villa had become an important mark of social status, and the *villeggiatura*—the leisurely time spent at the villa in the summer—became increasingly fashionable. Those who owned a villa would open it to family and guests for the season, which started in early July and lasted well into September. Those who did not would scramble to rent a property. And those who could not afford to rent frantically sought invitations. A rather stressful bustle always surrounded the comings and goings of the summer season.

Venetians were not drawn to the country by a romantic desire to feel closer to nature. Their rather contrived summer exodus, which Goldoni had ridiculed in a much-applauded comedy earlier that year at the Teatro San Luca,* was a whimsical and ostentatious way of transporting to the countryside the idle lifestyle they indulged in during the winter in the city. In the main, the country provided, quite literally, a change of scenery, as if the *burchielli*, the comfortable boats that made their way up the Brenta Canal transporting the summer residents to their villas, were also laden with the elaborate sets of the season's upcoming theatrical production.

Consul Smith had been an adept of the *villeggiatura* since the early twenties, but it was not until the thirties that he had finally bought a house at Mogliano, north of Venice on the road to Treviso, and had it renovated by his friend Visentini. The house was in typical neo-Palladian style—clear lines and simple, elegant spaces. It faced a small formal garden with classical statues and potted lemon trees arranged symmetrically on the stone parterre. A narrow, well-groomed alley, enclosed by low, decorative gates, ran parallel to the house, immediately beyond the garden, and provided a secure route for the morning or evening walk. The consul had moved part of his collection to adorn the walls at his house in

*Goldoni wrote his *Villeggiatura* trilogy for the Carnival season of 1756.

Mogliano, including works by some of his star contemporaries—
Marco and Sebastiano Ricci, Francesco Zuccarelli, Giovan Battista
Piazzetta, Rosalba Carriera—as well as old masters such as Bellini,
Vermeer, Van Dyck, Rembrandt, and Rubens. "As pretty a collec-
tion of pictures as I have ever seen,"[6] the architect Robert Adam
commented when he visited Smith in the country.

The consul had often invited the Wynnes to see his beautiful
house at Mogliano. Now, in the late spring of 1756, he renewed his
invitation with a more urgent purpose: to pay his court to Giustiniana with greater vigor so that he could come to a decision about
proposing to her, possibly by the end of the summer. Mrs. Anna,
usually rather reluctant to make the visit on account of the logisti-
cal complications even a short trip to the mainland entailed for a
large family like hers, decided she could not refuse.

The prospect of spending several days in the clutches of the
consul did not particularly thrill Giustiniana. She told Andrea she
wished the old man "would just leave us in peace" and cursed "that
wretched Mogliano a hundred times." But Andrea explained to her
that Smith's invitation was a good thing because it meant he was
serious about marrying her and was hopefully giving up on the
spinsterish Betty Murray. Giustiniana continued to dread the visit—
and the role that, for once, both Andrea and her mother expected
her to play. Her anguish only increased during the daylong trip
across the lagoon and up to Mogliano. But once she was out in the
country and had settled into Smith's splendid house, she rather
began to enjoy her part and to appreciate the humorous side of her
forced seduction of *il vecchio*—the old man. The time she spent
with Smith became good material with which to entertain her real
lover:

> *I've never seen Smith so sprightly. He made me walk with him
> all morning and climbed the stairs, skipping the steps to show his
> agility and strength. [The children] were playing in the garden
> at who could throw stones the furthest. And Memmo, would you
> believe it? Smith turned to me and said, "Do you want to see me
> throw a stone further than anyone else?" I thought he was kid-
> ding, but no: he asked [the children] to hand him two rocks and
> threw them toward the target. He didn't even reach it, so he*

blamed the stones, saying they were too light. He then threw more stones. By that time I was bursting with laughter and kept biting my lip.

The visit to Mogliano left everyone satisfied, and even Giustiniana returned in a good mood. Smith was by now apparently quite smitten and intended to continue his courtship during the course of the summer. As this would have been impossible if the Wynnes stayed in Venice, he suggested to Mrs. Anna that she rent from the Mocenigo family a pleasant villa called Le Scalette in the fashionable village of Dolo on the banks of the Brenta, a couple of hours down the road from Mogliano. Smith himself handled all the financial transactions, and since the rental cost would have been high for Mrs. Anna it is possible that he also covered part of the expenses.

Needless to say, Giustiniana was not happy about the arrangement. It was one thing to spend a few days at Mogliano, quite another to have Smith hovering around her throughout the summer. Meanwhile, where would Andrea be? When would they be able to see each other? She could not stand the idea of being separated from her lover for so long. Andrea again tried to reassure her. There was nothing to worry about: it would probably be simpler to arrange clandestine meetings in the country than it was in town. He would come out as often as possible and stay with trusted friends—the Tiepolos had a villa nearby. He would visit her often. It would be easy.

In the meantime Andrea decided he needed to spend as much time as possible with the consul in order to humor him, allay his suspicions, and steer him ever closer toward a decision about Giustiniana. It soon became apparent that the consul, too, wished to keep his young friend close to him. He said he wanted Andrea at his side to deal with his legal and financial affairs but he was probably putting him to the test, observing him closely to see if he still loved Giustiniana. Never before had he seemed so dependent on him. The two of them became inseparable—an unusual couple traveling back and forth between Venice and Mogliano, where Smith's staff was preparing the house for the summer season, and making frequent business trips to Padua.

Giustiniana was left to brood over her future alone. She complained about Andrea's absences from Venice and dreaded the uncertainty of her situation. She did not understand his need to spend so much time with that "damned old man." She felt they were "wasting precious time" that they could be spending together. Yet her reproaches always gave way to words of great tenderness. During one of Andrea's overnight trips to the mainland with the consul, she wrote:

> *You are far away, dear Memmo, and I am not well at all. I am happier when you are here in town even when I know we won't be speaking because I always bear in mind that if by happy accident I am suddenly free to see you, I can always find a way to tell you. You might run over to see me; I might see you at the window. . . . And so the time I spend away from you passes less painfully. . . . But days like this one are very long indeed and seem never to end. . . . Though I must say there have been some happy moments too, as when I woke up this morning and found two letters from you that I read over and over all day. They gave me so much pleasure. . . . I still have other letters from you, which I fortunately have not yet returned to you—those too were brought out and given a "tour" today. And your portrait—oh, how sweetly it occupied me! I spoke to it, I told it all the things that I feel when I see you and I am unable to express to you when I am near you. . . . My mother took me out with her to take some fresh air, and we went for a ride ever so lazily down the canal. And as by chance she was as quiet as I was, I let myself go entirely to my thoughts. Then, emerging from those thoughts, I looked around eagerly, as if I were about to run into you. Every time I saw a boat that seemed to me not unlike yours, I couldn't stop believing that you might be in it. The same thing happened when we got back home—a sudden movement outside brought me several times to the window where I always sit when I hope to see you. . . . The evening hours were very uncomfortable. We had several visitors, and I could not leave the company. But in the end they did not bother my heart and thoughts so much because I went to sit in a corner of the room. Now, thank God, I have retired and*

I am with you with all my heart and spirit. This is always the happiest moment of the evening for me. And you, my soul, what are you doing in the country? Are you always with me? Tonnina now torments me because she wants to sleep and is calling me to bed. Oh, the fussy girl! But I guess I must please her. I will write to you tomorrow. Wouldn't it be sweet if I could dream I was with you? Farewell, my Memmo, farewell. I adore you. . . . Memmo, I always, always think of you, always, my soul, yes, always.

As the *villeggiatura* approached, Giustiniana's anxiety increased. Andrea still spent most of his time with the consul, working for their future happiness, as he put it. But there was no sign that the consul was any closer to a decision. Furthermore, the idea of spending the summer in the countryside deceiving the old man disconcerted her. She grew pessimistic and began to fear that nothing good would ever come of their cockamamie scheme. Andrea was being unrealistic, she felt, and it was madness to press on: "Believe me, we have nothing to gain and much to lose. . . . We are bound to commit many imprudent acts. He will surely become aware of them and will be disgusted with both you and me. You will have a very dangerous enemy instead of a friend. As for my mother, she will blame us as never before for having disrupted what she believes to be the best plan she ever conceived." The two of them carried on regardless, Giustiniana complained—she by ingratiating herself to the consul every time she saw him "as if I were really keen to marry him," thereby pleasing her mother to no end, and Andrea by "lecturing me all day that I should take him as a husband." But even if she did, even if the consul, at the end of their machinations, asked her to marry him and she consented, did Andrea really think things would suddenly become easier for them or that the consul would come to accept their relationship? "For heaven's sake, don't even contemplate such a crazy idea. Do you believe he would even stand to have you in his house or see you next to me? God only knows the scenes that would take place and how miserable my life would become, and his and yours too."

In June, as Giustiniana waited for the dreaded departure to the countryside, Andrea's trips out of town increased. There was more to attend to than the consul's demands: his own family expected him to pay closer attention to the Memmo estates on the mainland now that his uncle was dead. As soon as he was back in Venice, though, he immediately tried to comfort Giustiniana by reiterating the logic behind their undertaking. He insisted that there was no alternative: the consul was their only chance. He argued for patience and was usually persuasive enough that Giustiniana, by her own admission and despite all her reservations, would melt "into a state of complete contentment" just listening to him speak.

Little by little she was beginning to accept the notion that deception was a necessary tool in the pursuit of her own happiness. But the art of deceit did not come naturally to her. When she was not in Andrea's arms, enthralled by his reassuring words, her own, more innocent way of thinking quickly took over again, and she would panic: "Oh God, Memmo, you paint a picture of my present and my future that makes me tremble. You say Smith is my only chance. Yet if he doesn't take me, I lose you, and if he does take me, I can't see you. And you wish me to be wise. . . . Memmo, what should I do? I cannot go on like this."

"Ah, Memmo, I am here now and there is no turning back."

In early July, after weeks of preparations, the Wynnes had finally traveled across the lagoon and up the Brenta Canal and had arrived at Le Scalette, the villa the consul had arranged for them to rent. The memory of her tearful separation from Andrea in Venice that very morning—the Wynnes and their small retinue piling onto their boat on the Grand Canal while Andrea waved to her from his gondola, apparently unseen by Mrs. Anna—had filled Giustiniana's mind during the entire boat ride. She had lain on the couch inside the cabin, pretending to sleep so as not to interrupt even for an instant the flow of images that kept her enraptured by sweet thoughts of Andrea. Once they arrived at the villa and had settled in, she cast a glance around her new surroundings and had discovered that the house and the garden were actually very nice and the setting on the Brenta could not have been more pleasant. "Oh, if only you were here, how delightful this place would be. How sweetly we could spend our time," she wrote to him before going to bed the first night.

The daily rituals of the *villeggiatura* began every morning with a cup of hot chocolate that sweetened the palate after a long night's sleep and provided a quick boost of energy. It was usually served in an intimate setting—breakfast in the boudoir. The host and hostess and their guests would exchange greetings and the first few tidbits of gossip before the morning mail was brought in. Plans for the day would be laid out. After the toilette, much of which was taken up by elaborate hairdressing in the case of the ladies, the members of the household would reassemble outdoors for a brief walk around the perimeter of the garden. Upon their return they might gather in the drawing room to play cards until it was time for lunch, a rather elaborate meal that in the grander houses was usually prepared under the supervision of a French cook. After-noons were taken up by social visits or a more formal promenade along the banks of the Brenta, an exercise the Venetians had dubbed *la trottata*. Often the final destination of this afternoon stroll was the *bottega*, the village coffeehouse where summer resi-dents caught up with the latest news from Venice. After dinner, the evening was taken up by conversation and society games. Blind-man's bluff was a favorite. In the larger villas there were also small concerts and recitals and the occasional dancing party.

Giustiniana did not really look forward to any of this. As soon as she arrived at Le Scalette she was seized by worries of a logisti-cal nature, wondering whether it would really be easier for her to meet Andrea secretly in the country than it had been in Venice. She looked around the premises for a suitable place where they could see each other and immediately reported to her lover that there was an empty guest room next to her bedroom. More important: "There is a door not far from the bed that opens onto a secret, nar-row staircase that leads to the garden. Thus we are free to go in and out without being seen." She promised Andrea to explore the sur-roundings more thoroughly: "I will play the spy and check every corner of the house, and look closely at the garden as well as the caretaker's quarters—everywhere. And I will give you a detailed report."

The villa next door belonged to Andrea Tron, a shrewd politician who never became doge but was known to be the most powerful man in Venice (he would play an important role in launching Andrea's career). Tron took a keen interest in his new neighbors. As an old friend of Consul Smith, he was aware that the death of Smith's wife had created quite an upheaval among the English residents. Like all well-informed Venetians, he also knew about Andrea and Giustiniana's past relationship and was curious to know whether it might still be simmering under the surface. He came for lunch and invited the Wynnes over to his villa. Mrs. Anna was pleased; it was good policy to be on friendly terms with such an influential man as Tron. She encouraged Giustiniana to be sociable and ingratiating toward their important neighbor. In the afternoon, Giustiniana took to sitting at the end of the garden, near the little gate that opened onto the main thoroughfare, enjoying the coolness and gazing dreamily at the passersby. Tron would often stroll past and stop for a little conversation with her.

Initially Giustiniana thought his large estate might prove useful for her nightly escapades. She had noticed that there were several *casini* on his property where she and Andrea could meet under cover of darkness. But thanks to her frequent trips to the servants' quarters, where she was already forming useful alliances, she had found out that Tron's *casini* were "always full of people and even if there should be an empty one, the crowds next door might make it too dangerous" for them to plan a tryst there.

In the end it seemed to her more convenient and prudent to make arrangements with their trusted friends, the Tiepolos: their villa was a little further down the road, but Andrea could certainly stay there and a secret rendezvous might be engineered more safely. Giustiniana even went so far as to express the hope that they might be able to replicate in the countryside "another Ca' Tiepolo," which had served them so well back in Venice. She added—her mind was racing ahead—that when Andrea came out to visit it would be best "if we meet in the morning because it is easy for me to get up before everyone else while in the evening the house is always full of people and I am constantly observed."

As Giustiniana diligently prepared the ground for a summer of lovemaking, she did wonder whether "all this information might ever be of any use to us." Andrea was still constantly on the move, a fleeting presence along the Brenta. When he was not with the consul at Mogliano, he was traveling to Padua on business, visiting the Memmo estate, or rushing back to Venice, where his sister, Marina, who had not been well for some time, had suddenly been taken very ill. Giustiniana might hear that Andrea was in a neighboring village, on his way to see her. Then she would hear nothing more. Every time she started to dream of him stealing into her bedroom in the dead of night or surprising her at the village *bottega*, a letter would reach her announcing a delay or a change of plans. So she waited and wrote to him, and waited and wrote:

I took a long walk in the garden, alone for the most part. I had your little portrait with me. How often I looked at it! How many things I said to it! How many prayers and how many protestations I made! Ah, Memmo, if only you knew how excessively I adore you! I defy any woman to love you as I love you. And we know each other so deeply and we cannot enjoy our perfect friendship or take advantage of our common interests. God, what madness! Though in these cruel circumstances it is good to know that you love me in the extreme and that I have no doubts about you: otherwise what miserable hell my life would be.

A few days later she was still on tenterhooks:

I received your letter just as we got up from the table and I flew to a small room, locked myself in, and gave myself away to the pleasure of listening to my Memmo talk to me and profess all his tenderness for me and tell me about all the things that have kept him so busy. Oh, if only you had seen me then, how gratified you would have been. I lay nonchalantly on the couch and held your letter in one hand and your portrait in the other. I read and reread [the letter] avidly, and for a moment I abandoned that pleasure to indulge in the other pleasure of looking at you. I pressed one and the other against my bosom and was overcome by waves of tenderness. Little by little I fell asleep. An hour and a half later I awoke, and now I am with you again and writing to you.

Andrea was finally on his way to see Giustiniana one evening when he was reached by a note from his brother Bernardo, telling him that their sister, Marina, was dying. Distraught, he returned to Venice and wrote to Giustiniana en route to explain his change of plans. She immediately wrote back, sending all her love and sympathy:

> *Your sister is dying, Memmo? And you have to rush back to Venice? . . . You do well to go, and I would have advised you to do the same. . . . But I am hopeful that she will live. . . . Maybe your mother and your family have written to you so pressingly only to hasten your return. . . . If your sister recovers, I pray you will come to see me right away. . . . And if she should pass away, you will need consolation, and after the time that decency requires you will come to seek it from your Giustiniana.*

In this manner, days and then weeks went by. Eventually, Giustiniana stopped making plans for secret encounters. There were moments during her lonely wait when she even worried about the intensity of her feelings. What was going on in *his* mind, in *his* heart? She had his letters, of course. He was usually very good about writing to her. But his prolonged absence disoriented her. She needed so much to see him—to see him in the flesh and not simply to conjure his image in a world of fantasy. "I tremble, Memmo, at the thought that my excessive love might become a burden on you," she wrote to him touchingly. ". . . I have no one else but you. . . . Where are you now, my soul? Why can't I be with you?"

While she longed for Andrea to appear in the country, Giustiniana also forced herself to be graceful with the consul. He called on the Wynnes regularly, coming by for lunch and sometimes staying overnight at Le Scalette, throwing the household into a tizzy because of his surprise arrivals and the late hours he kept. He took Giustiniana out on walks in the garden and spent time with the family, lavishing his attention on everyone. There was no question in anybody's mind that the old man was completely taken with Giustiniana and that he was courting her with the intention of marriage. Even the younger children had come to assume that the consul had been "tagged" and already "belonged" to their older sister, as Giustiniana put it in her letters to Andrea.

As she waited for her lover, Giustiniana watched with mild bewilderment the restrained embraces between her sister Tonnina and her young fiancé, Alvise Renier, who was summering in a villa nearby. "Poor fellow!" she wrote to Andrea. "He takes her in his arms, holds her close to him, and still she remains indolent and moves no more than a statue. Even when she does caress him she is so cold that merely looking at her makes one angry. I don't understand that kind of love, my soul, because you set me on fire if you so much as touch me." She was being a little hard on her youngest sister. After all, Tonnina was only thirteen and Alvise little older than that; it was a fairly innocent first love. But of course every time Giustiniana saw them together she longed to be in the arms of her impetuous lover.

Mrs. Anna, unaware of the heavy flow of letters between Le Scalette and Ca' Memmo, could not have been more pleased at how things were developing. With Andrea out of the way, the consul seemed increasingly comfortable with the idea of marrying Giustiniana. It was not unrealistic to expect a formal proposal by the end of the season. The other summer residents followed with relish the comings and goings at the Wynnes'. The consul's visits were regularly commented upon at the *bottega* in Dolo, as was Andrea's conspicuous absence. Were they still seeing each other behind the consul's back, or had their love affair finally succumbed to family pressures? Giustiniana's young Venetian friends often put her on the spot when she appeared to fetch her mail. However circumspect she had to be, she could not give up the secret pleasure of letting people know, in her own allusive way, that she still loved Andrea deeply. "Today we were talking about how the English run away from passions whilst the Italians seem to embrace them," she reported. "I was asked somewhat maliciously what I thought of the matter. I replied that life is quite short and that a well-grounded passion for a sweet and lovable person can give one a thousand pleasures. In such cases, I said, why run away from it? The same person pressed on: 'What if that passion is strongly opposed or if it is hurtful?' I answered that once a passion is developed it must always be sustained. . . . Must I really care about what these silly people think? I have too much vanity to disown in public a choice that I have made."

The consul's repeated visits—and Andrea's continued absence—created an air of inevitability about her future marriage that took its toll on Giustiniana. In public, she did her best to put on a brave front. But as soon as she was alone the gloomiest premonitions took hold of her. The hope that when it was all over—when the marriage had taken place—she would be free to give herself completely to the man she loved sustained her through the performance she was putting on day after day. But she could not rid herself of the fear that for all their clever scheming, once the consul married her she would not be able to see Andrea at all. As an English friend summering by the Brenta whispered to her one day, "I know my country well, and I am quite sure the first person Smith will ban from his house will be Memmo." She wrote to Andrea:

Alas, I know my country too! So what is to be done? Wait until he dies to be free? And in the meantime? And afterward? He might live with me for years, while I cannot live without you for a month. . . . True, any other husband would stop me from seeing you without having the advantages Smith has to offer, including his old age. . . . But everything is so uncertain, and it seems to me that the future can only be worse than the present. Of course it would be wrong for the two of us to get married. I wouldn't want your ruin even if it gave me all the happiness I would feel living with you. No, my Memmo! I love you in the most disinterested and sincerest way possible, exactly as you should be loved. I do not believe we shall ever be entirely happy, but all the same I will always be yours, I will adore you, and I will depend on you all my life. . . . So I will do what pleases you, [but remember] that if Smith were to ask for my hand and my Memmo were not entirely happy about it I would instantly abandon Smith and everything else with him, for my true good fortune is to belong to you and you alone.

In August Marina's health briefly improved and Andrea was finally free to go to the country to see Giustiniana. He was not well—still recovering from a bad fever that had forced him to bed. But he decided to make the trip out to Dolo anyway and take advantage of the Tiepolos' open invitation. Giustiniana was in a frenzy of excitement. "Come quickly, my heart, now that your sister's condition allows you to. . . . I would do anything, anything for the pleasure of seeing you." It was too risky for Andrea to visit her house, so she had arranged to see him in the modest home of the mother of one of the servants, thanks to the intercession of a local priest in whom she had immediately confided. "I went to see it, and I must tell you it's nothing more than a hovel," she warned, "but it should suffice us." Alternatively, they could meet in the caretaker's apartment, which was reached "by taking a little staircase next to the stables."

These preparations were unnecessary. Andrea arrived by carriage late in the night, exhausted after a long detour to Padua he had made on behalf of the ever-demanding consul. He left his luggage at the Tiepolos' and immediately went off to surprise Giustiniana by sneaking up to her room from the garden.

The following morning, after lingering in bed in a joyful haze, she scribbled a note and sent it to Andrea care of the Tiepolos: "My darling, lovable Memmo, how grateful I feel! Can a heart be more giving? Anyone can pay a visit to his lover. But the circumstances in which you came to see me last night, and the manner and grace you showed me—nobody, nobody else could have done it! I am so happy and you are wonderful to me. When will I be allowed to show you all my tenderness?"

Giustiniana fretted about Andrea's health. He had not looked well, and she feared a relapse: "You have lost some weight, and you looked paler than usual. . . . I didn't want to tell you, my precious, but you left me worried. For the love of me, please take care of yourself. How much you must have suffered riding all night in the stagecoach, and possibly still with a fever. . . . My soul, the pleasure of seeing you is simply too, too costly." Yet she was so hungry for him after his long absence that she could hardly bear not to see him now that he was so close: "Maybe you will come again this evening. . . . Do not expose yourself to danger, for I would die if I were the cause of any ailment. . . . If you have fully recovered, do come, for I shall be waiting for you with the greatest impatience, but if you are still not well then take care of yourself, my soul. I will come to see you; I will . . . ah, but I cannot. What cruelty!"

Andrea settled in at the Tiepolos' for the rest of summer. His health fully regained and his sister apparently out of immediate danger, he was anxious to catch up on the time not spent with Giustiniana. They were soon back to their old routine, working their messengers to exhaustion and conniving with trusted allies to set up secret meetings. Giustiniana's muslins were swishing again as she rushed off on the sly for quick visits to the "hovel"—which she now called "our pleasure house"—or to the caretaker's, to the Tiepolos', or even to the village *bottega* if they were feeling especially daring. When they were not together, they sent notes planning their next escapade. Giustiniana was in heaven. There were no worries in her mind, no dark clouds in the sky: "Am I really entirely in your heart? My Memmo, how deeply I feel my happiness! What delightful pleasure I feel in possessing you. There were times, I confess, in which I doubted my own happiness. Now, Memmo, I believe in you completely, and I am the happiest woman in the world. What greater proof of tenderness, of friendship, of true affection can I possibly want from you, my precious one? My heart and soul, you are inimitable. And it will be a miracle if so much pleasure and joy do not drive me entirely mad."

In the tranquil atmosphere of the Venetian summer, when the days were held together by card games, a little gossip, and an evening *trottata*, the sudden burst of activity between the Tiepolos' villa and Le Scalette did not go unnoticed. There was much new talk about Andrea and Giustiniana among the summer crowd. Even certain members in the Wynne household grew worried. Aunt Fiorina, always sympathetic to their cause, had been aware of the intense correspondence between the two lovers over the course of the summer but had refrained from making an issue of it. When she learned that Andrea and Giustiniana were actually seeing each other, however, she put her foot down and subjected her niece to "a long rebuke." The stakes with the consul were too high for them to be playing such a dangerous game, she explained.

Fiorina's alarm presaged worse things to come. Andrea went back to Venice on family business for a few days. Giustiniana wrote to him several times, but the letters never reached him; her messenger had been intercepted. Someone in the Wynne household— perhaps in the servants' quarters—had betrayed Giustiniana and handed the letters over to Mrs. Anna. The last lines of a frantic message to Andrea are the only fragment that has survived to give us a sense of the panic and chaos that ensued:

> . . . the most violent remedies. It is known that I have written to Venice, but not to whom! Everyone, my Memmo, is spying on me. . . . Don't abandon me now, and don't take any chances by writing to me. I won't lose you, but if something violent were to happen, I feel capable of anything. If you leave me I shall die, my soul!

Alas, Mrs. Anna knew very well to whom Giustiniana had written in Venice because she was also in possession of some of Andrea's letters—letters she had intercepted before they could be delivered to her daughter. She confronted Giustiniana, shaking with anger. "All day was an absolute hell—if Hell can really be that horrible," Giustiniana wrote to Andrea a few days later, when she was finally able to seclude herself ("I must write to you where and when I can"). At the height of her fury Mrs. Anna threatened to sue Andrea and "expose him as a seducer who upsets peaceful families," she raged, "for the letters I have in my hands prove that he is just that." Giustiniana pleaded for mercy with such force and conviction that eventually she managed to calm her mother down. In tears, Mrs. Anna withdrew her threat but warned her daughter there would not be another reprieve: "I will have you watched all the time, I will keep my eyes wide open, I will know everything. And remember that I have enough in my hands to ruin Signor Memmo."

The worst was avoided—what could have been more nightmarish than seeing their love story torn to shreds in a courtroom? But the betrayal had suddenly exposed the secret life of the two lovers. The places they met, their secret arrangements, their promises of lifelong love and devotion—everything was now known to Mrs. Anna. She had a list of the names of their messengers and accomplices. There was not much she could do about the Tiepolos except prohibit her daughter from setting foot in their house. But within the Wynne household, retribution was swift. The servants who had abetted the lovers were given a scolding and punished harshly. Alvisetto, who had been in on the whole thing from the start, was sent away.

There is something deeply sad about Alvisetto's dismissal, which reminds us to what degree a servant's life was in the hands of his *padrone*—his master. In general the master of the house and his wife had a formal, even distant relationship with the servants. But the younger members of the household had a closer rapport with the house staff. They would often appear in the servants' quarters to trade gossip or ask a favor. And it was not uncommon for a daughter of the house to confide some of her secrets to a maid (or for a son to seek sexual favors). But it was always an imbalanced and ultimately ambiguous relationship. And there was often as much room for treachery as there was for connivance—on both sides. After all, Giustiniana found her allies in the kitchen at Le Scalette, but she had probably found her betrayer there as well. Goldoni made fun of the complicated relations between masters and servants in one of his most popular plays. But poor Alvisetto was nothing like "the wily and dumb" Truffaldino, the main character in *A Servant for Two Masters*. One has the feeling that, all along, he had been forced by Giustiniana and Andrea to cooperate with them against his better judgment. Now he was being made to pay, very dearly, for a mess that was not of his making. And they could do nothing to save him.

The two lovers managed to resume communications within a

few days. Giustiniana barricaded herself in a kindly peasant's home on the property, where she hastily scribbled her notes to Andrea. But seeing each other was out of the question, given the circumstances. "Ah, Memmo, what must I do? . . . Will I ever see you again? I love you more than ever, but I am losing you! . . . Help me, tell me what to do." It was not long before they found a solution. Andrea suggested he write a letter to Mrs. Anna, professing his undying love for Giustiniana and offering to marry her in a couple of years if Consul Smith did not make an offer. It was a bluff: Andrea and Giustiniana both knew he was not planning to make good on the promise. But he thought it would convince Mrs. Anna that his intentions were honorable and she might therefore allow them to see each other. It was a risky strategy for a short-term gain. Nevertheless, Giustiniana agreed to the plan and decided to bring her aunt Fiorina in on it to a point—telling her about the letter Andrea wished to write to Mrs. Anna but without explaining to her that it was a deception. Aunt Fiorina responded with mixed feelings. "There is no denying that Memmo loves you and that he is a gentleman," she said to her niece. His proposal was "very reasonable." The problem, as she saw it, was getting Mrs. Anna to consider listening to him. But she was willing to help.

Even with Aunt Fiorina on their side, Giustiniana felt that, in the end, success or failure hinged on Andrea finding the right tone and words with which to address her mother. Her instructions to him were very precise—and they showed a considerable determination to take charge of the situation.

You will begin your letter by complaining that I have not written to you. You will tell me that you know in your heart that I love you deeply. You will assure me that you love me in the extreme and that to prove it you had written to my mother because you wanted her to hear an important suggestion you had to make—at which point you will copy the letter you have prepared for her. The most important thing (and here, my dear, you need to be artful and I want you to trust me) is to show yourself resolute in offering to write up a document in which, as you have said, you will promise to marry me in two years if Smith or some better party does not come along and propose to me. Give several reasons why it would be advantageous for me to marry you and add that it is your deep love for me that brings you to make this proposition, which you already know will be embraced by me with all my heart. And say you will have to wait because your present circumstances do not allow you to go through with the proposal at this time but in two years things should happen that could make us happy and comfortable for the rest of our lives. . . . [Add] that we would be very careful to keep this promise a secret.

It is hard to imagine that deep in her heart Giustiniana, though fully aware it was all a scheme, did not hope it would all actually come true, and that in two years' time she would be married to Andrea. If she did, she kept it to herself.

Andrea struggled over a first draft. Giustiniana showed it to Fiorina, who was "satisfied with [Andrea's] sentiments" but a little daunted by the resentment he expressed toward Mrs. Anna. "She told me to tell you that to seduce that woman one must flatter her—not be aggressive." She asked Andrea to try again. "My love," she added to encourage him, "what happiness will come our way if we manage to deceive her! Either Smith will marry me, in which case we won't need [the subterfuge], or he won't marry me, in which case she certainly won't take away from the man whom she thinks will one day marry me the freedom to be with me from time to time."

Andrea's second draft, however, was even more disappointing.

My Memmo, this is not the sort of letter that will get us what we want. . . . It is weak and useless, so you will understand why I haven't shown it to my mother and not even to my aunt. The other one was stronger and would have served our purpose wonderfully if you had simply deleted the few lines in which you insulted my mother. . . . In this one I see only the lover. . . . So write a new letter or rewrite the first one the way I told you to. . . . Send it immediately. . . . My aunt has already asked me if it had arrived, and it would be a pity if she saw us so unhurried in a matter of such importance.

Part of the problem was that Andrea was holding back in case their plan backfired. In his drafts, he committed himself to marrying Giustiniana only in the vaguest terms, because he feared the letter might get him into trouble with his own family if Mrs. Anna misused it. Giustiniana guessed what was bothering him and came to his rescue, suggesting that he tell the truth to *his* mother, even let her read a few of Giustiniana's letters to convince her that they had no intention of following through, that it was only a scheme to deceive Mrs. Anna, and that she—Giustiniana—would "never accept your hand" because she was well aware of the damage she would cause to the Memmos. There is no evidence, however, that he followed her advice.

In none of their letters to each other did either Andrea or Giustiniana suggest that they might actually marry one day. They stubbornly kept the thought at bay. This is somewhat ironic: Mrs. Anna was growing increasingly fearful that the two lovers were going to marry whether she liked it or not. Indeed, she came to suspect, in the paranoid state she had slipped into after intercepting the latest batch of letters, that the two lovers had already wed in secret.

In this sense Andrea's concocted letter, once it was finally approved by its exacting editor and delivered, must have provided some relief to Mrs. Anna. But there was little else in it to mollify her, and the deceit ultimately made matters worse. At first she thought the letter was a hoax. When her sister Fiorina finally convinced her in good faith that it was authentic, Mrs. Anna explained to Giustiniana in very sobering terms why she could not accept Andrea's proposition. This is Giustiniana's account of her mother's reaction:

> *I have read Memmo's letter and I believe he honestly wishes to marry you. You like Memmo, Memmo loves you, and your union would certainly be desirable. But, my dear Giustiniana, you cannot be his wife. I will now tell you something you might not have known the rest of your life. My dear daughter, the marriage contract would never be approved. Anyone but a Venetian nobleman would be good for you. Think about it and decide for yourself. Do you want to be shunned by all and barred from entering any*

nobleman's home, quite apart from being hated by the Memmo
family . . . and doing so much harm to that poor man? And what
about the harm you would inflict on the children you two would
have? Come, my child, take courage. I can feel your pain in los-
ing the man you adore just at the time you felt so close to possess-
ing him. But if you love him, surely you will not want to ruin him
or his sons. Marry, and then you may carry on a friendship that is
so dear to you.

Her savvy line of reasoning was, in fact, surprisingly similar to
Andrea and Giustiniana's own way of thinking. It was also the first
time she showed any degree of empathy toward her daughter.
Despite her severity and her terrible scenes, she apparently understood what Giustiniana was going through (did it perhaps remind
her of some painful separation in her own youth?). Of course, it
is impossible to be certain how faithful a transcription of Mrs.
Anna's reaction this really was. Certainly, according to the version
Giustiniana supplied to Andrea, her mother even seemed to be
sanctioning the possibility that their love affair continue once she
was safely married.

In any case, Mrs. Anna was not finished. She told Giustiniana that as soon as they returned to Venice (the season was now
over, and the Wynnes were getting ready to leave Le Scalette),
she wanted to discuss things directly with Andrea. Meanwhile, she
instructed her daughter to write a letter making a formal request
for the return of all her correspondence, in which she was also to
refuse Andrea's hand: for his own good and that of his family, and
for the good of her brothers, whose future in England might be put
in jeopardy if she married a Catholic.

Shortly after the Wynnes returned to Venice, Mrs. Anna and
Andrea met face to face. This was their first encounter since
Andrea's *cacciata funesta*, his fateful banishment two years earlier,
and it was not easy for either of them. Still, they managed to be
polite, and Mrs. Anna even showed a little compassion, assuring Andrea that she did not harbor ill feelings toward him. She
understood how much they loved each other, she told him, and
was convinced that in the future they could be together, but for the

time being it was out of the question. This was a very sensitive moment, she explained: as he well knew, the consul was interested in marrying Giustiniana and the future of her family was at stake. Again she demanded that Andrea cease all communication with her daughter.

Subtly, Mrs. Anna was, in effect, entering into a secret pact with her archenemy. If he agreed to step back and allow her to bring her delicate transactions with the consul to a successful conclusion, she, in turn, would not obstruct their relationship in the future. Andrea agreed to her demands—after all, he had had the same objective all along. He promised he would not write and would not see Giustiniana until her marriage with the consul was sealed. Upon Mrs. Anna's insistence, he also wrote a letter to Fiorina renouncing his intention to marry Giustiniana in two years' time—a request he found easy to satisfy. Separately, Andrea wrote to Giustiniana that, given the circumstances, it would indeed be prudent to cease all contact. Mrs. Anna had scored a complete victory.

Giustiniana was stunned by Andrea's betrayal. She could not believe he had acquiesced to her mother's demands so meekly. "Do you believe I can live without writing or seeing you? . . . You ask too much. . . . I would rather die." Andrea tried to placate her, but he remained adamant: "We are made for each other, and everyone will see it in the future, but believe me, this is not the time. . . . We have no choice. . . . If you need something, send someone for me . . . [but] for heaven's sake do not write to me. . . . The best answer you can give to this letter is not to answer it. . . . Love me, Giustiniana. . . . Have faith in me. . . . I leave you now."

Giustiniana could not stop the rage growing within her:

If you are willing to feel content, I am not. You do not know me yet. I feel the most violent passion and am capable of anything. You have reduced me to a horrible state. Do you think I will simply wait peacefully as you amuse yourself with the best company and the fairest women in the country? Put yourself in my position, and tell me if you would feel at ease. Of course you

probably would because you don't understand these things. . . .
Meanwhile, I am left to wait with indifference for an uncertain
marriage. What kind of love is this? . . . Your letter made me
shed so many tears that I had to hide my face all morning. . . .
How did you have the heart to ask me to break off our relation-
ship? How could you not take pity on me, on my heart, on my
love? Memmo, I have no one else in the world but you, and now
you tell me you will no longer be mine?

Andrea was exasperated by her reaction. Even though he was
"afraid to break the agreement" with Mrs. Anna, he sent Giustiniana an angry note: "You have managed to turn my pain into wrath.
What must I do for you? Pray tell me, you beast. What kind of
love is this that you are never happy with what I do? I adore you
and the desire to live with you kills me a little more every day. . . .
My one sin is that I do not write to you, but how can I write to you?
You know very well all the risks involved."

The only reasonable thing to do, he insisted, was to fix their
attention on the consul and help Mrs. Anna achieve her goal as
quickly as possible. It was still the surest path to their happiness.
Although Giustiniana never ceased to be skeptical, Andrea's hope
that things would work out to their advantage increased every day.
"The time will soon come," he declared, "when I shall be able to
enjoy your happiness and the pleasure of showing the world how
much I love you." Once again he broke the embargo he had
solemnly accepted in order to explain to Giustiniana that, in fact,
things could not be going any better:

By God, Giustiniana, we are lucky . . . because the only way
to bring this comedy to a happy conclusion is through Smith. . . .
And we are luckier still because he is old, because he is rich, because
he is my friend, because he stands in awe of society, because he
stands in awe of me . . . because he is vain, because he is crazy,
and because he has everything we can possibly need. Must I say
more? Listen, the truth is that our present misfortune—having to
bear with it for so long—is really our greatest fortune, provided it
comes to an end. . . . I ask: if Smith had married you when he

knew my love for you was still too hot . . . would it really have been possible for me to come to you? Believe me, it takes time to seduce an old cat and then play him for a sucker. But now I know that I have prepared everything well, that I have brought him closer to me, that he loves us all the more and that he trusts us. I have made a great deal of progress, and I hope at least we shall be happy.

The old cat wasn't napping, though. Back in Venice after his *villeggiatura* in Mogliano, it did not take long for Smith to learn about Mrs. Anna's confrontation with Andrea and, even more infuriating for him, about Giustiniana's prostration at the thought of not seeing her lover anymore. Andrea and Giustiniana did not make things easier for themselves: they were incapable of observing the ban on their correspondence, and messengers were once again shuttling between them. Soon they began to see each other, sometimes even in Piazza San Marco or Campo Santo Stefano during the evening stroll. It was only a matter of time before someone told Smith, and there was no shortage of people in Venice willing to trade on the misfortune of others.

One such person was the Abbé Testagrossa, a shady character who eked out a living in Venice by means of flattery and gossip. He had found employment as a secretary in the French Embassy but was still in the habit of crying poverty to cadge his lunches and dinners, for which he would sing whatever tune was required. For anyone with a secret, he was a man to be kept at a distance. One evening Andrea and Giustiniana were talking in a secluded corner near Campo Santo Stefano when the Abbé Testagrossa appeared from nowhere and passed by them, smiling. Andrea became so worried that the abbé might create a scandal that he went out of his way to be nice to him, and next time he saw him he even invited him to lunch at Ca' Memmo. "What could I do?" he sheepishly explained to an even more anxious Giustiniana. "I ran into him on the water near my house, and he said to me, 'I no longer have a kitchen, and I am forced to go out begging for a meal here and there.' " Andrea reassured her that he had "no intention" of being nice to Testagrossa again and would "treat him with so much formality it will be plain to him that this [lunch] does not represent the resumption of a friendship. But you wouldn't have wanted me to get on the wrong side of this indiscreet chatterer, would you?"

Still, he agreed with Giustiniana that the abbé would probably try to "hurt" them anyway because of "the sheer weirdness of his character." Given what we know of Testagrossa, it is certainly plausible that he casually told the consul—perhaps over a meal at Palazzo Balbi—that he had seen the two lovers alone near Campo Santo Stefano.

August turned into September, and still the consul made no official proposal. Andrea grew desperate to know what might have been said to Smith. Was it enough to undo all the work he had accomplished over the summer? Somehow the whole enterprise seemed to be more difficult to manage in the city, with its malicious whispers and knowing conversations. Andrea sought the consul's company to keep a close eye on him. But he could not read him as well as in the past. At times Smith seemed his usual old self. At others, his voice would take on a tone of sarcasm that worried Andrea. Here is a fragment of a conversation he had with Smith, which he transcribed for Giustiniana:

> *"What is the matter, dear Memmo, that you should sigh so heavily?"*
> *"I don't know. I'm not feeling very well. Maybe the sirocco . . ."*
> *"Ah, but it must be something else. These are not sirocco sighs . . ."*

Had he discovered their plot? "And yet the man treats me kindly, in his islander's sort of way," Andrea mused.

There was increasing pressure at home as well. The Bentivoglios, a rich family from the mainland, had spoken to Pietro and Lucia Memmo, offering the hand of one of their daughters for Andrea. The Memmos had agreed to initiate a preliminary round of negotiations through the offices of an intermediary. At first

Andrea went along with it, hoping the talks would bog down on their own, as was so often the case in these complicated matrimonial deals. He told Giustiniana not to worry, assuring her that in the end nothing would come of it.

Far more worrisome to him was the growing distance of the consul. He stopped talking about marrying Giustiniana, and his bantering tone vanished entirely. And he was cold not just toward Andrea but toward Mrs. Anna as well. The sudden change in his attitude threw her into a state of near panic. One night she took a gondola to Ca' Memmo and demanded to see Andrea. His servant woke him, and Andrea straggled downstairs: "I get in the gondola, she tells the gondolier to get out of the boat, and then she blurts out, 'You're killing me, you're murdering me. . . . Are you a gentleman or a traitor, Memmo?' " Andrea tried to placate her fury and claimed that in spite of his feelings he was not seeing Giustiniana anymore. He agreed to talk directly to Smith and tell him their affair was finished. As a further reassurance, he let her in on the secret marriage negotiations with the Bentivoglios. Neither she nor the consul had anything to worry about, he said.

But that was only a delaying tactic. Discussions with the Bentivoglios were going nowhere, the principal reason being that Andrea was now refusing to cooperate. He realized it was a very advantageous match—as he put it, "it contains all the elements I would not have found separately in other offers." But he belonged "entirely" to Giustiniana. As long as their situation was not settled one way or another, he was not going to marry anyone else. The Memmos were concerned that other prominent Venetian families might step in and make a deal with the Bentivoglios. Andrea's dillydallying irked them, and they pressed him for a straight yes or no. When he refused to give his consent, his mother, Lucia, exploded.

For months she had been under the impression that relations had cooled between Andrea and Giustiniana and that the consul was indeed going to marry her son's lover. Suddenly confronted with Andrea's recalcitrance, she was seized by a horrifying vision—as Mrs. Anna had been before her. All her son's talk about the consul marrying Giustiniana was really just a front to cover an unspeakable truth: Andrea and Giustiniana were already secretly married. "So all I heard about Smith was not true!" she yelled at him. "Oh, my God, Andrea, you've done it. Tell me the truth: you've married Giustiniana. Or you've given your word that you will. One of the two, I'm sure."

His mother's onslaught hurt Andrea. How could she believe him capable of dishonoring the family name? But it was the spectacle of his old and feeble father "with tears in his eyes" that really broke his heart.

The plan Andrea and Giustiniana had worked on since the spring finally spun out of control. Talks with the Bentivoglios collapsed at the end of September. Andrea's family put the blame entirely on him, and his life at Ca' Memmo became intolerable. When Smith learned that Andrea would not be marrying the Bentivoglio girl after all, he felt that all his suspicions about the two young lovers had been indirectly confirmed. In a dramatic and painful confrontation, he accused Andrea of plotting against him behind his back. He dismissed any further talk of marrying Giustiniana and abruptly sent him away.

It was a terrible blow for Andrea. As he expected, Mrs. Anna railed against him for scuttling what had seemed to her a done deal. But he was stunned by the amount of criticism he received from all sides for his embarrassing failure. "I have lost much more than my friendship with Smith," he wrote self-pityingly to Giustiniana. "Everyone accuses me of being imprudent, disloyal, not enough of a friend to you. If Smith has decided to renounce the project of marrying you—they say—it is on account of my lack of honesty and wisdom." Giustiniana's worst fears had come true. She was so crushed, so disoriented by all the mayhem that she did not know what to say to Andrea anymore and withdrew into silence.

Within days Smith proposed to Betty Murray, who had been waiting in the wings all along. "Old Consul Smith, who buried his wife nine months ago, has thrown himself at my sister's feet but has not yet bent her to his will,"[7] the Resident wrote at the beginning of October, savoring the moment with mischievous pride. Her resistance, if ever there was any, did not last long. They were married by the end of the month.

The winter of 1756–1757 was the coldest in living memory. By late October, autumn's golden light turned to a chilly gray. The *bora* blew in from the north. Snow fell early, swirling over the dark, brackish water. Some days the temperature dropped so low that the lagoon was frozen solid. A thick silence enveloped the city, pierced only by the mournful toll of church bells and the isolated cries of gondoliers. Inside the crowded *botteghe* and *malvasie,* the talk among Venetians was mostly about the war that had broken out in the summer.

Ever since Austria had lost the rich eastern province of Silesia to Prussia in the War of the Austrian Succession of 1740–1748, it had schemed to reclaim it for the vast Habsburg Empire. With that objective in mind, Vienna had worked successfully to bring France, Prussia's traditional ally, to its side. Russia and the Electorate of Saxony also joined the new coalition. Suddenly surrounded by this powerful array of forces, Frederick the Great of Prussia, the restless "philosopher-king," struck an alliance with Great Britain and its German appendage, the Hanoverian state. In late August 1756 he staged a surprise attack against Saxony, the weakest link in the enemy camp, and marched all the way to Dresden.

Frederick's assault was the opening shot of the Seven Years' War, the last great conflict between the European powers before the French Revolution and one that would redraw the balance of power in favor of Great Britain and Prussia. The Venetian Republic never took part in that drawn-out war fought on three continents. Her neutrality, however, owed more to her growing irrelevance on the European stage than to her once proverbial

diplomacy. The city remained at peace but still suffered the indi-
rect consequences of the conflict. Trade plummeted, and the
economy entered a period of decline. Venice would feel more and
more isolated as the war dragged on, and a numbing fear of the
future would creep into the population.

At Ca' Memmo the atmosphere was particularly gloomy that
winter. Andrea's beloved sister, Marina, after a short reprieve, had
died in terrible pain at the end of the summer. His father, Pietro,
old and weak, was devastated by the loss of his daughter. Andrea
found him "sitting alone by the fire" on a cold day. "He didn't
know whether he wanted to eat or sleep." All his life Andrea had
looked up to his uncle in a way he never had to his father, whom he
considered excessively ingenuous and impractical. But he knew
the tired old man hunched in the armchair by the fire loved him
dearly, and there were times when he felt that his father understood, perhaps better than others, the depth of his feelings for
Giustiniana. Andrea did not expect their relationship to change in
any fundamental way at this stage in their lives, but now his filial
devotion stirred in him more strongly than it had in the past. "His
stomach convulsions do not let him sleep all night," he worried,
"not to mention the gout and the fever. Poor old man! If only
he were as sensible as he is generous, how much more I would
love him."

Andrea had always been on more intimate terms with his mother,
Lucia, but he saw little of her during that winter. The halls of Ca'
Memmo were so cold that she hardly ever left her apartment. It
wasn't just the chill in the air that kept her so withdrawn. The
Smith imbroglio had offended her deeply, and for months she continued to brood over Andrea's embarrassing actions in the frosty
confinement of her rooms.

Giustiniana herself remained so distant Andrea feared he would
lose her as well. "Our love has not vanished no matter how much it
has been threatened," he reminded her, gently suggesting new
approaches to deal with her furious mother. But Giustiniana was
still too dejected to give him anything more than passive, perfunc-
tory replies. He felt her slipping away. "Why don't you defend
me?" he complained. "Your mother hates me. . . . She slanders

me. . . . Why don't you show her how wrong she is? . . . Because you don't love me anymore. . . . Oh God, I am lost. My soul, my sweetest soul, think hard before you ruin me."

Despite the biting temperatures, Andrea came by the house at Sant'Aponal regularly. He stood shivering under Giustiniana's window while his gondola sloshed about in the freezing water. Sometimes she did not even come to the window. She left Andrea's letters unanswered for days and seldom went out, usually only walking the short distance to church with her mother when she did. Andrea's pleading became increasingly desperate: "Oh God, if you want me to cease tormenting you, let me at least believe that we part as good friends and that you would still consider me worthy of you if circumstances were different."

Winter seemed to drag on endlessly, but in early spring Venice gradually regained her scintillating colors. The narrow streets again bustled with activity. The canals filled with boats of every size. After months of hibernation, the chattering crowds returned to the Listone for their daily stroll. Giustiniana was not immune to the changes around her. She responded a little more warmly to Andrea's letters. Warily, she agreed to see him again in secret. Andrea was grateful and extremely solicitous. He fretted over her health and her diet and was full of practical attentions as well. "I must look for some reed matting so that room of Rosa's will be less uncomfortable," he wrote in a touching display of domesticity. "My heart, how much I love you. I'm so full of you and so happy you will be mine forever."

On the surface, things gradually went back to the way they had been before. Of course, Alvisetto was no longer on the scene, but a replacement had been found: Martino, the bellboy at the Regina d'Inghilterra, the fashionable inn in the Frezzeria where Andrea sometimes stopped for a quick bite at lunchtime, now handled most of their secret correspondence.

Yet their relationship was not as it once had been. At the time of the conspiracy against Consul Smith, Giustiniana had given herself to Andrea with abandon because, in the end, she had allowed herself to believe in the success of their preposterous scheme.

Now, as they met like thieves in Rosa's unadorned little room, what prospect did their love have? "You will be mine forever," Andrea kept assuring her. But how was this to be? Again Giustiniana had nothing to look forward to: only uncertainty and more pain seemed to lie ahead. She gave in to Andrea's entreaties, spurred by her own physical desire to be in his arms, yet she remained emotionally aloof. Moreover, on the practical side she felt her mother was right: her marriage prospects *had* been seriously damaged. So there were a number of reasons why she was wary of following her lover along another tortuous path of deception. She preferred to live her passion day by day, avoiding her own thoughts about the future.

Andrea, however, had changed. It had been a painful winter for him, and the possibility of losing Giustiniana in the aftermath of the Smith debacle had made him even more aware of the depth of his feelings for her. As their clandestine relationship entered its fourth year with no hope of finding a practical arrangement that would allow them to be lovers in a less secretive manner, he began to contemplate what until now had been unthinkable. He loved her deeply. He wanted to be with her, to have children with her. If marriage was the only way they could be together, perhaps the time had come to take that bold step while trying to minimize the negative consequences as much as possible.

Without telling Giustiniana, Andrea had approached Clemente Sibiliato, a prominent lawyer, and the Abbé Jacopo Facciolati, a legal scholar and close friend of the family, to discuss the idea of submitting a marriage contract to the Avogarìa di Comun, the powerful three-member panel that had jurisdiction over such matters. The conversations were less discouraging than Andrea had feared, and he had come away with new hope. In the past, he had not even considered this possibility on the assumption that such a contract would never have been approved and the effort would only have discredited the two families. The same line of reasoning had led Mrs. Anna to banish Andrea in the first place. But circumstances had changed rather dramatically in the meantime, and with no serious alternative in sight, marriage did not seem such an unreasonable solution anymore. In many ways, it had become the only possible one.

Andrea grew increasingly convinced that the Venetian authorities would accept the petition, provided the two families preempted the veto of the Avogarìa di Comun by agreeing to endorse the marriage contract before it was presented. After all, he reasoned, the role of the Avogarìa was to protect Venetian customs and institutions and therefore, by extension, the interests of the ruling oligarchy. Where would the three *avogadori* find the legal authority to reject a marriage contract endorsed by one of the founding families of the Republic? All he had to do was persuade the two families. The rest would take care of itself.

Andrea figured he could bring his father over to his side. To convince his uncle—the old Procurator Andrea Memmo, hero of Constantinople and stern guardian of Venetian tradition—would have been an entirely different proposition, but the gentle Pietro Memmo, ailing and deeply loving, would not disappoint him, and his mother, despite their frosty relations, would follow in the end. The great obstacle, Andrea realized immediately, was Mrs. Anna. Giustiniana would have to work hard on her mother to bring her to agree, after all that had happened, to negotiate a marriage contract with the Memmos.

Despite his growing optimism, Andrea never lost sight of the fact that such a course of action was very risky for everyone involved. If in the end the Avogarìa rejected the contract, the Memmos' reputation would be tarnished for years to come. As for Giustiniana, her prospects of finding a husband would be so badly damaged that the Wynnes would probably have to leave the city. But a lucid assessment of the situation, combined with a good dose of wishful thinking, brought Andrea to rely on the ultimate wisdom of the *avogadori*. "I am sure," he told Giustiniana when he finally suggested to her this new course of action, "that if your mother gives in even only an inch, the path ahead will clear."

Giustiniana balked at Andrea's bold new plan. She feared confronting her mother, and furthermore she had little faith in the success of the petition. All through the spring and summer of 1757, as Andrea continued his talks with the lawyers, he cajoled and tried to reassure her. "I understand how mortifying it must be for a young girl to reveal her passion to her own mother—and a mother with such a temperament, who has already forbidden that passion," he told her. "But you are not like other girls, and this is the reason I speak to you the way I do." She resisted for months, and for a brief moment in the summer of 1757 they seriously contemplated going behind the back of his parents and Mrs. Anna and marrying in secret.* But in the end Andrea always went back to the idea of giving their best effort to a proper marriage, and Giustiniana's refusal even to broach the subject with Mrs. Anna started to wear him down. He complained gently at first: "My imagination and my heart grow warmer every day, and I think about you all the time, but alas you are so distant in every way. My precious life, give me the comfort of seeing you do as I say in such an important matter." Then, in the face of her obduracy, he grew more impatient: "All this time you've wanted to do things your own way, but what have we gained?" He could not understand why Giustiniana was so fearful. Did her resistance reflect a woman's congenital incapacity to plan ahead? he wondered, attempting to apply a philosophical veneer to his exasperation. "For [a woman] never thinks about the future. And not because of any fault of hers but because of her internal organization, which does not allow her to bear for very long the effort needed to work out a complicated scheme."

Giustiniana's letters from that period are missing, so we do not know how she reacted to these misogynistic thoughts. But it is easy to imagine her eyes glazing over as she read Andrea's pompous reflections on the character of women. Their secret encounters became tense again and were often the scene of more arguments.

However, Andrea was relentless, and in the fall of 1757, more than six months after he had first suggested the plan, Giustiniana finally mustered the courage to tell her mother that she and Andrea were still in love and wanted to get married with her consent. Andrea was euphoric, and he became even more so when Giustiniana reported to him that Mrs. Anna, after initially stiffening, had been surprisingly receptive to the idea. "How much effort and pain

*In July 1757 Andrea and Giustiniana contacted the religious authorities at the Patriarchal Chancery in order to begin the process leading to a clandestine union (choosing witnesses, gathering sworn statements), but it is unclear how far they went before giving up on the idea. In the archives of the Patriarchal Chancery there is a folder with their names in the register of secret marriages, but the contents have been removed.[1]

it has cost me to bring you back on the right track!" he exclaimed at his victory.

Mrs. Anna's volte-face was not without reason. After all, she had opposed the relationship with Andrea because she was convinced the Memmos would block a marriage contract by any means possible; if this was not the case, the matter would be worth pursuing. Prudently, she decided to wait for the Memmos to make the first move.

At Ca' Memmo, Andrea's optimistic prediction was borne out. Relations between him and his parents had improved, thanks to his deliberate efforts to be accommodating and helpful in the daily running of the house and their estate on the mainland. His diplomatic maneuvering led to an emotional family summit at which Pietro and Lucia Memmo agreed to a preliminary negotiation for the submission of a marriage contract to the authorities. Now it really looked as if Andrea's gamble might pay off. News trickled out and became grist for Venice's inexhaustible rumor mill. "Everyone in town speaks of our marriage as a done thing," he reported happily to Giustiniana.

The two sides had to agree to the terms of the contract, which usually consisted of lengthy and very detailed documents, filled with financial statements and numerous clauses and conditions. Once the contract was drawn up, it was presented to the *primario,* a sort of general secretary, of the Avogarìa di Comun for a preliminary review. If the review was successful, the contract was submitted to the three-member panel for final approval.

Mrs. Anna insisted that Andrea and Giustiniana should not see each other or be in communication during the negotiation. She decided to accompany Giustiniana to Padua, where they were to be the guests of Bernardino Renier, the prominent patrician whose son Alvise was still wooing the lackadaisical Tonnina. The rest of the children stayed in Venice with Toinon. Before leaving, Mrs. Anna hired a lawyer, Signor Faccini, to handle the negotiations with the Memmos while she and her daughter were away. Discreetly, she also turned to Consul Smith for financial advice. A full year had gone by since he had married Betty Murray, and Mrs. Anna felt it was time to renew a precious friendship.

It was hard on Andrea and Giustiniana to be separated now that

things were looking so hopeful. But it was harder still to have to
cease their correspondence at such a critical juncture. Andrea had
felt very much in charge, directing the course of events. He
needed to remain in touch with Giustiniana, if only to know what
decisions were being made on the other side. At the same time he
realized that if a compromising letter were found the entire plan
would be instantly derailed. A strategist to the core, he concluded
that the only solution was to develop a secret cipher. He spent several sleepless nights rearranging dots and lines and circles and tri-
angles to create a coherent alphabet and sent it to Giustiniana so
she too could master their secret language. This was the final combination they agreed on:

a	b	c	d	e	f	g	h	i	j	k	l	m	n	o	p
ө	....	?	!	:	,	.	z	∶			ω	υ	t	∷	s
q	r	s	t	u	v	w	x	y	z	’					
r	q	p	n	⫶	m			h	˜o						

At first they used their cipher only to dissimulate the most sensitive information: names, places, details of their plan or their own
intimate messages. But eventually they became so fluent they
could shift back and forth between the standard alphabet and the
secret one with ease. Sometimes they would slip in one or two
words in cipher and then carry on in Italian; other times they
would cover an entire page with their tiny hieroglyphs, giving a
rich and mysterious texture to the letter.

When she was in Padua, however, Giustiniana was still trying
to learn the symbols Andrea had submitted to her, and she did not
really have the strength for daily practice. Soon after arriving at
the Reniers' with her mother, she took to her bed complaining of
fevers and stomach pains and general weakness. The doctors tormented her with a succession of bleedings that sapped what little
energy she had while her mother forced her to follow a punitive
diet that consisted mostly of garlic. Andrea was "devastated" by
the news of her ill health and weighed in with some medical advice
of his own: "More bloodletting will surely do you good, but at

least wait until you are not so weak and are feeling a little better."
He also reproached her for not standing up to her mother: "Garlic
is very bad for you, and yet you keep eating it."

Away from home, bedridden and feverish, Giustiniana struggled to find some peace of mind. Was her mother sincere about
wanting to go ahead with the marriage contract? Despite Andrea's
frequent coded messages, she felt isolated from him and lonely.
Once more, she was overcome by waves of jealousy and mistrust.
Was he seeing his old girlfriends Marietta and Lucrezia in Venice
while she was stuck in Padua, half a day's journey away from her
loved one? Even more troubling to her was talk that the Memmos
were contemplating yet another marriage offer.

This time there was none of Andrea's old defensiveness in his
attempt to reassure Giustiniana: "My dearest one, . . . how do you
think I spend my days so far away from you? I spend them thinking about our tender passion. And still you think I am lost in
thoughts about Mariettas and Lucrezias! One is so precious, the
other so flighty. . . . One day I will paint a true picture of their
character for you so that you will be able to judge for yourself
if there ever was any reason to harbor doubts about me." As for
what she was hearing about another marriage proposal, Andrea
explained that a relative of the Memmos had indeed approached
his parents with an offer from a wealthy family, the Baglionis,
which included a handsome dowry of 12,000 ducats. "But rest
assured," he told Giustiniana, "I paid no attention, and neither did
anyone else in my family."

Andrea was being truthful. Once his parents had agreed to
go ahead with the marriage, they had embraced the idea whole-
heartedly and were now working hard to ensure the contract was
approved: their prestige, as well as their son's future, was at stake.
Lucia Memmo, who had looked down on the Wynnes ever since
Giustiniana had come into their lives, now became one of her most
ardent supporters. "She's crazy about your portrait!" Andrea
exclaimed, hardly recognizing his mother but delighted at how
sentiments were changing all around. Even more important, from
a practical point of view, was the change in his father. In an
extraordinary gesture of goodwill toward his eldest son, Pietro
Memmo had secretly lifted the *contraddizione*—the power of veto a

patrician family had over a marriage contract until it was signed—before the negotiations had even begun in earnest. This move was very generous but also imprudent; Andrea's uncle would never have approved it had he still been alive. Although Andrea was grateful to his father for removing a major obstacle before the talks had started, the future statesman in him must have winced. Using their code, he told Giustiniana about the new development and asked her to keep the secret. It would be humiliating for the Memmos if the news became public. Worried about a possible leak, Andrea's mother and brothers went to the Patriarchal Chancery and told the officials in charge of the case to inform anyone who asked that the *contraddizione* was still in place and to refuse to show the official ledger containing Pietro Memmo's declaration. Andrea explained to Giustiniana that this was "the only way to protect us as well as my parents, who have already been condemned by all of Venice for not having prevented our union so far." He was moved by Pietro and Lucia's flouting of convention for their sake and lost no opportunity in his letters to Giustiniana to remind her how grateful they should be to them.

The mood was now upbeat. Pietro's decision was bound to speed up the process. Andrea told Giustiniana not to worry: "The contract will be approved, and once it is, all the rest will fall into place." He ran into Signor Faccini, Mrs. Anna's lawyer, who assured him that their side of the contract would soon be completed and taken over to the designated *primario*, Signor Bonzio, a man apparently well disposed toward the two lovers. Andrea was also getting inside information from a well-placed source: Signor Bonzio's secret lover, Donada. "There will be important news in a few days," he informed Giustiniana. "And then who will dare keep me separated from my spouse?" He added a short note in cipher: "Tuesday or Wednesday you will return to Venice by order of the inquisitors."

Giustiniana's brief exile in Padua thus came to an end. The lovers were still not allowed to see each other, but it was impossible for them to remain apart now that they were both in Venice. The sense that negotiations were moving swiftly to a conclusion increased their desire to be together at whatever cost, and their physical love blossomed again as another frigid winter set in. "I am writing to you from home," Andrea told Giustiniana before he left the house for Rosa's. "But when you receive this envelope I shall already be where you know. . . . Run, for I am there already, waiting for you with open arms." Now Giustiniana gave herself to her lover more freely than ever before. Andrea was overwhelmed. He confessed to being *"ingiustinianatissimo"*—completely enthralled by her.

They made love in Rosa's dank little room, swaddled beneath layers of woolen clothes to keep out the cold. These encounters were necessarily hurried—there was always the fear of being found out, and, anyway, it was too icy to linger among the hardened sheets. They left their alcove still filled with desire for each other, and their lovemaking continued in their compulsive letters and notes—protected by the shield of their secret language:

> *When I left you, I came home and went straight to bed. As soon as I was under the covers my little nightingale felt an urge to fly back to you. I wanted to keep him here. I wanted him to stay quiet until the morning. But as much as I tried to distract him with fantasies about the nice legs of Cattina Barbarigo, the soft little tummy of Countess Romilii, and the pretty cheeks of Cattina Loredan, he would have none of it. He wanted satisfaction. Would you believe he even convinced me you had ordered him not to let me sleep if I did not satisfy his every desire? Thankful at last, and generous toward me, he wished to produce on this piece of paper the evidence of his satisfaction so that I in turn could prove to you, at the first opportunity, my blind obedience to all your wishes.*

Such playful but rather extreme displays of affection were not always to Giustiniana's taste. Yet he developed a habit of sending small samples of his semen to her as a tangible sign of his love. He would spread them on a piece of paper, which he then folded into what he referred to as his special *"involtini"*—borrowing a common Italian culinary term. At first, Giustiniana reacted with disgust to those sticky little envelopes that had traveled across town in the hands of their messenger. But she grew accustomed to them, even indifferent, and eventually Andrea gave up sending them while lamenting the fact that he had never received similar tokens of her love. "They would have caused such transport," he sighed.

There were changes at Rosa's. The two lovers were saddened to learn that "their" room was now being let out to other clandestine couples. The traffic around the house also made it more likely that they would be recognized. It was imperative that they both keep their mask on whenever they visited. But even that precaution was not always enough. For Andrea certainly had his mask on when he stepped out of Rosa's house alone one day (they were always careful to leave separately), wearing a bright red cloak over many layers of warm clothes and the typical Venetian three-cornered felt hat. It should have been very difficult for anyone to know who he was, especially since his face was entirely hidden. Yet when he suddenly found himself face to face with Giacomo Zandiri, a friend of Mrs. Anna's, he had the sinking feeling he had been found out by just the wrong person.

Zandiri, like Mrs. Anna, had emigrated as a child from one of the Greek islands. His brother worked as a butler for the Bragadins, a well-known Venetian family. Giacomo, on the other hand, had no fixed employment. He had managed to weasel his way into Mrs. Anna's home by being on hand to help out with the daily chores necessary to running a large household. A nosy fellow by nature, he also kept an eye on Giustiniana's comings and goings, and on several occasions he had provided Mrs. Anna with secret intelligence about her oldest daughter. "Stay away from him," Andrea had warned her many times, "and never forget how much he has hurt you in the past."

After his chance encounter with Zandiri, Andrea dashed off a note to Giustiniana in cipher: "Giacomo found me at Rosa's doorstep just as I was leaving. I am convinced he recognized me because he acted surprised and stopped to look at me for a while. I pretended not to know him and hid from him as best I could. But I feel it is nearly impossible that he won't tell your mother, even on the strength of a mere suspicion."

What to do? Andrea needed a convincing alibi in case Zandiri mentioned having seen him coming out of Rosa's. Giustiniana, meanwhile, should deny very firmly that she had been with him there and suggest that the man Zandiri had seen at the door might have been Lucatello Loredan, a friend of Andrea who also met his lover at Rosa's and "who wears a hat similar to mine and white stockings and has thin legs like I do." Andrea then remembered an important detail: upon leaving Rosa's he'd realized he had left his *manizza,* the fur hand warmer Venetians wore in winter, in their room, but he hadn't gone back to fetch it "because I didn't want [Rosa] to know we had been together for so long." Since the man Zandiri saw on Rosa's doorstep was obviously not wearing a *manizza,* Giustiniana should convince her sister Bettina to say she had seen Andrea pass in his gondola on the Grand Canal wearing his red coat *and his manizza.* "What I fear the most are the stupid answers Rosa and her servants might give if they are asked. So tomorrow morning you must make sure [they] deny I was ever there."

The following morning Andrea waited in vain for a letter to reach him at Ca' Memmo. Then he checked at the various *botteghe* he and Giustiniana used as mailboxes. Nothing. Finally, in the evening, his gondolier brought him the news: no one had dared deliver Giustiniana's letters to Andrea because of the "the terrible uproar" that had taken place at the Wynnes' after Mrs. Anna had discovered that the two had seen each other. So he'd been right about the wretched Zandiri, and none of his efforts to cover his tracks had made the slightest difference.

They stopped seeing each other at Rosa's. It was too risky. Meanwhile, the negotiations had stalled. The times called for maximum prudence. Yet Andrea continued to write, mostly in cipher now, to keep Giustiniana abreast of developments.

Even before the Zandiri incident, Mrs. Anna had made a series of demands that were clearly at odds with the goodwill displayed by the Memmo family. Andrea was especially incensed by her insistence on the inclusion of a clause stating that if the contract were not approved, all correspondence between Andrea and Giustiniana would have to cease by order of the court. Mrs. Anna was trying to protect her daughter's chances of marrying someone else, and Faccini told the Memmos she insisted on having her way on that point. Andrea protested vehemently: "What a foolish request! If I agreed to it, my family would immediately think: Ah, then Andrea is not so attached to Giustiniana after all."

It was not so much the specific clause that worried Andrea. He felt that Mrs. Anna's attitude was self-defeating: by negotiating as if the contract would never be approved, she would inevitably undermine the whole effort. He sent Giustiniana a message explaining that the Memmos would not respond to Mrs. Anna's requests until she had made clear the names of all her counsels. "Then I will reason with them. . . . Don't worry, my beloved wife. . . . I have thought of everything." Andrea had in fact lost all confidence in Faccini, who kept him out of the loop and came to Ca' Memmo "his belly sticking out, asking to speak to my mother alone without having talked things over with me first." Not only was he hurt, he thought his exclusion unwise: he, more than anyone else, could help finesse the agreement since he knew what both families wanted.

The difficulties raised by Mrs. Anna made the Memmo camp nervous because they had already put their reputation on the line. "My mother is now desperately worried that the news that she has lifted the *contraddizione* will become public too soon," Andrea complained, twisting the facts a little. His father, of course, had lifted it—he was the titular head of the Memmo clan and was the only person entitled to do so. To tell Giustiniana that his *mother* had done it was technically incorrect but rather revealing about who was really in charge of the negotiation. Lucia Memmo, however, was no longer as optimistic as she had been. She feared her family would be dragged into quicksand. Why was Mrs. Anna not pressing for the contract to go forward? Andrea's mother feared "very much" that she was stalling simply because she was afraid it would not be approved—which Mrs. Anna had in fact already said to several people outside the negotiating circle.

To make matters worse, the dreaded Morosinis were once again poking around, advising Mrs. Anna on what course to take. Encouraged by her mother, Giustiniana had continued to visit their *palazzo* despite Andrea's old plea that she never be seen with his "enemies" again. For a long time he had turned a blind eye, but now the negotiations were so precarious that he insisted the Morosinis stay out of the picture. "I absolutely do not want [them] to meddle in our affairs." And why was Mrs. Anna consorting with them anyway? Was she having second thoughts? Despite the persistent optimism he displayed to Giustiniana, Andrea, like his mother, became wary of Mrs. Anna's true intentions.

While she privately continued to pursue a deal with the Memmos, in public Mrs. Anna became so negative about the chances of success that she even began to question the benefit of going forward. "She tells everyone that we are crazy, that I am a rogue, a liar, and a cheat, that it is not true that my parents are happy, and that I made it up in order to deceive you and your mother," Andrea wrote in bafflement. "Luckily my parents could not be any sweeter. . . . By God, they are true heroes."

Yet more mischief on the part of Mrs. Anna was on its way. A young Frenchman who went by the name of Comte de Chavannes arrived from Paris intending to spend part of the long Carnival season in Venice. He was charming and good-looking and had an air of sophistication about him that thrilled young Venetian ladies. He was immediately taken with Giustiniana when he was introduced to her. He plied her with gallantries, escorted her to the theater, danced with her, and took her to the Ridotto for some cardplaying. Mrs. Anna was delighted to see such a fine young man lavish her daughter with attention. Behind the scenes she did her best to facilitate Chavannes's courtship even as she continued to be engaged—formally at least—in marriage negotiations with the Memmos.

The worst part for Andrea was that Giustiniana was not insensitive to the charm of the *soi-disant* Comte de Chavannes.

The Carnival of 1758 offered Giustiniana a pleasant break from the drama and the draining intensity of her relationship with Andrea. By the mid-eighteenth century the Carnival had become "a less raucous, more polite affair than its Rabelaisian antecedent."[2] Plebian celebrations like human pyramids and the war of fists, bullfights and regattas had been suppressed. Still, the streets and bridges were packed with jesters, fire-eaters, and prodigies of all kinds. Music and dances and drinking went on late into the night. The throngs were so thick that it was always a struggle to move from one place to another, but it was also easier to move anonymously through that crowd of dominoes.

Chavannes, who had decided to stay on through the festivities, was thrilled by the excitement and the licentiousness that filled the air, and Giustiniana could finally indulge the more coquettish side that she had repressed for so long. She enjoyed her time with the young Frenchman—the air of Paris always went to her head, even when she breathed it in Venice. And she did not shy away when he kissed her at the end of a happy evening—not just a French kiss on the lips, as Andrea later reminded her, shocked by her slovenliness, but a deep, long kiss "in the much more fervent Italian manner," according to witnesses who had been quick to tell him. Didn't she know people talked? Didn't she realize her behavior risked jeopardizing all their plans for the future? What was she *thinking* "as she chatted continuously" with Chavannes in public? They were the talk of the town, Andrea reported reproachfully. Many people were already saying that Giustiniana was risking "losing her husband just to gallivant with a silly Frenchman who will soon be leaving Venice anyway." And what about the pain she was inflicting on him? The last time he had seen them together, at the theater, he had had to run away in order not to see Chavannes "offer you his arm and you getting into his gondola and maybe even going to the Ridotto with him." Not to mention those awful Italian kisses Andrea felt he would "never have the heart to erase" from his memory.

Andrea's nightmare ended at Lent, when the Frenchman returned to Paris, apparently still pining for Giustiniana. The tireless Mrs. Anna pressed her daughter to keep up a correspondence with Chavannes and sit for a portrait to be sent on to him in Paris. But after the initial thrill Giustiniana had lost interest in her French suitor, wrote lazily to him, and looked for excuses every time the portraitist came by the house. His courtship had been a distraction for her, and now that all the craziness of Carnival was over she was ready to throw herself back into the arms of her true love. Andrea was relieved, but he could not resist carving out his pound of flesh in a long and rambling letter he wrote late into the night:

> *Listen to me: we all saw your mother rise from an unhappy and miserable station to become the wife of an English chevalier. Your mother does not have the best reputation. You have nasty relations and little dowry. You are a Catholic, and therefore one*

assumes nobody will want you back in England or in any case you will choose not to go. Your education does not please. The liberties you take are viewed with suspicion. You are a bright girl. How easy it would be for anyone—a man, or better still, a woman— to believe that all this time you have cultivated me out of self-interest when they see a nice young Frenchman . . . make love to you and be gallant and draw sighs from you at a time when you should appear particularly respectful of me. For heaven's sake, it would have cost you nothing to tell that silly young fellow off— your reputation would have gained so much. Of course a scene with your mother would have been costlier, but that too would have been manageable. And you would have earned so many points with me, my blessed Giustiniana. . . . Oh, never mind, but let this be the last "distraction" before our wedding. This time I will consider you innocent—I will not infer from this episode an easy yearning to please on your part or an overconfident attitude toward your Memmo in love, always good to you, full of respect for you, and blindly faithful. But if it happens again I promise nothing. . . . I still don't know whether I will be a victim of the weakness husbands in love often fall prey to—jealousy. So far, my respect for you and the low opinion I have had of my rivals have spared me this curse, but who can tell what will happen in the future. . . . Remember that I marry you out of boundless love and deep esteem, and for this very reason I am convinced that my eternal happiness can come only from you. And that the only dowry you bring to me is your love, so perfectly sincere, and a character worthy of all my admiration. Remember that I give to you the love of my father, my mother, my brothers, my parents, my friends, the esteem . . . of the rest of my world, the advantages that come with me and my house, and maybe even more.

Giustiniana must have shown some regret for the forwardness she had displayed with Chavannes, for in his next letter Andrea was glad to declare the hostilities between them officially over. *"Trêve donc des inutiles querelles,"* he joked, using French to communicate the truce in their pointless quarrels. "I couldn't be happier about it; stick to your resolutions, and everything will be fine." He snickered at the portrait being shipped to Chavannes in

Paris. Such poor quality, so few sittings . . . should he worry about the bad impression it might make among Parisians?

His truce with Giustiniana, however, did little to improve their overall prospects. Six months had gone by since the first contact between the Memmos and Mrs. Anna, and after initial encouraging signs, very little movement had occurred. The draft of the wedding contract had not even been presented to Signor Bonzio at the Avogarìa. Mrs. Anna was still dragging her feet and looking out for other options. The Memmos could not allow the negotiation to languish any longer: their prestige was in danger. Andrea felt it was time for another bold move: he decided to call on Consul Smith, who was again exerting a great deal of influence over Mrs. Anna.

Relations between Andrea and the consul had not improved since the previous year's embarrassments. Though civil to each other in public, they had maintained their distance. Now Andrea realized he needed to have the consul on his side. Besides, he was happily married to Betty, and Andrea was no longer a threat. There was no reason why they should not be friends again. Except pride, of course; but in his dealings with the consul, Andrea had learnt that his pride could be overcome with the right amount of flattery. "We must work on the consul until he does our bidding," he wrote to Giustiniana. "We must help him rid himself of that special dourness he harbors toward us."

Andrea knew that the consul was facing serious financial and legal difficulties and could use some help from a well-connected patrician like himself. In his old age Smith had lost his keen commercial touch. A series of business deals had gone sour. Quite apart from the loss of money, these setbacks had tarnished his reputation. It was said in Venice and London that he had resorted to dishonest practices to patch up his damaged finances. While it was certainly true that his affairs were in disarray, Consul Smith seems to have been the victim of his own ingenuousness more than the avid perpetrator of shady schemes, as some of his enemies claimed. The consequences of one particular deal, in which he had been brazenly duped by a professional swindler, had been worrying him for many months.

The previous year a man who went by the name of Captain

John Wilford had taken over a merchant ship belonging to an English trading firm, changed her name from *Nevis Planter* to *Fuller,* and crisscrossed the Mediterranean buying and selling goods. Wilford had arrived in Venice to unload merchandise and, needing a large sum of money to finance his next expedition, had asked the consul to advance it. The unsuspecting consul had obliged him with a maritime loan drawn against the value of the ship. Wilford, however, had had no intention of paying him back. Upon his return to Venice he had secretly registered the *Fuller*—which wasn't his to begin with—in the name of his fictitious children. The consul had sued Wilford, as had the legitimate owners of the ship, but to no avail. Wilford had taken advantage of a loophole in the Venetian maritime law to keep the boat. His "children" had materialized out of nowhere to produce a tearful performance at the trial, and the consul had never recovered his money. Wilford had added insult to injury by bragging all over town about how he had tricked the old man. It had been a trying experience for Smith.[3]

Andrea approached the consul in the aftermath of the Wilford incident, at a time when the old man felt distraught and vulnerable. He was glad to make peace with his young friend and promised to help sway Mrs. Anna. Andrea informed Giustiniana that the consul would soon be calling on her mother. He added that, in order to test his goodwill, he would ask him to give Giustiniana a small enameled snuffbox as a gift from him "so that your mother won't realize it is from me. . . . Consider it my present to you on the day of my *festa,* which is tomorrow." A few days later the consul called on Mrs. Anna as promised but failed to speak in defense of the two lovers. Andrea backed up his new ally, explaining to Giustiniana that "even though he came by your house expressly to speak to [your mother], in the end he decided not to push the point because he felt it was inopportune. But he did ask her how the contract was going . . . and she told him things were as good as they could possibly be at this time." Andrea continued to press him. A few days later, he informed Giustiniana that the consul had finally "sworn" to him that he had had "a very long conversation with Mrs. Anna and that he had gained quite a lot already and was now confident he could bring her completely to our side, having shown the care and the zeal with which he continues to protect your house and you in particular."

Andrea himself was not quite as sanguine as Consul Smith. Mrs. Anna's attitude toward the lovers remained cold, and he was irritated by the way she spoke about his family in public and felt strongly that her behavior was not helping their cause. "You do remember, don't you, how your mother went about saying that my close relations were horribly critical about us and how they were slandering her behind my back. Smith asked her what those accusations were based on since he knows the Memmos to be upright and wise and he is very much aware of our thinking on this whole matter. She was quite embarrassed and admitted she had no proof. She had heard . . . she had thought . . . so there. It turns out we Memmos are gentlemen after all, we have not dishonored her, we have not caused her family's ruin, its collapse, its violent death."

As Andrea drew the consul into the picture, he also edged himself back into the consul's life, offering advice on how to disentangle himself from new legal disputes. Once again Andrea was at his most Machiavellian. He instructed Giustiniana "to cultivate Mr. Smith and his wife," bearing in mind that "they probably believe we are already married one way or another, for I have done my best to excite their suspicion without ever stating things clearly." Soon Andrea was able to report that he was once more "at the very center" of the consul's activity. "Here I am, necessary to him, willing and helpful."

There was a cruel edge to Andrea's treatment of the consul. It was not just the arrogance of the young dealing with the old. There was a lingering hint of resentment, a suggestion that all was not entirely forgotten. Their rapprochement was borne of mutual convenience, and the two did not really recover their close relationship. Here is how Andrea described him to Giustiniana in a particularly mean-spirited letter: "I tell you: Smith is bound to do all he can for us unless he is the most ungrateful man on earth. For he surely would have lost at least fifteen thousand sequins, not to mention his peace of mind and his honor, if it had not been for my advice, which was the opposite of what he and his counselors had argued. So I will not ease the pressure on him. The worst part of it is that he really is an ass, that he doesn't know how to handle a deal, that he's English and old."

The consul may have lost his ability to handle a deal, but his word still carried weight with Mrs. Anna, who was mindful that the young Chavannes had been sucked back into the Parisian whirlwind and no longer seemed seriously interested in Giustiniana. Besides, she had found out that, contrary to his claim, he was not really a count. After a long winter lull, negotiations suddenly began to move forward again. In the early spring of 1758 Mrs. Anna, under pressure from the Memmos, finally instructed Signor Faccini to present a draft of the marriage contract to Signor Bonzio, the *primario,* for preliminary scrutiny. Andrea was thrilled: "How happy we shall be. Yes, I am sure of it now, my little one."

Anticipating a wedding agreement, the lovers' temptation to see each other became irresistible. Andrea paraded up and down the Grand Canal in his gondola two or three times a day. He was delighted to see her at her balcony again: ". . . and with that nightcap of yours, oh dearest, oh my rarest Giustiniana, my desire for you. . . . I feel I cannot resist it." Yet a treacherous winter chill was still in the air, and he warned her to be careful. " For heaven's sake, don't come to the window," he pleaded one morning. "It is still too cold." A few days later he sent another worried note: "Ask one of the maids or a houseboy to watch for me in your place. They can call you as soon as they see me from afar. Otherwise I will worry too much."

It started with a splitting headache. Then a fever set in and Giustiniana's temperature rose, and then came the dreaded stomach pains. Andrea followed the progress of the illness from the window at the Tiepolos' with increasing agitation: "You seemed to be burning last night, and the way you repeatedly put your hand to your forehead gave me so much grief." Andrea was in a state of great agitation. It was the second time Giustiniana had fallen seriously ill in the space of six months. She was again subjected to a debilitating cycle of leech-induced bloodletting by Dr. Trivellati, one of Venice's leading physicians. Her mother force-fed her the usual supplement of garlic, which Andrea insisted was "really very bad" for her. It was hard for him to communicate with her and to get credible news on her health. His sister Marina's death was recent enough that a creeping fear reinforced Andrea's anxiety about Giustiniana's health. Most nights he returned home late after wandering aimlessly around town, stopping at friends' "and talking about you while the others played cards." In his room he would battle the cold and his sleeplessness by pacing back and forth in front of the fire. Or he would wrap himself in blankets and stay up writing by the stove until the chiming of the first call to mass. Images of Giustiniana kept him awake: "You cannot imagine how my heart is filled with worries and endless pangs of anxiety and how my mind is full of thoughts of terrible things that surely will not happen. . . . Now I see my Giustiniana in a bed, her head so hot, her body wracked by fluxions and fever and pains and debilities of all sorts . . . without her Memmo, without a hope of having him near even for a moment."

A chance encounter with Dr. Trivellati in the street provided the first relief: "He told me your pulse had slackened after the last bout of fever. He said he had decided to go ahead and draw more blood now that your headache has subsided somewhat and you have had a copious clearing out. How his words, so precise and truthful, have consoled me."

In spite of all the bloodletting, which probably weakened Giustiniana more than the actual ailment, her health gradually improved. As the weather warmed, she returned to the balcony. She looked pale and thin under her beribboned nightcap, but she smiled in the bright sunshine and squinted and waved to her lover down below. As she recovered, deeper stirrings came back to her as well, and with them the usual logistical problems. Ever since Andrea was spotted leaving her house, Rosa had been reluctant to help the two lovers. She claimed to be ill and made herself generally unavailable. Andrea pleaded with her so forcefully she finally agreed to let them use their room "one more time," with the understanding that it would be the last.

Other friends now willingly stepped in. Johann Adolph Hasse, the German composer, and his wife, Faustina, the celebrated diva, had always had a tender spot for Andrea since the days when Uncle Andrea, the old patriarch, had still been alive and they had been frequent guests at Ca' Memmo. Their daughters, Beppina and Cattina, had grown, and now they too had become friends of Andrea and Giustiniana. The Hasses were a joyous, fun-loving family, and they were more than happy to connive with the two young lovers. On the appointed day, Giustiniana would tell her mother she was going to pay a visit "to the Hasse girls." Andrea would arrive there shortly before her, to be whisked up to the girls' room on the second floor. This way Giustiniana could go upstairs and meet Andrea even if she had the misfortune of being accompanied by her mother.

More surprisingly, the consul himself agreed to give Andrea the keys to his box at the Teatro San Giovanni Grisostomo, a rather traditional establishment with an uninspiring program—which suited Andrea and Giustiniana just fine. They met there at their leisure and made sure the little curtain was drawn. They were seldom tempted to watch the play. "Of course it has become my favorite theater," Andrea now said after having criticized the San Giovanni Grisostomo for years. "That box is very comfortable indeed. Oh, I hope we shall go there often. . . . There is such peace and quiet. . . . And of course the privilege of not having to listen to the performances, which are usually so bad."

Now that the marriage cavalcade was moving again, Andrea was "immersed in the pleasure of our present condition." He could not get enough, even when they were not together:

> As I lay in bed alone for so long I thought of the days when we will be together, comforting each other at night. This idea led to another and then to another and soon I was so fired up I could see you in bed with me. You wore that nightcap of yours I like so much, and a certain ribbon I gave you adorned your face so sweetly. You were so near to me and so seductive I took in your tender fragrance and felt your breath. You were in a deep sleep— you even snored at times. You had kept me company all evening long with such grace that I really didn't have the heart to wake you up . . . but then a most fortunate little accident occurred just as my discretion was exhausting itself. You turned to me at the very moment in which you dreamed of being in my arms. Nature,

perhaps encouraged by habit, led you to embrace me. So there we were, next to each other, face to face and mouth to mouth! Your right leg was leaning on my left leg. Little by little the beak of the baby dove began to prick you so forcefully that in your sleep you moved your hand in such a way the thirsty little creature found the door wide open. Trembling from both fear and delight, it entered oh so gently into that little cage and after quenching its thirst it began to have some fun, flying about those spaces and trying to penetrate them as far as it could. It was so eager and made such a fuss that in the end you woke up.

The greatest intimacy came naturally to them. The playful tone softened the raw sexual desire. And the writing too, one feels, prolonged and completed their pleasure. Andrea returned to his room at Ca' Memmo one evening, his head filled with sexual thoughts about Giustiniana. He considered masturbating but then thought better of it: "I felt terribly in love with you. . . . But I didn't want to force nature for a third time, having it forced with such profit in the morning."

During the spring of 1758 Andrea's letters were filled with a mixture of sexual exuberance and serious talk about their future life as husband and wife. When the lighthearted side of his personality took over, Andrea reveled in the pursuit of pleasure. But his serious side, which carried the weight of tradition and family responsibility, was never far behind. He begged Giustiniana, for the sake of his reputation as well as her own, to be more circumspect in her public demeanor and always wary of that "malicious world" out there, which preyed on the smallest glimmer of gossip. Sometimes this sanctimonious carping irritated Giustiniana's rebellious spirit, but Andrea pressed on regardless, teaching her the ways "of this Venetian world of ours, as a good friend would." When he did not write to her as a playful lover, he took the approach of a philosopher-husband whose passion should always remain firmly fastened to reason: "Believe me, my little one, a simple rapture would not have led me to risk everything I have in order to marry you. What led me to do it was the clear and perfect picture I have of my Giustiniana, the deep and well-founded respect I have for her, and a sentiment far stronger than the most virtuous and sincerest of friendships. And all of this has led me to pursue my goal with as much prudence and patience and industry and foresight as I could muster." Had he been more fickle, had his love been "not as deep as it is," he might have tempted her "to run away" with him during one of their many moments of despair. Or he could have found "an honorable way" out of their relationship: "Yet these thoughts never even entered my mind. I have remained constant. I feel as strong and resolute as I did on the very first day—before which I had already reflected on our fate far more than you could possibly imagine."

In early summer Venetian society prepared itself once again for the yearly ritual of the *villeggiatura*. But it was hard for the Memmos and especially the Wynnes, who did not own an estate in the country, to firm up their plans at a time when the negotiations on the marriage seemed to be reaching a critical stage. Mrs. Anna discarded the idea of renting a place, instead accepting another invitation from the Reniers to spend some time at their house in Padua. Andrea decided he would stay in Venice, where Signor Bonzio would be examining the marriage contract, and made plans to ensure he and Giustiniana could be in constant communication while they were apart. After four and a half years of subterfuge, Andrea had become a master at handling the intricacies of maintaining the flow of their correspondence: "I will draw two small lines under the name of the county. That will tell the postmen in Venice [the letters are from me]. . . . They will deliver them in the morning. . . . If anyone should check at the Padua post office or the Venice post office, they will find nothing—it will not be your writing, the letter will be addressed to a Venetian gentleman, there will be no *poste restante,* hence no reason to suspect anything."

The rest of the Memmo family left town to seek respite from the heat. Pietro was so frail that Andrea wondered if he'd make it through the summer. He gave Giustiniana a touching description of their leave-taking: "I think he will stay out at our villa for a long time because it is good for his health. . . . After lunch I kissed his hand, which is not something we Memmos usually do. After that blessed moment we were unable to speak because our eyes filled with tears."*

Life in the city slowed down considerably. Except for the great Festa del Redentore on the third Sunday of July, there were no major festivities. The theaters were closed. The palaces on the Grand Canal were empty. The *botteghe* and the *malvasie* were less crowded than usual. Andrea did not have much to do except run a few errands, browse among the picture dealers, and make sure Signor Bonzio had everything he needed. "Early this morning I went by Tonnin Zanetti's shop† to see some drawings by Titian and cultivate a priest who might prove useful to us one day. As I savored those magnificent drawings I thought, 'If only I could have Giustiniana, who is so far away from me.' That's the way it always is. You're always in my heart, and I would feel so undeserving of you if I did not think about you constantly." Alone in the stifling heat of the city, he marveled at how things were turning their way: "Do you know that it is nearly impossible to be blessed by that good fortune that God is preparing to bestow upon us after all our grief? To discover such kinship between us, to see reason and virtue guide our love and give true and everlasting pleasure . . . these are things that don't often come along. Oh, when will we be together, my dearest little one? And what delight I shall feel in pleasing you, in making you happy, in loving you! How sweet your company will be."

His happy thoughts soured, though, when he was told about a sudden change of plans: the Reniers had invited Giustiniana and a few other guests to leave Padua and travel to their villa at Mirano, another little town by the Brenta. Mrs. Anna would have to remain in Padua with Tonnina, who was convalescing after a brief illness, and it was a little odd that Giustiniana should have been asked to go without a chaperon. Andrea was miffed. After all, the Reniers knew very well that he and Giustiniana would soon be married. Even more irritating to him was the fact that Giustiniana herself felt inclined to go. "Do as you please," he wrote to her peevishly,

*Though frail, Pietro went on to live until the age of 93. He died on February 14, 1772.[4]
†Antonio Maria Zanetti was an important collector and dealer of Venetian artists. He was a friend and at times a rival of Consul Smith.[5]

"but I want you to know that I don't like this idea at all. . . . It is never a good thing to generate suspicions, and it would be utterly foolish to do so given our circumstances. . . . [Renier] should respect the fact that I don't like you to go around without your mother." He then took his complaint directly to Alvise Renier, listing "all the reasons why I dislike the idea of this little trip" and lamenting the indifference with which he felt Alvise could abuse him. Andrea expected to be treated with greater respect by Alvise, who was quite a bit younger than he. To treat his wife-to-be in such a fashion, he concluded bitterly, was nothing less than "the act of an uncivilized lout."

Giustiniana was in a difficult spot. She wanted to please Andrea but felt he was being excessively protective of her and making things difficult. The Reniers had been kind to her family, and she didn't see the point of making such a fuss. Andrea sensed that Giustiniana had neither the strength nor the inclination to say no to the trip to Mirano. He made some mild threats: "You will not have any news from me until you return to Padua. . . . And you will not see me until you come back to Venice." In a final taunt he asked her to please tell him quickly whether she was going to Mirano or not so that he could make arrangements "to spend the next fifteen days or so in some other place and get some exercise, which I really need." He added a postscript that was typical of Andrea. If there was no way out, if she really *had* to go to Mirano, "then I hope you will at least make the effort of staying close to Bonzio's lover, that woman Donada, and to Bonzio himself if he should also come out there. Cultivate them as much as you can, and remember to always call him 'Your Excellency.' "

In the end Giustiniana went to Mirano. Andrea swallowed his pride and informed her that he had little choice but to join her there as soon as possible: "I've explained to my young friend Renier that he cannot treat me like a radish. . . . I am sorry for everything I said to you. . . . It was all on account of the pain I felt. . . . To calm you down, and to bring you completely onto my side . . . I see no other solution but to come straight to Mirano." Before leaving Venice, he made arrangements to take a room above the haberdashery in the main square of the little town and sent new instructions to Giustiniana: "As soon as you get [to

Mirano], go to the *bottega* in the square and ask the owner for a letter addressed to a certain Battista. . . . I love you, my soul, I love you to excess. For this reason I will come to Mirano. . . . I must run now, hopefully to hear good news about our papers. . . . Everyone says we are already married. . . . Our wedding is all people are talking about."

As soon as he reached his destination, he dashed off a note to Giustiniana, who had only just arrived at the Villa Renier herself: "I love you so much that I had to come despite all the objections. I am writing to you from Mirano, my soul, I am here, at the *bottega*, on the right-hand side of the arcade, near Signora Laura Angeloni's haberdashery, just as I had said to you. I will not move from here. I don't want to cause a scene that might make people talk about us. . . . I cannot wait to see you. Forgive my sloppy writing, my love, but I sleep as I write."

The following morning Giustiniana arranged to walk by the arcade during the promenade. Andrea could hardly contain the joy of seeing her after so many weeks: "My God, what consolation. . . . I am out of my wits now that I am near you again, that I have seen you. I actually felt I was holding your hand tightly and talking to you and kissing you. . . . You can imagine the state I'm in right now! What shall we do, my little one? . . . Tomorrow is market day. If possible, I would like to see you at the very least. How are you? My God, this is killing me. . . . My mind, my soul, my entire body are in such turmoil now. . . . Oh Christ, I have this huge desire to press you against my chest! By God, I cannot stand it anymore. . . . I wish we could be alone for half an hour and live out our love's apotheosis."

That night Andrea let himself into Villa Renier. At last he felt Giustiniana in his arms again, shivering with happiness and desire. This was how it was going to be—a life together, filled with their love for each other.

News from Venice suddenly shattered Andrea and Giustiniana's dreamy world in Mirano. The examination of the marriage contract had come to a halt. This time it had nothing to do with Mrs. Anna's demands or hesitations: her own past had surfaced to cast a disreputable shadow over her daughter's future. Sifting through old records, Bonzio had discovered that in the early 1730s, before Sir Richard had arrived in Venice, Mrs. Anna had been "deflowered by a Greek"—these were the actual words the *primario* later used with Andrea. She had become pregnant, and nine months later a baby boy had been handed over to an orphanage. Mrs. Anna's family had apparently taken the Greek man to court, but it was unclear whether the trial had ever taken place because Bonzio's office had been unable to locate all the documents.

Andrea was stunned. Now it was clear to him why Mrs. Anna had been so shifty and difficult. All the while, as she had bad-mouthed Andrea and his family and made up excuses to slow the process, she had in fact been hiding this secret. Andrea was furious with her. He rushed back to Venice to see the *primario*. "The meeting lasted for two hours," he reported back to Giustiniana, who was, if possible, even more distraught about the revelation than he was. "Bonzio had an extremely serious expression on his face. He seemed disgusted . . . and very well informed about everything that can be prejudicial to us: the year of the trial, the name of the Greek, the place where the suit was filed, the intervention of the *avogadore*, the boy sent to the orphanage, and, especially, every detail about your mother's life."

It is possible that the unctuous Bonzio had his own reasons for being upset. At the start of such negotiations it was expected—and certainly the Memmos had assumed the same in this case—that at some point it would be necessary to oil the bureaucratic machine a little by passing a few sequins to the *primario* under the table. Indeed, the general feeling among those who knew about the Memmo-Wynne negotiations was that with a bribe of one hundred sequins "the contract will surely be approved." Over the previous months, however, Mrs. Anna's delaying tactics had disheartened Bonzio and his colleagues to such an extent that, according to Andrea, "they did not expect to receive a single coin from her." She had added insult to injury by telling people such as Zandiri, who had spread the word, that the Memmos would get the contract approved only by "drowning" Bonzio in gold. According to Andrea, the *primario*'s conclusions, while delivered to him in the most obsequious manner, could not have been more discouraging:

"Your Excellency," Bonzio had said to him, "if we were to find a document in which Mrs. Anna herself publicly declares to have been deflowered by that Greek, what could Your Excellency possibly want us to do? These are not matters for arbitration. We depend on the laws absolutely, and they are very strict, and if it turns out there was a public dispute at the Quarantìe* a mere twenty-five years ago—for it seems there was an appeal at the Quarantìe even if the case was never actually examined there— well . . . what would Your Excellency expect us to do in that case? Our honor is publicly committed, and we would find ourselves publicly exposed, and people would be right to assume that Your Excellency 'is drowning the *primario* in gold,' as they say."

The message was clear, and the concluding allusion to Mrs. Anna's comment made Bonzio's little speech even more devastating. Once again, all their painstaking work had been torn apart. But unlike the Smith imbroglio, this storm would never blow over. Everyone knew that. The damaging court papers Bonzio referred to in his talk with Andrea were never actually produced. It is possible the *primario* did not even look for them. It was not worth his trouble anymore; enough of Mrs. Anna's story had been resurrected from the dusty Venetian archives to seal the fate of the marriage petition, which never even reached the final stage.

"This is our situation," Andrea summed up sadly. "Could our misfortunes be any worse?"

*The Republic's judicial council. It was made up of forty patricians.

On the morning of October 2, 1758, Mrs. Anna and her five children, accompanied by Signor Zandiri and Toinon, left the familiar city of Padua in two hired carriages—one for luggage, one for passengers—and took the road to Vicenza, their first stop on the long, uncomfortable journey across Europe. It would take them three to four days just to reach the end of Venetian territory, which extended westward all the way to the city of Brescia and a little beyond. Then they would travel through the Duchy of Milan and the Kingdom of Piedmont, make the arduous crossing of the Alps, descend toward Lyon, and finally head straight north for Paris. It was a daunting prospect, and not just because of the length of the journey (three to four weeks) and the size of the party. The cramped circumstances and the loud clatter of the carriage as it sped along the uneven dirt track made travel by coach an exhausting experience. The posts along the road, where horses were changed and the passengers could stretch and take a breath of fresh air and have a meal, were often rather seedy places. There were bound to be delays as well—a wounded horse, a broken wheel, a sudden rainstorm. And then there was the tedious everyday paperwork: rooms had to be booked and horses hired, and the right documents—passports, entry permits, exit permits—had to be in order every time one crossed a border. Zandiri was there for that; Mrs. Anna, believing it was more prudent and practical to travel with an adult male, had asked him to come along and manage the trip as far as Paris.

Huddled inside the crowded coach, Giustiniana was oblivious to her physical discomfort. As the city walls of Padua gradually disappeared from view, she drifted into melancholy thoughts. She was leaving the world she had lived in all her life. And she was leaving the man who for so long had been at the center of that world as her lover, her best friend, her guiding hand. As the carriage barreled down the road, she fixed her mind on Andrea to keep herself from feeling lost.

When the negotiations on the marriage contract had collapsed, Mrs. Anna had decided to leave Venice at once and seek a new life for herself and her children in London. What would be the point of staying on in the wake of the scandal? Giustiniana's prospects of finding a husband in the Republic were ruined. And Mrs. Anna's past, which she had fought so hard to bury and forget, had suddenly resurfaced to humiliate the whole family. So she had packed her belongings and uprooted her children with the same determination she had shown in the past, as she had struggled to preserve the respectability Sir Richard had bequeathed to her upon his death.

She was in a hurry now to cross the Alps before winter set in. The onset of the war would make their journey even more uncertain than it might otherwise have been, since they would be traveling through France as British subjects—and France and Great Britain were enemies. But Mrs. Anna counted on the good auspices of the Abbé de Bernis, the former French ambassador to Venice who was now foreign minister. Once they were safely in London, Lord Holderness, the children's guardian, would introduce them to their English relatives and help them settle down. He might possibly arrange a presentation to Court. Seven years after Sir Richard's death, his family was going home.

During their final days in Venice, Andrea and Giustiniana had been inseparable. Mrs. Anna's hostility toward Andrea had mellowed as the separation neared, and she had allowed him to take the boat trip from Venice to Padua with the family. In Padua, where the Memmos owned a large property, he had escorted Giustiniana around town as last-minute preparations were made for the trip. Andrea had even taken his meals with the Wynnes in an atmosphere of general reconciliation. After his final, wrenching farewell with Giustiniana, he had galloped ahead of the carriage to wave one last time from the bridge at the Gate of Santa Sofia. But Giustiniana had already withdrawn into her shell.

The Wynnes arrived at their inn in Vicenza very late that night. Giustiniana felt drained and completely disoriented. After a light dinner she went to her room and wrote to Andrea about the confusion in her heart:

> *Mon cher frère,*
>
> *Where am I, sweet Memmo? How awful is my pain! What desperation! Oh I do love you, alas; and I cannot cease telling you even in the first moments of our separation! How I have penetrated your being. . . . How I have felt! Ah, there is no point in telling you. I am desperate. . . . I did not have the strength to call you back when you drew away from me, so I followed you with my soul. I heard you stopped at the Bridge of Santa Sofia, but I did not see you.*

From the very beginning of their new life apart, Giustiniana addressed her letters to "Mon cher frère," my dear brother—a semantic device designed to put some distance between them and somehow ease the disentanglement of their feelings. She was quick to admit it was a weak subterfuge: "I will call you mon cher frère, but you will still be everything to me."

In reality this new form of address masked a deeper change in their relationship, which had actually occurred a few weeks before her departure from Venice. Giustiniana never spoke very openly or clearly about the matter in her letters to Andrea; she never mentioned a name or a place or a specific date. But she said enough to leave us in no possible doubt. At some point in 1758, either shortly before the revelations about Mrs. Anna or, more probably, in their aftermath, she had tired of the endless waiting game. She had tired of being isolated, tired of being shuttled back and forth between Venice and Padua, tired of being forcefully kept away from the man she loved. For a moment she had even tired of Andrea and his seemingly futile machinations. She had felt the utter hopelessness of her situation just as she had two years before, after their dramatic failure with Consul Smith. And for a short period of time—

she called it her "moment of weakness"—she had given in to the gallantry of another man.

For all we know it was a brief affair, probably a matter of a few weeks. Her feelings for Andrea had not died, however, and when her fling was over she had gone back to him more in love than she had been in a long time. Andrea himself had learned of the deception only later that summer. After Mrs. Anna's sudden decision to drag the family to London, Giustiniana had confessed her betrayal to Andrea, believing, in a contorted sort of way, that by painting herself as fickle and weak she would somehow diminish "the terrible pain" he would feel at their separation.

Andrea had forgiven Giustiniana—he was never a resentful man. But their relationship was not the same after her "cruel and spontaneous confession." Giustiniana had allowed someone else to come between them, and this shadow had lingered on. There had been lies, and then there had been remorse. But even after Andrea had forgiven her, even after their tearful farewell in Padua, Giustiniana continued to damn herself. "I despise my life and I despise myself even more," she wrote to him that first night in Vicenza, contemplating "the unhappy combination of events that has ruined me in your eyes."

Despite the changes in their relationship, Andrea and Giustiniana were still very much together when the Wynnes left Venice in the autumn. They saw themselves as a couple and intended to meet soon. They still talked about spending their life together—one way or another. In fact, they were already working on a new scheme.

Their most urgent goal was to thwart Mrs. Anna's plan to settle in London. Giustiniana had agreed with Andrea to try to extend their stay in Paris for as long as possible and hopefully to avoid reaching London at all. In Paris, Giustiniana was to aim her powers of seduction at Alexandre Le Riche de La Pouplinière, an aging widower, great music lover, and one of the richest *fermiers généraux*, the famously wealthy French tax collectors. It looked very much like a variation on the plan they had tried unsuccessfully on Consul Smith two years earlier.

Monsieur de La Pouplinière had been Andrea's idea. Exactly a decade before, the old tax collector had been at the center of the notorious *scandale de la cheminée*. The Duc de Richelieu, a powerful figure at the court of King Louis XV and a flamboyant womanizer, had seduced Monsieur de La Pouplinière's beautiful and much younger wife. The duke and the tax collector happened to be neighbors in Paris. To facilitate the secret encounters with his new lover, the duke had had a secret passageway built in a huge fireplace that led directly into Madame de La Pouplinière's music room. The tax collector eventually discovered the ploy and banished his wife from his household. The episode had caused a huge scandal at the time—as much because of the affair itself as because of what was perceived as La Pouplinière's unnecessarily cruel treatment of his wife. The *fermier général* had never remarried while his wife was alive, but she had recently died and Andrea had heard from his Venetian friends in Paris that the old man, now well into his sixties, was looking for a new young wife.

Monsieur de La Pouplinière was probably not uppermost in Giustiniana's mind the day she left Padua. But she had gone along with the idea when Andrea had discussed it before her departure. As at the beginning of their relationship, perhaps on account of the guilt she still felt for her "moment of weakness," she was again deferring to his judgment. She promised absolute transparency: "Let God separate us forever if I do not tell you everything that happens to me. And you must do the same with me even at the cost of hurting me." She yearned to please him in the hope of possessing him again completely. "You will know everything, and I shall win back your tenderness—you will see . . ."

Yet for all her resolutions, for all her valiant efforts to harness her feelings for Andrea, Giustiniana had little control over the sheer sadness that kept assailing her. If only she could give in to her emotions from time to time . . . "Your *tenderness*, Memmo! Oh God, may I speak to you this way? Do you allow me to do so? I have not shed a tear after those I shed with you in Padua, but I am immersed in desperation. Oh God! What will happen to me, and to you, Memmo? . . . I can only speak to you of love. Allow me to surrender for a few moments to my excessive feelings."

After a sleepless first night away from Andrea, she added this rambling postscript to her letter as she waited for their little convoy to get started again:

> *I wept a great deal [all during the night] and was inconsolable. I made a thousand plans to go back to you if you do not find a way to your Giustiniana. What misery is mine! You are always on my mind, and at this very moment I am kissing your little portrait. Let me speak to you about my passion. I shall be wiser when I will have persuaded myself that I am far from you; but will I ever be able not to talk to you about my passion? You allowed me to talk about it again, and now I feel it with such power that it is impossible for me to bury it. May I hope, mon cher frère, to find the words 'I love you' in the letter I will receive from you in Turin or Lyon? Write long letters to me, be my friend always, love me as much as you can. I owe you so much. I feel close to you in all those things to which my soul will always be sensitive. May God give me a fortune so that I can run off to live wherever you may be. . . . Farewell, my love. Take care of yourself for me, take care of yourself for Giustiniana, who is so unhappy now but will soon be near you and happy again.*

Andrea and Giustiniana found themselves in each other's arms much sooner than they could possibly have expected. A short distance outside Vicenza the axle of the carriage in which the Wynnes were traveling cracked and the vehicle crashed to the ground, damaging the luggage carriage as well. All the passengers came out of the wreckage unscathed, if a little shaky. Back at the inn, a dejected Zandiri informed the Wynnes that fixing the carriages could take as much as four days.

Giustiniana seized her chance: she summoned a messenger and dashed off a note to Andrea, who was still in Padua on business, telling him to join her in Vicenza immediately. "My mother thanks the Virgin for having saved us," she quipped. "I thank her because I am not moving from here." He could justify his sudden appearance in Vicenza, she added, by telling Mrs. Anna that having heard of the accident he wished to make sure Giustiniana and the rest of the family were all right. "If I get to see you again, I will certainly believe in miracles. Let me say no more. I want the lackey to fly to you immediately."

Andrea arrived at the inn the next day, wearing an appropriately worried expression, and inquired about the Wynnes. Mrs. Anna was resting, and she exploded when she heard that Andrea was downstairs, cursing him and even accusing him of having some-how orchestrated the entire incident. Zandiri, who was already beside himself because of the delay, slammed the door of his room in Andrea's face and refused to speak to him. Not to be outdone by Mrs. Anna, Zandiri then threatened to kill Andrea, who had already prudently retreated to a nearby inn. Giustiniana sent her lover a dramatic report of what had happened after he had quit the scene:

> *A firestorm, my dear Memmo, a terrible firestorm. My mother is so furious she says she wants to notify the authorities.... She treated me abominably and I suffered in a thousand different ways, but when all the composure I had in me was finally exhausted I gave in to my anger.... [Zandiri] said loudly that he wanted to knife you.... I told him you would have him caned very soon, and he answered he would have you caned first. Every-one in the next room heard each word, as there were no other noises in the house. We cannot see each other here anymore. Go to Venice, take legal action, and, if you can, try to arrange things in such a way that [Zandiri] will be arrested tomorrow. He did threaten to kill you.*

Andrea was utterly unprepared for the violent reaction his appearance had provoked—after all, Mrs. Anna and he had parted amicably in Padua only two days before. Then again, she had always been a difficult woman. But Zandiri's behavior really incensed him. Andrea would teach him a lesson, give him a scare he would not forget. The law was on his side: threatening the life of a prominent Venetian patrician was a serious offense, and for once Andrea had every intention of using the prerogatives of his rank. Besides, the bewildered clientele of the inn had overheard everything. Zandiri had sealed his own fate.

However, rather than taking legal action in Venice, as Giustiniana had pressed him to do, Andrea decided to seek justice on the mainland, away from the city gossips. He asked Giustiniana to provide him with signed statements from three patricians who had been present at the scene in the inn and had heard Zandiri's curses against Andrea, as well as sworn depositions by several servants attesting to the fact that Andrea had not provoked Zandiri—had not even been given the chance to speak to him. Once Giustiniana supplied the evidence, Andrea contacted the all-powerful Venetian *rappresentante* in Verona, who in turn ordered the chief of police to follow Andrea's instructions to the letter. In effect, the *rappresentante*, himself a member of the ruling oligarchy and a friend of the Memmo family, allowed Andrea to take justice into his own hands.

Mrs. Anna spent most of the following day in church. In her absence, the two lovers had ample opportunity to plan their legal offensive together. Brazenly, they even visited some of the architectural marvels of Vicenza, including Andrea Palladio's famous Teatro Olimpico. It was a good day, one of their best in a long time:

> *Seldom have we had a chance to be together as long and as sweetly as today. Alas, this good fortune comes to me now, ensuring that the pain of separation will be stronger still! It is my fate. . . . But oh my God, I cannot tell you more because my mother is calling me now. Tomorrow I shall be at the Due Torri [in Verona]. You will spy on us, I am sure, and I will be told everything. . . . I hope our time together will not be bad there either. Meanwhile, give the go-ahead to our great coup, and have a good trip. God! We are rushing simultaneously toward new bliss and new danger! If you love me, be passionate about everything, and fear nothing.*

It felt as if their conspiratorial days were back. Secret messengers shuttled between them as they prepared the "great coup": Zandiri would be arrested and thrown into jail. Giustiniana egged Andrea on, encouraged him to use all the powers in his hands to finally rid them of the "scoundrel."

As soon as Andrea left for Verona that evening, however, doubts began to creep into Giustiniana's mind, for she and her family now faced the prospect of a long and difficult journey without the protection of a man. Suddenly she wasn't so sure: "If [Zandiri] comes with us it will be hell, and if he stays we will have to deal with a thousand dangers."

That night a messenger sent by Giustiniana went looking for Andrea "all over Verona," shaking guards out of their slumber and even forcing the deputy mayor from his bed to deliver an express letter to him. On the envelope, Giustiniana had used their old cipher to write:

Don't be amazed, just laugh.

Sleepily, Andrea read on:

I cannot be entirely evil. I have worries and fears. My wish for revenge is giving in to my good heart, and I am about to ask you that yours give in as well for love of me. I foresee a thousand troubles if you have [Zandiri] detained. My mother would be so furious she would be capable of abandoning the family and ruining us all. Memmo, give in to me, give up your resentment to your Giustiniana, who beseeches you. Let me leave with a renewed admiration for your soul.

Andrea did not want to leave Zandiri rotting indefinitely in some godforsaken prison of the Venetian Republic. He only wanted to give the man a scare. A public apology, he reassured Giustiniana, was all that was needed to grant Zandiri's release. Meanwhile, the carriages in Vicenza had been repaired, and the next day, October 7, the Wynne party arrived in Verona and took up lodgings at the Due Torri, not far from where Andrea was staying.

The lovers managed to steal another full day together, roaming the streets and squares of the town while Mrs. Anna attended a succession of church services and Zandiri took care of travel arrangements. Before curling into bed, Giustiniana wished Andrea a good night:

Sleep well, my heart, for you will need it after all the walking we did. I could learn so much traveling with you! You've seen everything, you know everything, and you are so good at pointing out things and drawing distinctions. . . . I love you, yes, I do love you. Oh God! How much there is to say—more than I even dare to wish or say. . . . Good night. . . . Dream of me. . . . Love me much. Will you always let me ask you to love me?

The Wynne party started early the next morning on the road to Brescia, most of them unaware of the trap that Andrea and Gius-tiniana had laid for Zandiri in what was then the last major city of the Venetian State before entering the Duchy of Milan. They spent the night in the small town of Desenzano and arrived in Brescia the following afternoon. The two lovers kept in regular contact during the trip through brief express notes sent from the stations along the road; it was important to synchronize the steps that were to lead to what Giustiniana, perhaps not fully antici-pating the seriousness of the matter, was now calling "the great prank."

The Wynnes had barely settled into their lodgings in Brescia and were still unpacking when loud noises were heard in the foyer: police officers had arrived at the inn, shouting orders and creating great alarm among the guests. They summoned Zandiri down-stairs and, after questioning him briefly, dragged him away.

For all her conniving, Giustiniana was suddenly frightened.

God only knows what is going on. I tremble for my own sake as well. My mother is spewing fire at this moment. . . . If you love me, Memmo, try to be as prudent as you can. I never thought things would take such a turn. They tell me [Zandiri] is in jail!

That afternoon word came back to the Wynnes confirming that Zandiri had been roughly interrogated by the police and locked up in the Castello, Brescia's intimidating fortress in the Old City. Mrs. Anna became incandescent when she realized that her traveling companion would not be returning to the inn that night. She accused Andrea of acting out of spite and vowed to expose him in Venice. Then she turned on her daughter.

I warn you: my mother is in a fury, and she blames me for everything. She also says she will take her vengeance on me and plans to send all the letters she has—mine and yours—tomorrow morning by courier either to the [British Resident in Venice] or to someone else—I don't quite know; right now she swears she will ruin me. If she continues to insult me the way she has, I might have to make a decision. . . . I cannot stand it any longer.

Giustiniana hoped things could still be resolved the following morning with a simple apology by Zandiri, but she feared that his own pride and her mother's anger might conspire to make matters worse for everyone: "If he asks your forgiveness and if you grant it immediately, as you intend to," she wrote to Andrea before retiring that evening, "things will settle themselves. But if he behaves crazily, God only knows what we must fear!"

The next day Giustiniana awoke to find her mother's fury unabated. She had taken the affront personally, and she seemed determined to wage war on them even if it meant keeping Zandiri locked up a while longer. "My mother has sworn to ruin us," she told Andrea. "She doesn't want [Zandiri] to say he's sorry. . . . I'm desperate." It was pure theater: Mrs. Anna was in one corner of the room writing a letter to Murray, the British Resident, while Giustiniana was sitting across the room writing frantically to Andrea about Mrs. Anna writing to Murray. ". . . She makes it appear as if [Zandiri's] arrest were the result of some violent action on your part designed to keep us here. God only knows what else she will make up."

In open revolt against Mrs. Anna, Giustiniana decided to send her own version of events to the Resident in order to preempt her mother's letter to him.

Sir,

I will be in serious danger if you do not help me and grant me your protection in a case so clearly ruled by vengeance alone—not by justice. Hear me, sir, and save me.

When we arrived in Vicenza our carriages broke down, and we were told the repairs would take four days. I immediately informed Memmo with the sole purpose of bidding him farewell just one more time; and he, hoping for the same, rushed to Vicenza. My mother was asleep when he arrived at the inn. He waited for her to wake up in order to congratulate her on the fact that nothing distressing had happened to the family on account of the crash. Having observed that was the case with his own eyes, he was about to go back—as he had promised my mother and as she herself seemed convinced he would do, since he was without coffer and manservant.

Meanwhile, I called in Zandiri—the very stern and knowledgeable manager of our trip—to explain to him all that was going on. But he simply walked from one room to the next without greeting [Memmo] and even slammed the door in his face. That wasn't enough: when I went down, I was upbraided by my mother in the usual manner while Signor Zandiri hurled insults at Memmo and threatened to kill him even though he was by then far away. His insults were heard by three gentlemen and by many servants. Once Memmo was informed of all this he thought he would simply remind Signor Zandiri that such a rodomontade was very much to his own disadvantage, and in lieu of availing himself of the harsh instruments he had at his disposal, the use of which might have offended our family, he asked the three noblemen for their honest testimony and gathered more evidence of the fact that he had not even spoken to Zandiri; then he turned to the [Venetian] rappresentante *to obtain justice. The* rappresentante *happened to be out of town, and [Memmo], who, despite his gentle manner, was determined to make [Zandiri] feel his superior status and mortify him, went ahead of us to Verona, whence the* rappresentante *had in fact just left for Vicenza. This unexpected turn of events forced [Memmo] to go on to Brescia, where he was finally able to present his case and where Zandiri was reprimanded by the Tribunal in presence of the authorities as well as many gentlemen and then transferred to the Castello and put at [Memmo's] disposal.*

My mother went into a fury when she heard of the arrest and blamed me for everything and swore to ruin Memmo and me— again. She doesn't want [Zandiri] to tell Memmo he's sorry, even though that would put an end to everything. . . . We could resume our journey as early as tomorrow and Memmo could return to Venice. But no, she wants to move ahead and take her revenge on us for no fault of our own. As she is now writing to you, I have decided to inform you as quickly as possible of the facts, all of which can be proven by eye-witness noblemen.

I know, Mr. Murray, your sense of justice as well as your prudence. And I know that, once well apprised of all the facts, you will not encourage her unfair wrath. I have left Memmo to go to London in accordance with the orders my mother has received [from Lord Holderness]—though under the laws of my country no one could have forced me to had I decided to do otherwise.

Truth reigns in all I have said to you, and all I ask is that you consider it well. I have reason to be fearful, and I put myself in your hands for whatever future violence I might suffer. Whatever you have heard about me, I am sure you will do right. . . . My character is not tainted. You have had occasion to know me. Meanwhile I am fearful of everything, and the only prudent course of action I can take is to ask for your useful and experienced assistance. Use your best judgment in reading my letter written in the greatest haste. . . . I also beg for the protection of Lady [Murray], your wife, to whom I have the honor of being . . .

It was a remarkable letter, scribbled at top speed with one eye on the page and the other on Mrs. Anna sitting across the room. Her tone was respectful, even obsequious, but with just enough familiarity to give her appeal a personal touch, enhanced by her prudent inclusion of the Resident's wife in her plea.

The last thing Murray could have wished was to become embroiled in a dispute in a remote provincial town between an angry Anglo-Venetian lady with a rather stained reputation and a well-known member of a prominent Venetian family. Luckily, the confrontation was defused before it could escalate into a full-blown diplomatic incident.

Giustiniana told Andrea about the two letters that were due to leave for Venice, and he informed the *rappresentante*. The following morning, the police intercepted Mrs. Anna's messenger, who had been instructed to slip out of town unnoticed. Her letter to Murray and the accompanying documents—a selection from the two lovers' correspondence—were handed over to Andrea, who, in a magnanimous gesture, returned them to Mrs. Anna unopened. But the *rappresentante* stepped in to remind Mrs. Anna of a basic fact of life in the Venetian Republic: Andrea's word carried more weight than hers. There was really no point, he added, in pursuing the matter further. She would only damage herself and her family.

In the end, Murray did not receive either of the letters (Giustiniana's was held back after Mrs. Anna's had been intercepted), though he was probably informed about the incident in detail. Meanwhile, the *rappresentante* sent his military aide to the prison at the Castello to work on Zandiri, who finally caved in and wrote a submissive letter of apology to his sworn enemy. Andrea promptly pardoned Zandiri. Giustiniana was delighted and sent Andrea a short adulatory note: "You are a great man in every respect, my Memmo! And such cold blood, such dexterity, such quick and firm decisions in moments of great pressure! Oh, I shall never find another man like you if I live a thousand years."

The next day a grumbling Zandiri returned to the inn. "No one spoke," Giustiniana noted. "He and my mother appear to be fairly calm. . . . No secret meetings so far and no new letters." Victory made her bold again, even reckless. "I am dying to see you. . . . If per chance this evening you should feel inclined to come visit me in the same room as last night, be sure that I would feel infinite comfort in seeing you."

The lovers spent the night together—the last before they parted ways.

On October 12 the Wynnes headed for Milan. Ten days had passed since the carriage had broken down. Andrea and Giustiniana had to go through a painful separation all over again. "Everything that has happened in between has made me feel that I belong to you even more," Giustiniana wrote. "I feel this separation very deeply. . . . I've never felt such pain, my Memmo—not even in Padua." There, at least, they had had more time to take leave from each other. Their parting in Brescia was a rushed and brutal affair. After a long day on the road that left her exhausted and "completely battered," she began to take stock. As in her first letter from Vicenza, she reverted to addressing her lover as her dear brother:

Mon cher frère,

I am far from you, my dear Memmo, I will not see you again, and I am so sure of it now that all I feel is pain and desperation. It was so difficult to leave [this morning]! They had to call for me ten times because I had locked myself in a room and had spread out your letters and was crying and feeling completely desolate. But what's the point? In the end I had to leave, and now you are so far away that I have finally come to realize I will not see you for a very long time. But I had to tear myself away without even a farewell, an embrace, a few shared tears! Oh God! . . . Oh, my Memmo, why do I love you so? Your friendship is such a rare thing that I would have felt bound to you forever even without having any other feelings for you. Oh, wretched circumstances! And you, Memmo, will you still love me? Yes, you will; but do not tell me, or else just tell me with the coldest words. I feel I could become extravagant: so far away that I cannot lay a claim on you nor give in to my feelings. Ah, if only you knew how torn I am! The past, your kindness, your friendship. All this love I have for you, it startles me, it fills me completely. I love you more and more, and more and more I see the miserable difficulties ahead. . . . Oh God! Memmo, my Memmo, still forever mine, oh God, pity me. And you, my heart, how will you remember me? Forget the past; be generous to me the way only you can be, and promise to think of me only the way I will be from now on. I will tell you everything, do not doubt that; I will keep you informed of my conduct, my opportunities, my feelings, my prudence. Yes, I shall be prudent—you mustn't doubt that any longer. If only you knew how I feel now about caprice and weakness, I think you would be satisfied; but do not worry: my prudence will not be excessive; it is wise, well founded; and it will not vanish. Think well of me, if you still can, and expect to think even better of me yet. Tell me everything; continue to lend me your tender assistance. I will depend on it: I am yours. My dearest Memmo, mon aimable frère, you are such a rare being. Where else to find you if not in

you? And will I not look for you and find you again? Wait for me,
wherever you want.

It was typical of Giustiniana to address her letter to her *cher frère*
and ramble on for pages, as if the actual scribbling of all those
words dulled the pain and provided a small measure of relief.
Invariably, however, the indulgent musing stopped as she reminded
Andrea—and herself—that circumstances called for more disci-
plined behavior. After all, there were things to be done in Paris,
urgent matters to attend to:

> *I will also take a keen interest in La Pouplinière and my future*
> *state, which will depend entirely upon myself and my reputa-*
> *tion. . . . With my good manners, my cleverness, and my talent in*
> *eliciting the sympathy of others, I will make the catch; and then,*
> *Memmo, others will depend on me as I now depend on others, for,*
> *believe me, I will have a name and all the rest. . . . Trust me; I*
> *will tell you everything; I have given you my sacred word, and I*
> *intend to keep it. Look over me, my heart, and help me, but above*
> *all love me always.*

The Wynnes arrived in Milan on the evening of October 13 and
took rooms at Il Pozzo, a fashionable inn not far from the Duomo.
It was the first time Giustiniana had left Venetian territory since
her trip to London after her father's death, when she had been
fifteen. Once she was outside the Republic, her distance from
Andrea seemed even greater. In her thoughts she traveled back to
him constantly in order "to penetrate his being," as she was fond of
writing. She conjured, as a lover will against all odds, Andrea's
magical appearance in the most unlikely places: at street corners, in
shops, even in the foyer of the inn where she was staying. To free
herself from the suffocating presence of Mrs. Anna, Zandiri,
Toinon, and her four younger siblings, she went out to explore the
city in Andrea's imaginary company.

Squeezed between the Venetian Republic and the rising Kingdom of Piedmont and Sardinia, the Duchy of Milan was a shadow
of its former self—little more than a city-state on the southern rim
of the Austrian Empire, which had extended its authority over the

duchy after the War of the Spanish Succession. The city was fairly prosperous, yet its morale had long been sapped by the rule of the invaders. "There seems to be a provincial atmosphere everywhere here," Giustiniana wrote, complaining that people stared at her "as if they had never seen a foreigner."

She visited the Duomo, watched charlatans sell their miraculous balsams and unguents in the square, wandered around the streets, peered into fancy stores, observed the clothes people wore. She was struck by the great number of elegant carriages congregating in the main square for the evening stroll, and she also noticed the poverty and filth and the high number of beggars in the streets. As for the ladies, always the object of her special attention, her verdict was rather damning: "Mostly ugly, mostly clumsy."

One way or another, the Milanese always came up short in her running conversation with Andrea. "I had a different idea of Milan," she concluded petulantly. ". . . I make comparisons, and at present I like Venice in the extreme."

Giustiniana went to the theater with Mrs. Anna and thought the show so boring that she stared blankly at the stage until she was overwhelmed by a wave of nostalgia: "It occurred to me I was in a *theater,* and so I was taken over by the strongest melancholy. I remembered . . . Oh, what I remembered. . . . Do you remember all that I remember? If you can, then surely you will pity my state."

The Venetian Resident, Giuseppe Imberti, offered the Wynnes a seat in his box at the Opera. On her first night there, Giustiniana loudly complained that the singing was "dreadful." The Resident agreed, and since he knew Andrea well, he showed himself more eager to catch up on the latest twist of their love saga than to listen to the music. Mrs. Anna, still recovering from the jolting trip from Brescia, arrived late at the opera, so Imberti had plenty of time to tease Giustiniana.

> *I confessed to him that I love you, but I also told him we are now bound only by friendship. He asked me if I had your portrait. I showed it to him and kissed it in his presence. . . . Then he wanted to know how much I was willing to pay in order to see you and I said: Everything. And I said it with all my heart! He asked*

how much I would give him if he produced you in less than twenty-four hours. . . . In the end he only promised to show me a letter of yours tomorrow. Still, I hope to God he will. He then tried to make me believe that you were hidden somewhere inside the hall. At that point, I must confess, I began to fantasize that you might actually be there, and much to my embarrassment I started looking for you in every box. You can imagine my state when I couldn't find you! How terrible I felt until the opera was over! I feel miserable, Memmo. . . . If you love me, if you are my friend, arrange things in such a way that you can visit me soon, and I will not fail to come looking for you.

The Wynnes stayed three full days in Milan while their carriages were refitted for the next leg of the trip—straight west toward Piedmont and its capital, Turin. Giustiniana was incapable of reviving her initial curiosity about the city and grew more miserable with each day. She got up late, went to mass with Mrs. Anna before lunch, and took uninspired walks around the neighborhood. She had little interest in the people she met. "Everything bores me . . ."

For lack of anything better to do, she went to the "dreadful" opera again, figuring Imberti would be there—as indeed he was—and they could talk about Andrea: "I came home in the Resident's carriage, and I talked about you along the way, telling him, as always, part of our story. I had talked to him about you at the Opera as well—during the first act and the dancing part."

The solicitous Resident enjoyed Giustiniana's company, not to mention the whiff of Venetian intrigue she had brought with her. He gave a dinner party for the Wynnes on their last evening in town (since he knew they had not unpacked their trunks entirely and did not have their evening gowns available, he downgraded the formal dinner to a more casual affair—but still "with many guests"). Despite her melancholy mood, Giustiniana was a breath of fresh air in that musty Milanese crowd of retired generals and diplomats and crumbling aristocrats. She was the object of everyone's curiosity: even strangers came up to her and asked shamelessly about her "well-known passion." And when her mother was not within earshot, Giustiniana indulged in Andrea-talk, which invariably brought on a familiar mixture of pleasure and pain: "The few I choose to speak to all know I adore you."

Imberti was sorry to see Giustiniana leave. The night before the Wynnes' scheduled departure, he begged her to stay on a few days and even offered to hide Andrea in his house. Andrea was in fact on his way to Milan on business, but he was waiting for the Wynnes to leave Italy before making an appearance there. It was unthinkable that the two lovers should find themselves again in the same city so soon after the Zandiri incident—and with Mrs. Anna still in a rage. "I explained to him your justified worries, as well as the dangers for me." Still, Giustiniana now had a useful ally in the Resident, who agreed to handle their secret correspondence in the days ahead.

It was a gray, dreary afternoon on October 17 when the Wynnes drove away from Milan. Before leaving the inn, Giustiniana scribbled one more note to Andrea and pressed it into the hands of Imberti, who had come to say farewell:

> *If you do come to Milan and you don't stay at the Resident's, come here and take the room I was in. . . . Come to [Il Pozzo] and ask for the San Carlo room. There are two beds, and you must sleep in the one next to the wall. . . . Remember that from that bed I sent you a million sighs, and in that bed I shed a few tears as well. . . . Tell me everything about your life. . . . Be mine forever. . . . Love me as much as you can and as long as you can.*

And off they clattered toward the Alps. It took them three days and three nights to reach Turin, where they planned to rest a few days and make the inevitable repairs to the carriages. The journey was especially tiring and uncomfortable. "Always rain and always this awful cold," Giustiniana complained. They were knocked about against the hard wood of the coach till the bruising became "unbearable." Their feet were damp, their clothes splattered with mud:

> *And with all that, my mother still insisted on keeping a window open all the time. I pretended to sleep in order not to have to*

*talk or pray with the others, but I was always in the blackest
mood. I can only think about how to be near you again.*

Her mood did not improve. They spent one night in the "dreadful" village of Bussalova. The following day they stopped for an "awful meal" in Novara. They left the plains of Lombardy and drove through the soggy rice fields of eastern Piedmont. Giustiniana scarcely looked out the window. She had only one thing on her mind: Andrea's letter waiting for her in Turin.

*You will have received mine from Milan. When will I have
one from you? Can I hope to receive one the day after tomorrow?
Where are you? How many questions I have for you. Do you love
me now? Will you always love me? . . . Come to me, please. I
make myself crazy; I want my Memmo absolutely. The ambassador told me the other evening that we really are made for each
other. And it would be so true if only I had been a better person.
How much I have lost! But will I have your love again? I tell
everyone we have established a simple friendship between us; but
then I immediately add that I adore you . . . Yes, I adore you, and
with greater strength than I want to.*

In Vercelli, the Wynnes arrived haggard and exhausted in the middle of the night and left before dawn the next morning. They stopped for lunch and changed horses in the "wretched" hamlet of Livorno Ferraris and spent the last night in the old border town of Chivasso before making the straight run over the undulating plain of the Po valley, all the way to the bustling capital of Piedmont.

Turin was the center of a growing young state ably ruled by King Charles Emmanuel III. Giustiniana had visited it once already, on her return journey from London six years earlier. She loved this sturdy little city at the feet of the Alps. The avenues were neat and clean, the squares were pretty, the symmetry of the city's layout softened by the curves of the late baroque palaces and churches:

"The city has a beautiful appearance, and, though small, it is organized in the most graceful way possible. Beautiful streets, beautiful houses, beautiful setting, and charming surroundings."

Unlike the Venetians, Charles Emmanuel III had taken advantage of his kingdom's neutrality in the war to turn his attention to domestic improvements and reform. Political debate was lively. Intellectual and scientific associations were multiplying. True, social life was a little stiff, certainly by Venetian standards. But there was nothing provincial about the city. Giustiniana could not help but notice that, unlike Venice, Turin was a busy place with a growing sense of its own importance.

When she arrived there in the early afternoon of October 20, however, she had little desire for sight-seeing. She wanted to know whether Andrea's letter was waiting for her at the Venetian Embassy and what was the quickest way of getting her hands on it. The Wynnes were held up for several hours at customs outside the city gates because Mrs. Anna fussed and argued with the officers. Giustiniana grew so impatient that she convinced Zandiri to go on ahead and announce their arrival to the Resident, Giannantonio Gabriel. Zandiri returned clutching Andrea's letter. The irony was not lost on the poor man. "I was never your go-between in Venice," he hissed. "Now I am reduced to being one here."

Giustiniana stifled a laugh and ran off "trembling" to read the letter.

It was not what she had expected; certainly not what she had hoped for, and she replied heatedly:

> *Every sentence of that letter produced its share of tears! Oh yes, I am truly and completely unhappy. I have adored you, I have betrayed you for weakness, I have consequently deceived you, I have at times hated you, I have admired you, and I have fallen in love with you again and I love you now—and I am honest with you and I always will be. Do you doubt my friendship now? Come, Memmo, don't offend me; don't make me lose heart. I would like to be just a friend to you; I would like to harbor nothing but fraternal feelings; but I love you—even though I now understand I will never have a hold on your heart. What do you want me to do with your admiration for me if I love you? Hear it*

one more time: I am jealous, and I still expect from you what you will not give to me—out of deliberation as well as necessity.

Andrea's letters from this period are lost, so it is impossible to know what, exactly, he was writing to her, but Giustiniana's reaction to his words certainly gives us a sense of what they felt like to her. Clearly he did not respond to her outpourings with enough enthusiasm. He seemed evasive, perhaps even a little ambiguous. All she could think of was how to get her letters to him and stay in touch. He, on the other hand, was not nearly as meticulous. She did not even know where to send her next letter. Why was there no forwarding address? How could he be so forgetful? And then the needless cruelty of telling her he had met a young nun who would certainly have "reawakened his senses" if his heart had not been Giustiniana's: "The Nun! Why do you imagine she might awaken your senses? . . . You add: If Giustiniana were not so much in your heart. Oh believe me, Memmo, he who imagines feelings already has those feelings. The portrait you sketch for me is much too seductive."

Giustiniana was struggling to stay calm. She felt the need to declare her love loudly and incessantly and claimed the right to tell Andrea—her *cher frère* now, but still the man she loved more than anyone in the world—how afraid she was of losing him entirely:

> *Forgive me, but you must understand all my weakness even as I thank you for your sincerity—which I continue to beseech of you for a thousand reasons. I am always looking for tokens of your love; and I might still need to do so. Your character, your words, your noble actions are always such that whatever will happen to us you will always have the strongest, truest interest in me; but I fear that eventually your heart will be possessed by a much stronger feeling—and that I will not be the object of that feeling. I am crazy; I go looking for my own misery. Yes, but can anyone say it will not be that way? That is the only certainty. . . . Ah, Memmo, pity me. I really need your counsel.*

Giustiniana went to bed exhausted, lay awake all night, and the next morning continued to write:

I have not been able to stop thinking about our whole history together. I have lost a great deal, my Memmo . . . and nothing can possibly bring any consolation to me now except the knowledge that my confession (which probably no other woman would have been able to make) has at least eliminated the extreme pain you would have felt at the moment of our separation had you believed you were losing a faithful Giustiniana. . . . Yet I am sure that if they hadn't kept me away from you for so long I would never have given you an opportunity to accuse me of infidelity. . . . But let us not talk about this anymore.

Bad weather forced the Wynnes to stay in Turin a full week. The heavy autumn rains had swelled the Dora River outside the city, and there was the added risk of flooding. The high mountains west of the city were covered with snow, and Giustiniana feared a "difficult journey" over the Alps. She tried to make the best of the situation, though, and with the help of the Venetian Resident, Mr. Gabriel, she and her sisters blended effortlessly into Turin life. They received guests at the embassy, members of the small English community for the most part. They visited palaces and churches. Occasionally the skies cleared and they rode a carriage out to the Valentino Royal Park—"which is really more of a grand alley with a view of the Po and the hills in the background." In the evening, Mr. Gabriel took them to the opera.

Giustiniana found the Turinese to be "very sociable, though they adhere to the most rigid etiquette, and extremely reserved." She was struck by the fact that "ladies may not go out in their carriage in the company of a male escort." And gallantry, she added, perhaps with her old Venetian friends in mind, was "conducted terribly." The formality of Turinese society she ascribed to the influence of the court of Charles Emmanuel III, "which is most serious-minded."

Luckily the king and his family were at their country estate in Venaria, so Giustiniana could look around the Palazzo Reale at leisure. She wandered for hours in the grand halls, taking her time to inspect "every apartment," and although she did not particularly like the sumptuous rococo style of the furniture, she loved the openness of the space, the sweeping perspective, "the long enfilade of rooms that offers such a pleasant view"—an effect that was more difficult to achieve in the smaller Venetian *palazzi*. As royal palaces went, the Palazzo Reale was modest in size, in keeping with the sobriety of the House of Savoy, "yet it is certainly more beautiful than [Versailles]. Everyone says so."

Over the years the king had assembled an impressive collection of drawings and paintings by Italian and other European masters. He was very proud of his recent acquisition *The Woman with Dropsy*, a masterpiece by Flemish artist Gerrit Dou, which had received a great deal of publicity. Now that she was suddenly face to face with the famous painting, Giustiniana could compare it to a similar work of Dou's, *A Sick Woman Being Visited by the Doctor*, which belonged to Consul Smith.[1] She thought the latter far superior, perhaps out of loyalty to her old friend. "Next time you see Smith," she wrote to Andrea, "please tell him I defended his painting in front of many people who wanted to stone me to death."

Far away from Venice, Giustiniana looked for connections with the more familiar world she had shared with Andrea. And she sometimes found them in the most unexpected places. Shortly after arriving in Turin, she met Filiberto Ortolani, a young scholar and collector and a dear friend of Andrea's who had studied in Venice with Lodoli and had fallen under his spell. They connected immediately. "I told him I knew him well [through you], and he said he knew me well through the same channel, and we quickly became best friends in the world. I went to see his apartment, his rooms. . . . He gave me a few things to read, he talked about Lodoli, he talked about you a great deal. . . . He is a very good man." She could speak to Ortolani about Andrea "with great liberty," so she sought his company as much as possible. When they were together, deep in conversation and reminiscence, she easily lost track of the time.

Giustiniana had been spending the afternoon with her new friend one day when she suddenly realized she was late for the opera. She picked up Bettina and Tonnina and rushed to the performance wearing a large, frilly bonnet *à la française* (she wore her traveling dress under her cloak, as most of their trunks were still packed). The house was full when the three girls made their entrance (Mrs. Anna had stayed home), and the show was well under way. Not that the Turinese were paying much attention to the singing: "The three of us—my sisters and I—were the real show in the theater," Giustiniana bragged. "Everyone was staring at us." Not because they were more beautiful—she conceded that there were many beautiful women in Turin, "if horribly done up"—but simply because they were from out of town. "The mere fact of being foreigners here is enough to earn us praise."

Chevalier B., captain of the Royal Guards, stared at Giustiniana with such intensity he made her blush. He took a seat right in front of her, in the box that belonged to the Marquise de Prié, a lover of music and a prominent member of Turinese society, whom Giustiniana had briefly encountered in Venice some years before.

"Mademoiselle, do not move," the captain cried out. "You look exactly like the woman who was my very first passion."

Giustiniana curtsied and turned further away.

"Yes, I can see the very same features to which I am so sensitive," the captain insisted, calling on the marquise to take a look for herself.

Again Giustiniana curtsied, but the man wouldn't give up. So she finally blurted out in her uncertain French, "Sir, if what you say is true you put me in the odd position of having to either consider your taste to be poor or feel flattered by a vanity I don't believe to be justified."

Delighted by Giustiniana's reply, the marquise stepped in at her side: "Ah, *mon Dieu,* she is charming! How well she has answered! I was right to say that by the sheer look of her one could guess she had spirit."

The captain continued relentlessly to compare Giustiniana to his first love: "I can assure you, Countess Castelli was a beautiful dame. And here I see the same eyes, the same significant features, those eyelashes, that silhouette, that same serious yet seductive look . . ."

"She might well have been very beautiful," Giustiniana interrupted, by now rather enjoying this impromptu duet, "and I might indeed have some slight resemblance to her without of course having her charms, Monsieur. But I am surprised you should find the resemblance so perfect. I am of the opinion that one never encounters such resemblances to the people one loves."

"Well, Mademoiselle, you can therefore appreciate your own power over me if it is God's will that what I see in you is only an illusion."

By this time a small crowd had gathered under their boxes and clapped at Giustiniana's repartees while she feigned annoyance and made endless curtsies. The marquise laughed and applauded her new young friend. Nobody was paying much attention to the singers on stage.

"I know you, Mademoiselle," the marquise whispered to Giustiniana. "I had the privilege of seeing you in Venice, and people spoke well of you."

"And I, Madame, had the privilege of admiring you more than anyone else, even though everyone who sees you admires you." Turning to the besotted captain, she said, "Here is the most beautiful dame I have ever seen, and the most agreeable; so I question your good taste: How can you talk about an old passion in such gorgeous company?"

The captain was not to be daunted, and turned again to Giustiniana: "Mademoiselle, this particular triumph of yours is but a measure of your charm. Though I stand next to the most beautiful lady of the land, I only have eyes for you. If only God willed that you be my last passion just as your look-alike was my first! I am certain it would be so if you stayed on [in Turin]."

Giustiniana dismissed the hopeless suitor and turned again to the marquise, who wanted to know if she and her family were on their way back to Venice.

"No, no, we have left. We are going to London."

"I understand," the captain interrupted. "You are engaged to someone in Venice."

"It could well be, Monsieur."

"I knew it. . . . Those eyes are not meant to be useless; there is a fire in them that needs to be tended. Ah, who is the happy man? I must meet him, I must at least make myself useful to him. . . . Mademoiselle, please appoint me your personal secretary. . . ."

Giustiniana laughed off his histrionics, but the marquise, too, now wanted to know the name of the mysterious man in Venice.

"Madame, you know him very well, for he often had the honor of dining with you and Countess Romilii."*

"Ah yes, now I remember. It must be Monsieur Memmo, the eldest . . ."

How well the marquise spoke of Andrea! How good it was to hear such words! But the opera, alas, reached its conclusion "and we had to put an end to a conversation that had become so sweet for me."

The war had entered its third year when the Wynnes were in Turin on their way to Paris. The political atmosphere was less tense there than elsewhere in Europe, since the kingdom was not directly involved in the conflict. Still, the English in town did not speak to the French, as the two countries were at war. The French ambassador, Monsieur de Chevelin, on the other hand, was full of attention for the Wynnes and was often seen in their company, together with his young secretary, who had a weak spot for the eldest of the *demoiselles anglaises*.

One afternoon the British chargé d'affaires, Ralph Woodford,[2] and his party went out to the Valentino Park to join the Wynnes for a stroll. Giustiniana and her sisters were already in the company of a small French crowd, so the English simply greeted them from a distance and continued along. No matter: Giustiniana preferred to spend her time with the French anyway. On several occasions she complained to Andrea that the English in Turin "are really not much"—except for Woodford, who was in her view "the most relaxed Englishman" she had ever known.

Woodford felt at home on the Continent, having spent a happy time in Madrid, and he was now enjoying his post in northern Italy. He did not miss England and rather dreaded the day when he would be recalled to London, where, he told Giustiniana, he did not expect much happiness. "In fact, he says I shall not be able to stand it." Especially young English men. "As long as you stay in London," he assured her, "you will certainly remain faithful to your worthy lover because you are not likely to meet anyone

*See p. 98.

among our young men who can show such tenderness in affairs of the heart."

The young chargé d'affaires had a refreshing spontaneity that set him apart from the rest of his countrymen in Turin. When Mr. Gabriel gave a farewell dinner for the Wynnes at his home, he did not invite the stuffy English contingent. They all took offense, except for Woodford, who happily "invited himself over."

During her week in Turin, Giustiniana took advantage of the French ambassador's interest in her to practice a little diplomacy. The Wynnes' travel papers allowed them to spend only a few days in Paris, but Giustiniana's long talk with Woodford had made her even more determined to stay in the French capital for as long as possible. The first order of business in Paris would be to make a formal request for an extension of their permits, which would not be easy to obtain; they were, after all, subjects of Britain, at war with France. But Monsieur de Chevelin had assured Giustiniana he would inform the French authorities of their arrival in Paris and write a personal letter of recommendation to the Abbé de Bernis, the French foreign minister, whose help in this matter Giustiniana was already counting on.

The Abbé de Bernis had first met the Wynnes during his tenure as ambassador to Venice from 1753 to 1756. In those years he had also befriended Casanova and the two had shared a lover, a very intriguing and beautiful nun who used to escape under cover of darkness from the nunnery on the island of Murano to meet the two men in a *casino* rented by Bernis. (Casanova later claimed that the abbé had not always been an active participant in their sexual escapades, preferring to indulge in his taste for voyeurism.) Upon his return to Paris, Bernis had quickly risen to power under the sponsorship of Louis XV's mistress Mme de Pompadour and had played a key role in the sudden redrawing of European alliances, which had led to war in the summer of 1756. But the vivid memories of his Venetian days had stayed with him even during his meteoric ascent at Versailles, and he had kept in touch with his old friends in Venice. So he had probably heard through the grapevine that the Wynnes were on their way to Paris. Given his interest in gossip and intrigue, he was also likely to know quite a bit about the ill-fated love story of Andrea and Giustiniana. There was no real need for an introduction from the French ambassador in Turin— Giustiniana was certainly aware of that. But she must also have felt that a letter of recommendation would be a useful reminder of their imminent arrival at a time when Bernis was surely distracted by grave affairs of state. In any case, she expressed her deep gratitude to the solicitous M. de Chevelin when she saw him at the theater on the eve of their departure. "He came to visit us in our box, and despite the presence of the English chargé d'affaires, he praised me very much and assured me he had written to Bernis."

At last the Wynnes departed. The traveling plan decided upon by Zandiri was to head northwest for the town of Susa, then veer sharply to the west and upward over the pass of Mont Cenis, at seven thousand feet. The party would then travel down the steep road that led to the valley of the Are, along the river to Modane, and west to where the Are meets the Isère, a few miles north of Chambéry. From there it would be a fairly easy ride to Lyon.

Giustiniana did not feel well the day they left—bouts of nausea, mostly, as well as an incipient cold. The weather was not promising, and she was apprehensive about the passage over the Alps, even a little fearful. "I will write to you from Lyon," she scribbled to Andrea as the carriage was being fitted out. "Remember to tell me everything with the same precision I use with you. . . . Dear Memmo, am I still your little one?"

Giustiniana's cold got progressively worse as they climbed toward Mont Cenis, and by the time they reached the rocky pass it had settled in her chest. The ride downhill into France was even more miserable. The wind kept blowing snow into the post chaise through cracks and openings, and as they made their uncomfortable descent she was wracked by a violent cough.

> *The cold was so extreme I could no longer use my legs and feet and hands. I spent a whole day in that state, and by the time we got to [Lanslebourg] I couldn't stand up anymore. I was sat down near the fire with other travelers, and soon I felt a fever coming*

on. We had to stay there for two whole days, as our luggage had not yet arrived, and I was in a most pathetic state the entire time. My nose bled profusely. I lost my voice. And I felt a terrible pain in my chest, together with the coughing and the fever. Still, I did not want to linger in that place, for the Savoyard doctors scared me even more than their unbearable mountains.

At the height of her delirium, as the snow fell on the tiny mountain village, she dreamed of Venice and Andrea:

I waited for you at the dock [at Ca' Memmo], and after a long time you came into my boat. I reproached you for your scarce love, and full of passion I told you a thousand things. You apologized, my Memmo, by shedding many tears and holding me tightly in your arms without a word but with that rare expression on your face that I noticed when you arrived in Vicenza. What a moment! My tears joined yours, and I woke up. If this were the price to pay, I would want to be ill all the time. . . . You would be so tender with me, so loving. Oh Memmo, Memmo.

The carriage with their luggage finally caught up with them at Lanslebourg, and the Wynnes continued their journey through Modane and Chambéry and on to Lyon. The skies gradually cleared. Giustiniana's health improved every day, and as she regained her color, the daunting mountains behind her receded until they were little more than an unpleasant memory. "Mountains and more mountains. Terrible beds and awful food. . . . What a life!" she exclaimed. But at last she was in France. Lyon, where they planned to stay a few days, was known for its theater, its shops, and especially its beautiful silks. And beyond Lyon was Paris, a mere ten to twelve days away by regular coach.

Giustiniana missed Andrea terribly, and she was disappointed to discover that the letter she was hoping to find in Lyon was still stuck in Geneva because he had not put enough stamps on it. (She had money sent to Geneva to have it forwarded to Paris.) "You can imagine the pain. . . . I reached Lyon longing for a letter from you, longing to hear whether poor Giustiniana still reigns in your heart as you reign in hers. . . . Ah, my Memmo, what are you up to?

Where are you? . . . If only I had a compass that could tell me where you are."

Yet there was a lightheartedness in her tone that hadn't been there in a long time. She sounded less frantic, her feelings less jumbled. It was as if the physical barrier, concrete and inexorable, that had come between them after the passage of the Alps allowed her to focus more easily on the road ahead.

"Here all people talk about is fabrics," she quipped after her first tour of the city. She bought two dresses, a formal one with an autumnal motif of yellow leaves and green velvet ribbons and a simpler one of striped satin with flowers, "which will do just fine for a *déshabillé*."

She was already in Paris.

CHAPTER *Six*

"I had my hair done," Giustiniana proudly announced in her first letter from the French capital.

She had not even finished unpacking, and already she had summoned the coiffeur and his little army of stylists. "Don't laugh: the hairdresser kept me in his clutches from ten in the morning until six in the evening, with no interruption for lunch." He had snipped and trimmed and shaped her hair until about noon. Then his three assistants had planted "at least four hundred curling papers" about her head. In the afternoon, when the curls had set, the hairdresser had removed the papers, combing and puffing Giustiniana's hair carefully while his wife prepared her unguents for an extra-large chignon: "She mixed eight ounces of cream with as many ounces of powder. I'm not teasing you. It's absolutely true. They rub the mix into the hair, and thanks to the powder it grows into an enormous mass." Giustiniana was thrilled with the result: "In truth no hairdo has ever suited me so well." In Venice she had let her dark curls fall naturally around her face. Now she wanted to experiment with new styles, "and my hairdresser told me he will try a new one every time he combs me."

Alas, Parisian society was still officially in mourning for the death of the Duc de Luynes,[1] the former governor of Paris and a distinguished member of the Court at Versailles, and she was not allowed to parade her new coiffure beyond the confines of their hotel.

Upon arriving in Paris, Mrs. Anna had rented furnished rooms at the Hôtel d'Anjou, a comfortable house on the rue Dauphine, in the heart of the Faubourg Saint-Germain. To the right, their street led to the Seine, and then to the Tuileries Palace on the other side of the river. To the left, rue Dauphine wound its way past the bustling market and toward the old Church of Saint-Germain-des-Prés. The Wynnes occupied a large apartment on the ground floor. They had their own living room and dining room and were attended on by servants "with liveries, braids, and silver buttons."

During the journey to Paris, Giustiniana had always shared a room with Bettina or Tonnina, and sometimes with both. Now she fought hard—and successfully—to have one of her own. She was given a small "cabinet" with just enough space for a bed and a writing table. It had the disadvantage of being next to Mrs. Anna's boudoir but came with a nice view of the inner court and garden. Besides, it was somewhere she could finally have a little privacy after living in such close quarters with the rest of the family ever since they had left Venice.

The innkeeper lived on the first floor with her three daughters, who were "rather coquettish and not all that ugly," according to Giustiniana's preliminary reckoning. They often invited their guests for a meal or some musical entertainment. Among the other lodgers, Prince Dolgorouki and another Russian aristocrat, whom Giustiniana rather mysteriously referred to as "the Muscovite," immediately stood out: they dressed with flair, talked loudly in their native tongue, and brought a touch of cosmopolitan panache to the atmosphere of the hotel. Giustiniana also noticed a French officer, a royal *mousquetaire*. She thought him rather intriguing and not a bad-looking fellow, either. Unlike the noisy Russians, he spoke little and kept mostly to himself.

The arrival of the Wynne girls at the Hôtel d'Anjou did not go unnoticed, of course. But they behaved discreetly during their first days in Paris, as much on account of their own uncertain status in France as of the official mourning. Their loyalty to Britain was not very deeply felt—certainly Giustiniana never took sides in her letters to Andrea. Nevertheless, they were strangers in the land of the enemy and anxious to obtain an extension of their residency papers before venturing out into society. The Venetian ambassador, Niccolò Erizzo, was supposed to speed up matters, but he received the Wynnes with no great enthusiasm. He vaguely promised he would soon have them over for dinner and would talk to Bernis, the minister of foreign affairs on whom they had pinned their hopes, about obtaining permission for them to stay through the winter. But Giustiniana had the clear impression that Erizzo was not about to make a major effort on their behalf. "So far he has given me no reason to be satisfied with him," she complained to Andrea, trading haughtiness for haughtiness. "His superficial and patronizing tone does not suit my character at all." Erizzo's behavior so piqued her, she added, that she was tempted to tell him not to bother with the papers at all. Bernis had always been courteous to them in Venice, and he would surely grant them the "small favor" they were asking, even without Erizzo's intercession. She checked herself in the end, believing, like all proud Venetians, that an official step by their ambassador "means something after all."

Despite the "curfew," Giustiniana wasted little time in preparing for her first sortie onto the Parisian scene. After the hairdresser's visit, it was the dressmaker's turn. She bought winter capes and shawls, equipped herself with many "ornaments," and had a new morning *déshabillé* made of batavia, a delicate fabric she had purchased in Lyon. To keep herself warm, she added a muff and a stole in matching leather, with a fashionable motif of "birds from Lake Geneva." In the privacy of her small room, Giustiniana tried on her new clothes.

She also applied rouge to her cheeks for the first time.

The late fall of 1758 was one of Paris's strangest seasons. The war, now well into its third year, was not going well for France. The Grande Armée had suffered defeat after defeat at the hands of the Prussians. In America, the French were losing their colonies to the British. In India, too, they were retreating before the Union Jack. These endless military campaigns had defeated the Treasury. France was on the verge of bankruptcy, and the government was squeezing the people with intolerable taxes. Louis XV had benefited from a brief surge of sympathy in the wake of the assassination attempt against him the year before, when a deranged man by the name of Robert François Damiens had walked out of the crowd and stabbed him. The reprieve was over now, and his popularity was falling again. Mme de Pompadour, still the most influential force at court, was increasingly the object of public scorn. Posters denouncing her and the king appeared mysteriously around the city. The police cracked down ruthlessly on the populace. A person could be hanged for speaking the wrong word.

At Versailles, the crusty aristocracy lived on a diet of whispers and murmurs about who was in favor at Court and clung to the tired daily rituals dictated by royal etiquette. But in the city, society life carried on more splendidly than it had in a long time, as if the gloom spreading from the battlefields needed to be exorcized with special éclat. Every night there were lavish dinners, the theaters were full, and the public *bals de l'Opéra* were such crowded affairs they often turned into glittering stampedes.

Giustiniana could not resist the call for very long. When the period of mourning ended a week after her arrival in Paris, she was already dressed and coiffed *à la française* and eager to take a quick peek around and do a little showing off. After attending Sunday mass at the Church of Saint-Sulpice, she went for a spin in the Tuileries Gardens with Bettina and Tonnina. A crowd of carriages was out parading on the grounds despite the bitter cold. Later, when Giustiniana returned to the hotel, the flush of excitement still lingered. "We went around only twice in our *déshabillé*, and yet we were much looked at, and heard we were the most beautiful and best-looking women there," she reported proudly. She thought her rivals unimpressive: "Not a single beauty, many average-looking women, and an infinite number of ugly ones." But she was startled by the audacity of their *décolletés:* "All of them are naked . . . with nothing but a *petit collier* around their neck, covered by a *tour de gorge.*"

She had been out only a couple of hours, but she had surveyed the scene with a reporter's eye, noticing how the delicate silk scarves always matched the dresses. There were fewer hoops than when she had been in Paris six years earlier, and they were not as wide. "And all the ladies wear muffs that are covered with capon feathers that also match the color of their dress." She was certainly relieved that she had made her purchases in Lyon and did not have to go out in her old and rather passé Venetian dresses.

If she indulged in these descriptions, it was because, apart from her own love of beautiful fabrics and clothes, she knew of Andrea's

keen interest in the latest Parisian fashions. "The men are magnificent," she assured him. "Their velvet suits are adorned with rich
embroidery. Most wear black velvet with a gold or silver waist-
coat and no frills. But the really fashionable men wear a *pensée* suit
lined with the soft black wool of baby lambs taken straight from
the mother's womb. Muffs are lined with Siberian wolf's hair,
which is very long and white and bristly." She also kept Andrea up
to speed on the latest in men's hairstyles: a large toupee, combed *à
la cabriolet*—"wavy, without many curls, ending with a *frisé* and
firmed up with a small metal bar in the back." And if he really
wanted to impress his friends at the Listone, Andrea should consider having the heels of his black buckled shoes painted bright
red—a little touch she found especially chic.

The gorgeous clothes, the stylish hairdos, the sheer luxury and
flamboyance of the spectacle she had glimpsed outside the hotel
dazzled Giustiniana. Even the carriages she found "truly beautiful," so finely lacquered in black and gold, with "painted bouquets
of flowers that seem embroidered onto them." If only she could
share that splendid stage with Andrea. Together they would charm
Parisian society with their youthful good looks and clever conversation. "Why are you not with me?" she asked from the quiet of
her room in Paris.

In moments of greater lucidity—and greater melancholy—
Giustiniana saw clearly how the great distance that now separated
them made "my longing for your love all the more ridiculous."
From her new vantage point she was also able to appreciate more
fully all that Andrea had meant to her: "You revealed all the mys-
teries of life to me. You gave thunder to my soul. You made my
spirit delicate and noble. . . . You were my guide in everything, my
Memmo, a huge presence in me always." Her own "foolhardiness"
in once deceiving him haunted her still. There were times when
she longed to regain "the innocence of when you first met me."
Yet despite her "despicable" behavior of the previous summer, she
still dared "to claim those feelings you had for me in another
time." She was not about to give up on him, no matter how irrational her enduring love seemed to her at times. And so she was left

to contend with the confusion in her heart: "I love you; I am afraid; I am angry with myself; I call upon Philosophy to help me, yet I also despise her; and so my soul is torn."

Initially Giustiniana's letters from Paris took time to reach Andrea because he had not yet returned to Venice and she was never quite sure where she should mail them. After their final separation in Brescia, he had lingered on the mainland, visiting friends and building up his contacts. In recent years he had neglected his political career to the point that his younger brother Bernardo had already entered government service while Andrea still had no official occupation. Now Andrea's first appointment by the government appeared to be imminent—word had it he would be named *savio agli ordini,* a junior commissioner with responsibility for maritime affairs (the position was also used to train promising young patricians in the art of administration). He needed to redirect his energies toward the duties and responsibilities that befitted a young member of the ruling class. True to his character, he also indulged in what Giustiniana teasingly called his "amusements and distractions" during his tour of the Venetian mainland territories. As the rising hope of an old and prestigious family, he was fêted everywhere he went, and he was also, inevitably, introduced to young women looking to be married—though he dutifully assured Giustiniana that none of them could replace her in his heart.

Curled up in her cabinet at the Hôtel d'Anjou, Giustiniana read Andrea's reports on his "little travels" with a mixture of delight and apprehension. All those young ladies he glibly mentioned in his letters . . . was it true she had not been replaced in his heart? And what about the beautiful and mysterious "nun" he wrote about? Giustiniana was having nightmares about her: "You were in her arms. . . . Yes, I even heard you shout your happiness. . . . You had penetrated the convent, you had struggled to get through the iron bars. . . . And finally there was the beautiful nun. . . . Ah, I can see you now with her. . . . I only wanted to put an end to your delight, to upset your pleasure; instead I suddenly fainted and went completely numb. Then I woke up, and I was soaked with tears and sweat."

In general, she did her best to strike a lighthearted tone when she touched on Andrea's relationships with other women. Nagging would do no good. She knew from experience how much she had to lose by appearing excessively jealous. Yet even her bravest attempts at dissimulation were marked by the fear of dispossession:

> *What is keeping you in the provinces? At times I do not read through you, and the words you tell me are not enough to calm my wary soul. . . . I know that on the mainland, perhaps even more than in Venice, you are bound to stand out. You will set the tone, you will set the fashion, and so inevitably you will be master of all the ladies. You tell me all of this does not touch you. But is it really possible for a young man so good-natured and lively and open to new possibilities as you are to resist temptation for very long . . . ? Do not speak to me of what is impossible. Speak to me with sincerity. I can see you now* en petit Sultan, *bothering all the ladies, expertly casting your glances around and negotiating with skill the favors you must surely bestow. Nothing could be more amusing, and I honestly hope that this will in fact be your behavior. It is in my interest that you act like a* petit-maître *[dandy]. . . . I much prefer to see you wasteful than moody and even melancholy. I allow your head to play as much as you wish; but your heart . . . Oh God! Your heart . . . I know it is uncorrupted still; and you are keeping it for me even though you might not even realize it. I notice you are happy with all women and therefore undecided. . . . I believe you have more than one woman by now, and I will not take seriously any declarations to the contrary. . . . You say you like the lively one with the beautiful eyes and that she is willing but you hold back? Ah, Memmo! She does not stir you? How can that be since you admit to liking her? In the end, I do not wish to second-guess you, and even less do I wish to quarrel. Will you be my friend? Alas, it may well be the only thing you will ever be to me. . . . Ah, it would be so much better if you remained fickle and seductive and vain and crazy.*

Giustiniana's own future seemed so uncertain that the notion of returning to Venice just to be close to Andrea was never far from her thoughts. Once her brothers had settled in England could she not make her way back, unmarried and unmarriageable perhaps, and therefore free of the burden that had forced her to abandon Venice? "I will come to live there in whatever circumstances," she wrote. "In the end I need little and much prefer peace and a quiet life to all the efforts I would have to undertake to change my situation; anyway, what good would I ever be capable of away from you?"

The fantasies faded as quickly as they formed. It was enough to look up from the paper she was writing on to remind herself that she was in Paris with a mission. Although her heart was not really in that far-fetched plan to seduce La Pouplinière, the old *fermier général*, Andrea need not worry: she had not forgotten it. "I will attend to it because I promised you I would. I will set my thoughts on him as soon as I am allowed out. But returning to be with you—forgive me—will always be my primary aim."

However, their *démarche* with Bernis to obtain residency papers did not look promising: "We are anxiously awaiting a reply, but it might be difficult to get permission to stay." There was even talk of "a new edict against the English." (In September ten thousand British troops had landed in Brittany, and they had frayed French nerves considerably before being pushed back to sea.) Cooped up at the Hôtel d'Anjou, Giustiniana and her family lived in fear of a sudden expulsion from the country. There was a great deal of tension, and as usual Mrs. Anna was taking it out on everyone, including the faithful Zandiri: "She's become unbearable. . . . Even Giacomo she cannot stand anymore. She torments him to the point that I have come to pity him."

Each day the sense of isolation increased. The Wynnes had no life outside the hotel. Ambassador Erizzo's invitation to dinner had failed to materialize even though they had been in Paris nearly a month. To make matters worse, Giustiniana had lost a batch of letters of recommendation Andrea had written for her before her departure from Venice—and she suspected her mother had taken them. Even the one person she had been confident would rush over to see her—young Chavannes, her former suitor—did not come to visit. "Perhaps he is still upset that we stopped writing to him when he revealed to us that he was not a count," she ventured. "I don't much care about that really . . ."

In December Bernis finally sent word to the Wynnes. He begged their forgiveness for the tardiness of his reply "with very graceful expressions." Unfortunately, he could grant them permission to stay in Paris for only another fifteen days, twenty at the most. It was depressing news. What the Wynnes did not immediately realize was that Bernis himself would remain in Paris for even less time.

As Ambassador Erizzo explained to the Wynnes, Bernis was a "creature" of Mme de Pompadour. He had risen to power in large measure because he had agreed to become the instrument of her new policy of friendship with Austria at the expense of Prussia, France's traditional ally. That momentous switch in alliances had set the stage for the bloody conflict that was now raging in Europe, North America, and the Indian subcontinent. Bernis, however, had never been an enthusiastic supporter of the war against Prussia and England, which was proving very costly. He agonized over French losses and looked for ways to reach an honorable peace. Mme de Pompadour, backed by Louis XV, felt it was impossible to come to terms from a position of weakness. The war effort had to go on—at least until France's negotiating position improved. The mere sight of Bernis's glum round face at Versailles had become intolerable to the king and his mistress. He had to go. Louis XV arranged for him to be raised to the purple by Pope Clement XIII and then dismissed him from his post. "Cardinal de Bernis's health, which has not been good for some time, makes it impossible for him to keep the position of minister of foreign affairs," it was announced in the authorities' official *Gazette de France*.[2] A few days later, on December 13, the king exiled the new cardinal to his estate at Vic-sur-Aisne, near Soissons, a full day's trip north of Paris. His demise had been even swifter than his rapid climb to power three years earlier.

"Now, here is a lost cause," Giustiniana noted wistfully. "What is the use of having memorized all his works to learn to think like him and say the right things when we met?" Overnight, people ceased talking of Bernis except in the most derisive manner. "The *bon mot* currently making the rounds," she told Andrea, "says he was given a cardinal's cap so as better to take his bow."

The Wynnes' petition was passed on to the new minister of foreign affairs, the Duc de Choiseul. There was little else Giustiniana could do during that cold December except bide her time and avail herself of the distractions offered by the house. "I have a whole crowd of the most unbearable worshipers here," she wrote to Andrea, hoping perhaps to make him jealous. "I laugh with them, but I never give them any hope. I make them despair over me. This is my amusement."

The main protagonists in this amorous siege were the two Russian aristocrats, Prince Dolgorouki and the Muscovite. They were distant cousins and quarreled constantly, bad-mouthing each other at every opportunity. The two of them were friends of Princess Galitzine, the wealthy wife of the Russian ambassador, who lived not far from rue Dauphine, surrounded by a circle of expatriates who frequently dropped by the Hôtel d'Anjou, bringing with them an air of Russian exuberance. The French *mousquetaire* still lurked in the background, though Giustiniana had managed to draw him out a little. "He's not a bad type," she wrote Andrea. "He speaks to me often, but when the Muscovite approaches he moves away." Lesser characters "tormented" her as well, including "a rather grand individual" whose "endless sighs" she really could not stand, and "a foreigner who is here with his wife. Imagine . . ."

Among this eclectic band of *innamorati* Giustiniana had a marked preference for the Muscovite, a tall, handsome twenty-seven-year-old, "magnificently dressed and quite a gentleman." He said he was related to Princess Galitzine but explained, perhaps taking a swipe at his less prepossessing rival Dolgorouki, "that he does not wish to use his own title because he considers it a ridiculous affectation some Russian aristocrats tend to indulge in, especially here in Paris." Giustiniana knew little about him except that he had arrived in Paris ten months earlier, had already spent a fortune, and had conquered the hearts of many French ladies. Her frequent updates from the Hôtel d'Anjou made it clear to Andrea that she herself was not insensitive to his charms:

> *Last night the innkeeper's daughters asked us to stop by their apartment because a woman was going to sing* chansons poissardes, *songs about the Pont Neuf that I enjoy very much. So we*

went and found ourselves among a large company. The Muscovite came over to me and showered me with expressions of love. I was in a good mood and I made fun of the things he said to me, insisting that his little speech was very old style and his bleeding heart and all the rest were quite unfashionable. I must say, he does have a sense of humor, and he handles himself well.

A few days later she was still on the lookout for the handsome Russian:

I was lying in bed this morning when I heard a few shots in the garden. The Muscovite was target shooting with a Frenchman. I went down with the innkeeper's daughters. I took a few shots myself and won the round. I then recalled that day in Padua when I was trying my hand with a pistol and nearly killed you by mistake. Do you remember?

After a couple of weeks the Muscovite was clearly enlivening her confinement:

He spends most of the day here at the hotel, he leaves the shows early to come back as soon as possible. He is happy when he can be with me. . . . Every morning when I wake up I see him either in the garden or at his window, across the garden; he waits until my windows are opened, and he comes to me as soon as I get up.

Then he spoiled things by losing control of himself:

The other evening, after I left the innkeeper's apartment, the Muscovite took my hand in a small passageway and started to hug me tightly. He used his strength, his prayers, and all his weapons of seduction to take liberties with me; he touched my breast, and he pressed me; but I held him back despite his insistence—and the natural temptation I might have felt for a man who was quite beside himself over me—until I saw that he was in quite a state, trembling and loving at the same time. I managed to run away from him, not without first having torn his sleeve and scratched his hands.

The following day Giustiniana avoided the Muscovite as much as possible. "I just gave him the opportunity to make a thousand apologies and blame everything on love, as you men are wont to do." But the Hôtel d'Anjou was a small establishment, and unless she locked herself up in her room it was unlikely she could keep the Muscovite at a safe distance for long, especially since he gave every indication that he was eager to go back on the offensive. Indeed it appeared his Russian heart pounded faster than ever after his clumsy assault outside the innkeeper's apartment. He sought Giustiniana out in the hallways of the hotel and whispered "a thousand things" to her.

As he read her reports, Andrea must have wondered how much longer she could possibly resist the *avances* of the handsome Russian. Hadn't she just mentioned in passing the temptation she had felt during her scuffle with the Muscovite? But then he knew her well enough to appreciate the way in which she was trying to get even with him for the anxiety he had caused her with his careless talk about the beautiful nun.

One night Giustiniana had been sleeping for several hours when she was suddenly awakened by the sound of scratching at the end of the bed. In the darkness she did not immediately realize that she was lying in her nightdress completely uncovered, her blankets bunched up by her feet. "I did not move," she later wrote to Andrea. "I did not breathe. After a short while I heard the sound of footsteps—someone walking away and lowering himself into the garden. I was shaken. I pulled my blankets up, got under the covers, and thought: the Muscovite must have come to my window from the garden and, seeing that a pane of the window near the end of the bed was broken, he had grabbed the blankets from outside and pulled them toward him, uncovering me."

Giustiniana went back to sleep thinking she would let him have it the next morning. Fifteen minutes later she felt her blankets slip away again and the bed begin to shake.

"Who's there?" she cried out.

"Not a peep, Mademoiselle; just come to the window and hear

me." To her complete surprise, she recognized the voice of the *mousquetaire*.

"How do you expect me to listen to you at this late hour? Leave at once."

"I have come to tell you I adore you, and I intend to prove it to you."

"You are mad, Monsieur. Your brain has gone soft. So leave the window at once and don't bother me anymore, or else I shall look upon you as the last of the scoundrels."

The *mousquetaire* insisted she come to the window until he realized the key to the glass-paned door next to the window had been left in the outside lock. He let himself in "and threw himself on the bed in an instant."

"You villain, what do you want to gain with this violence?" Giustiniana lashed out. "I detest you. Leave at once!"

He took off his dressing gown and forced himself into her bed.

"I felt only anger and contempt," she told Andrea. "I defended myself with all my strength, using my nails and my cape, which luckily I had used as a cover. He gradually relented and began to use kind words to seduce me. He whimpered and begged. Contemptible man! . . . I hate violence and I hated him, but how could I get rid of him?" If she yelled, her mother, who was sleeping next door, would have come rushing in "and God knows what would have happened if she had found me with that man." She struggled and prayed and covered him with so many insults that after a while the *mousquetaire* saw "the impossibility of success." He got up, begged her not to say a word about his failed incursion, and sheepishly left the room.

Giustiniana ran to the door, locked herself in, went back to bed, and lay awake until morning wondering how best to handle the episode. What if the *mousquetaire* spread "his own version of the story" among other guests in the hotel, distorting the facts to make it sound as if his pathetic assault had been a success? Upon returning from mass the next day she found the Muscovite waiting for her at the hotel with the hairdresser, who had come to prepare a new chignon for her. On impulse, she took the Muscovite aside and told him what had happened "in order to have a witness on my side." He was only mildly surprised, for it turned out that the *mousquetaire* had informed him in advance that he was planning a nocturnal visit. Suspecting it was just talk, the Muscovite had not bothered to warn Giustiniana. Now he advised her to "vent all her resentment" by giving the *mousquetaire* a serious dressing-down and then let the matter rest.

As soon as she took her leave to join the hairdresser, the Muscovite raced off to tell everyone the story. The *mousquetaire* was so embarrassed he did not show his face for nearly a week. Giustiniana claimed to be annoyed by the Muscovite's indiscretion but decided it was punishment enough for her aggressor and forgot all about it.

The Muscovite lost interest in her. "He is too much a man of the world to be wasting his time with me after what happened," Giustiniana noted with sarcasm. But then how could these comedy characters, these good-for-nothing half-men, possibly be compared to her Memmo? Her feelings for him were undiminished, and though they caused her sadness they also brought her comfort when she felt low: "I love you, my Memmo. Yes, I love you so much. Too much for my own sake and perhaps even for yours, because if you know your feelings for me are not as strong as mine are for you, my love will surely be a heavy burden." But if he still loved her, he needn't worry: "I am as well behaved as you may possibly desire. . . . And I have not forgotten my financier. If perchance we are allowed to stay [in Paris], I will arrange to meet him, and, with enough time to do the job, I will do with him what you want."

The week before Christmas, when hope for a favorable word from the French authorities had faded and the time left on their permit was running out, Choiseul informed the Wynnes that they would be allowed to stay through the winter and possibly even beyond. Giustiniana was greatly relieved. She had Prince Dolgorouki to thank for the permits: he had brought the case to the attention of a powerful general in the Grande Armée, Prince de Clairmont, under whom he had fought at the beginning of the Seven Years' War. All her friends at the Hôtel d'Anjou received the news with delight, especially Prince Dolgorouki, whose courtship of Giustiniana had become more pressing since the Muscovite had withdrawn from the field.

The nod from Choiseul instantly gave the Wynnes a more respectable status, and the elusive invitation to dine at the Venetian ambassador's residence duly materialized. True, it was not the fanciest occasion—the only other guests were Tommaso Farsetti, a dour Venetian poet then living in Paris, and Signor Pizzoni, first secretary to the embassy. But Giustiniana managed to make the most of the small Venetian soirée by lavishing her attention on Farsetti, who claimed to know Monsieur de La Pouplinière very well. "Deftly, I hinted that I would be happy to meet [the old man]," she boasted to Andrea.

While she waited for Farsetti to come through, she renewed her old love of the theater, though the first thing she discovered, to her embarrassment, was that in Paris, unlike in Venice, it was "not considered *bon ton* to arrive late at the show." On the whole, Parisians were just as obsessed with the stage as Venetians were. The Comédie Française and the Comédie Italienne, the two most popular theaters, were full to capacity every night. Many spectators had a genuine interest in the performance, but many more went to see and be seen. In their flamboyant suits and with their elegant coiffures, they put on such colorful and lively displays that it was sometimes hard to distinguish the stage from the floor.

The hit of the 1758–59 season was a tragedy in verse called *Hypermnestre,* by a young author, M. Lemierre, who was sponsored by the *Mercure de France,* the widely read monthly on culture and current affairs. Giustiniana made her Russian friends take her to the opening night. "All Paris was there," she wrote to Andrea, who was keen to hear the latest on French theater even though his own project had never seen the light. "The tragedy was divine, and the applause went on forever. I was very moved and cried. The entire theater was moved. How well the French act!" The star of the evening was Mlle Clairon, the most celebrated, ambitious, talented, and spoiled prima donna of her day. Giustiniana had heard about her back in Venice, and she was glad to report that the great actress was indeed "a true prodigy."

Giustiniana was eager to explore the city in earnest. Two months after she had arrived in Paris, her world had still not expanded far beyond the Hôtel d'Anjou. Mrs. Anna did not encourage her daughters to broaden their circle of friends and was constantly reining them in. So when Giustiniana did go out with her sisters, it was usually in the company of their Russian friends.

Princess Galitzine was the main organizer of their evenings at the theater. It was an open secret that she was smitten with Mlle Clairon. "People say she loves her with a tender passion," Giustiniana wrote. "She trembles when she sees her, she becomes pale, she is beside herself. . . . She always has her over for dinner. . . . People say she has spent more than a thousand francs on this *comédienne*." The princess commissioned Charles Van Loo, first painter of the king, to do a portrait of Mlle Clairon. He painted her as Medea standing atop a chariot, a dripping dagger in her hand, her two dead children at her feet, and Jason's expression filled with terrible wrath. The unveiling of the painting at the artist's studio at the Louvre became an event in itself. "A crowd of admirers has seen Van Loo's masterpiece, and never has a painting been praised so unanimously," glowed the art critic of the *Mercure de France*, quite mesmerized by Jason's "fiery eyes" and the slain bodies of the two infants "that still tremble before us."[3] Giustiniana went to see the painting with the princess and her large train of squabbling Russians, and she was not quite so impressed. "It cost six thousand francs," she remarked. "The colors are pretty, the characters meaningful; still, there *are* defects."

Yet despite her criticism, indeed despite the affected annoyance that often filled her descriptions of her friends, the pleasure of feeling more and more connected to the Parisian scene began to come through her weekly reports to Andrea. True, she occasionally tired of running around town with the Russians. She wanted to shine in the famous literary *salons* and at the elegant dinners she kept hearing about. "I would like to meet ladies, I would like to meet men of intelligence, literary people as well as members of the Court. I would like to be received in the good houses of Paris. But with my mother here, and two sisters in tow, it's impossible. . . . Ah, if only we were traveling together, you and I, what a difference it would make! But who knows? That day may yet come." Waiting for the day when she and Andrea might converse with Diderot and the Encyclopédistes in the drawing room of a Mme du Deffand or show themselves off among the *crème de la crème* of French aristocracy, Giustiniana could nevertheless console herself with the fact that she saw plays everyone talked about, read the new books, and was up to date with the latest gossip at Versailles. The trusty *Mercure de France* kept her abreast of the great debates of the day, whether they touched on the celebrated polemic between Rousseau and d'Alembert about the corrupting influence of the theater, the controversial vaccine against small-pox, or even the imminent appearance of Mr. Halley's comet in the eastern sky. As for pure distraction, she could always count on the latest installment of the unending comedy unfolding at the Hôtel d'Anjou.

Around Christmas, Prince Dolgorouki and the Muscovite quar-reled badly over Giustiniana, and events took a grave turn. She was frantic—and perhaps a little thrilled as well—"at the thought that very shortly I will be the topic of every conversation in Paris."

The row blew up shortly after the *mousquetaire* episode. Dol-gorouki was ten years older than the Muscovite and had neither his grace nor his good looks. He was making little progress in his pursuit of Giustiniana. She found him charmless, meddlesome, and excessively irascible—a real nuisance at times. Dolgorouki was under the impression—not an entirely false one—that he was making little headway because Giustiniana was still attracted to the Muscovite. So he told her that he had heard the Muscovite slight her in public and that he had been compelled to come to her defense. Giustiniana quickly informed the Muscovite, "and he had a fit, protesting his innocence and insisting [Dolgorouki] was only acting out of jealousy. . . . He stormed off in a fury."

After dinner that night a doleful Dolgorouki told her that he and the Muscovite were to fight a duel. He added, in a rather macabre voice, that he was "happy about it." Giustiniana begged him to give up such a crazy idea. He and the Muscovite had been the closest friends; they were even related. Besides, had he not considered how it would affect her reputation? She enlisted the help of the innkeeper and the other guests in the hotel, but Dolgo-rouki remained deaf to their pleas. So she went to the Muscovite and "with tears in my eyes" implored him not to fight. After much pleading and cajoling on her part, he agreed to avoid Dolgorouki for four or five days to see if his rival would calm down and the episode could be forgotten. This did not work. On Christmas Day, Giustiniana wrote to Andrea in a state of great agitation. The Muscovite had tried to stay away from Dolgorouki, but the latter had become a "beast." He had provoked and attacked the Muscovite at every opportunity. He had accused him in front of the other guests of being "fickle and thoughtless" and "unworthy" of courting her—this at a time when the Muscovite had already put an end to his clawing ambushes in dark corners of the hotel.

One evening the two Russians came to blows in the common room, up in the innkeeper's apartment. Guards had to be called in, and both men were put under surveillance. Under pressure from the Russian Embassy, Dolgorouki and the Muscovite agreed to sign a document renouncing their intention to duel. But the matter did not end there. Though dueling was illegal in France, many people still felt it was the only honourable way of resolving a conflict of that nature. "They will either fight or face infamy," Giustiniana worried. "Surely they will lose the respect of their regiment if they don't." The Russians kept quiet, but word had it that the duel had simply been postponed. They would travel secretly to Flanders to fight, and if that became impossible they would wait until spring and duel after they returned to Russia. Thus the dramatic *dénouement* was postponed just in time for the New Year's visit to Versailles.

The Court had announced that on the first of January the king would bestow the prestigious Cordon Bleu on eight new members of the Order of the Holy Spirit. The Wynnes planned to attend the ceremony with Ambassador Erizzo and remain in Versailles until evening to witness the *dîner du Roi*. On the appointed day, Mrs. Anna and her three daughters (the boys stayed in Paris with Toinon) left the Hôtel d'Anjou dressed in their very best gowns and beautifully coiffed. The ride took about an hour. Once in Versailles, they stopped at an inn to refresh themselves and pick up Ambassador Erizzo before going to the palace. He was running late, so they arrived halfway through the mass. The crowd was so thick that they couldn't reach the inner chapel. But even from afar the youthful, forty-eight-year-old king looked magnificent. "He is a very handsome man . . . very grand and majestic," wrote Giustiniana. Despite the distance between them, she was sure he had cast "the most graceful and unaffected glance" upon her and her sisters.

The Wynnes and the ambassador went back to the inn in the town of Versailles to wait for the next ceremony. There they were joined by the Russian contingent minus the Muscovite, who was still avoiding Dolgorouki. A Galitzine prince, cousin of the princess, had come in his place but fell asleep upon arriving and snored through the meal, which Giustiniana predictably found "bad, long and very boring. . . . Nobody had anything amusing to say. Everyone yawned or slept." At last they returned to the palace and filed into the Antichambre du Grand Couvert, where the king and queen, their backs to the fireplace, dined with their immediate family as a crowd of visitors slowly rustled by. "The room is rather small, not very well lit, and rather unremarkable," she later wrote to Andrea. "There were so many people we were not directly in the king's view; yet he saw us and observed us attentively. . . . He has very beautiful eyes, and he fixes them on one so intently that one cannot sustain his gaze for long."

At around eleven, while the crowd still milled about in the palace, Giustiniana went to rest in the carriage. It had been a long day, and she was tired. While she waited for the others in the dark, her thoughts drifted back to the handsome king and the way he had looked at her. "Then I closed my eyes and slept until Paris."

Shortly after the New Year, Giustiniana was with her mother at the Comédie Italienne when she heard loud cheers coming from a box near theirs. It was her old friend Casanova, "making a magnificent appearance." She pointed him out to Mrs. Anna, who smiled and beckoned to him with her fan. Mrs. Anna had not seen him since he had preyed on her sixteen-year-old daughter. Five years later and so far away from Venice, she was not unhappy to see him again. Besides, he was now a celebrity. Everyone wanted to meet him.

Back in November 1756, sixteen months after he had been thrown into jail thanks to Andrea's mother, Casanova had staged a spectacular escape from the prison of the Leads. With the aid of a rudimentary pike he broke a hole in the ceiling of his cell, clambered onto the roof of the Ducal Palace, worked his way down to an adjacent canal, and left Venice under cover of darkness. He walked for days across the Venetian mainland territories, steering clear of the police patrols sent to hunt him down. Famished and exhausted after covering more than two hundred miles, he eventually reached the northern city of Bolzano, where he rested for a week. He then crossed the Alps at the Brenner Pass, traveled to Munich, and from there went on to Paris—this last leg in comfort, having found a means of transport and pleasant company. He arrived in Paris on January 5, 1757— the very day of the assassination attempt on the king.

The first person he went to see was his old "comrade in arms," the Abbé de Bernis, then at the height of his power. The foreign minister gave him a warm welcome and filled his pocket with a roll of louis d'or, and later that year he sent him on an intelligence-gathering mission to Dunkirk. Upon his return, Casanova convinced the cash-starved French government to launch a national lottery, which he had devised with Giovanni Calzabigi, a financial wizard working for the ambassador of the Kingdom of the Two Sicilies. The project was a success, and Casanova's cut of the ticket sales brought him a steady income.

The following year the government, desperate to revive the sagging price of French bonds and stave off financial collapse, entrusted him with a highly sensitive mission. The idea was to sell twenty million francs' worth of those rapidly depreciating bonds on the Amsterdam market at a limited loss and use the cash to purchase securities from a country with better credit. After several weeks of negotiations with Dutch brokers and frantic exchanges with the French government, Casanova pulled it off by convincing his counterparts that a peace treaty between the Great Powers was imminent and it therefore made sense to buy French bonds at a discount. He raised a huge amount of cash for France and in the process helped to revive the French securities market.

He returned from Holland a hero. During his absence, however, Bernis had been removed from power. Casanova went to see him the day he returned to Paris. "You have performed miracles," his old friend told him. "Now go and be adored."[4] It was that night, when Casanova went to bask in acclaim at the Comédie Italienne, that he saw Mrs. Anna and Giustiniana waving at him. Surprised by the warmth of their greeting, he went over to their box "at once" and promised to visit them the next day at their hotel. The sight of Giustiniana, fully grown and beaming in the lights of the theater, stirred his old yearning. "She looked like a goddess," he wrote decades later, an old man hunched over his desk in the castle of Dux. "After a sleep of five years my love [awoke] again with an increase in power equal to that which the object before my eyes had gained in the same period."[5]

In early January the Wynnes left the Hôtel d'Anjou. Mrs. Anna felt it had become "too noisy and crowded," and she didn't like the way the innkeeper tried to meddle in their family affairs, with her indiscreet queries and her unsolicited advice. They moved to the Hôtel de Hollande, just around the corner, in rue Saint-André-des-Arts. Casanova was among the first to visit them in their new lodgings, and he quickly made a habit of stopping by. "He is with us every day even though his company does not please me, and I don't think these visits are in our interest," Giustiniana complained to Andrea. "He has a carriage and lackeys and is attired resplendently. He has two beautiful diamond rings, two tasteful pocket watches, snuffboxes set in gold, and always plenty of lace. He has gained admittance, I don't know how, to the best Parisian society. He says he has a stake in a lottery in Paris and brags that this gives him a large income. . . . He is quite full of himself and stupidly pompous. In a word, he is unbearable. Except when he speaks of his escape, which he recounts admirably."

Ambassador Erizzo strongly disapproved of these visits—Casanova was a Venetian fugitive, after all. Quite apart from the requirements of his office, the ambassador felt a deep aversion for the man and an even deeper distrust. He warned Mrs. Anna about the corrupting influence Casanova would have on her daughters and sons. She listened to Erizzo, and her old wariness gradually resurfaced, but Casanova was so persistent it was hard to keep him at a distance. The other Venetian in their circle, the poet Farsetti, had a strong dislike for Casanova as well. His feelings for Giustiniana, however, were even stronger, so he took his *merenda* (afternoon meal) every day at the Hôtel de Hollande with the Wynnes, even if it meant he had to sit through Casanova's performances.

The two men irritated each other to no end. Casanova flirted incessantly and played to the gallery with elaborate accounts of his adventures that kept everyone spellbound—especially the two boys, Richard and William, who stared at him with envy and growing admiration.* Farsetti meanwhile sipped his chocolate and looked on in disapproval. "I think Farsetti is a little in love with me," Giustiniana confessed to Andrea, begging him not to gossip about it with their friends in Venice. "He grows pale when he sees me, he shakes when we are alone, but he has yet to make me laugh." Farsetti held her attention by bringing daily assurances that the invitation to the house of Monsieur de La Pouplinière, which he had promised, was imminent. He also brought his "little poems and plays" in the hope of softening Giustiniana's heart. "But I don't tell him whether I find them good or bad . . . and if he doesn't deliver on his promise, I shall treat him harshly."

A few days later her patience with Farsetti was rewarded. "It is arranged at last," she wrote to her lover and accomplice. "I am going to La Pouplinière's this evening with the rest of the family."

The old *fermier général* was indeed, as Andrea had assured Giustiniana, one of the richest men in Paris, having raked in millions of francs by collecting taxes for the king. He lived in a splendid house on the rue de Richelieu and owned a country estate at Passy, just outside Paris. Chamber music had become his passion, and the exquisite concerts he hosted every Saturday were favorite rendezvous of Parisian society. The playwright Jean-François Marmontel, a frequent guest, later wrote that the house was always

---

*Richard and William, fourteen and thirteen, often sneaked out of the hotel to get their own taste of Paris. Richard in particular was having his first sexual experiences and often relied on Casanova to get him out of trouble. "He showed me a chancre," Casanova recounts, "of a very ugly kind, which he had acquired by going all by himself to a place of ill fame. He asked me to speak to his mother and persuade her to have him treated, complaining that Signor Farsetti, after refusing him four louis, had washed his hands of the matter. I did as he asked, but when I told his mother what the trouble was she said it was better to leave him with the chancre he had, which was his third, for she was sure that after he was cured of it he would simply go and get another. I had him cured at my expense, but his mother was right. At the age of fourteen his profligacy knew no bounds."[6]

filled with the sound of music: "The players lived there. During the day they prepared in beautiful harmony the symphonies they executed in the evening. And the best actors and singers and dancers of the Opera were there to embellish the dinner parties."[7]

Now sixty-six years old, semiretired, and still recovering from an illness that had nearly killed him two years earlier, La Pouplinière had lost much of his joie de vivre. Ten years had passed since he had banished his beautiful wife in the wake of the infamous *scandale de la cheminée*. Yet he had never forgotten her, and obviously she had not forgotten him. When he had fallen ill she had returned to Paris to nurse him, even though she herself was already ravaged by cancer. In the end he survived and she did not. A year after her death he still carried the burden of her loss.

During the years of his wife's banishment, La Pouplinière had had a succession of mistresses. When he was finished with them he would either pay them off, take them in, marry them off, or a combination of all three. It was the job of M. de Maisonneuve, who was half secretary, half pimp, to take care of the arrangements. In the meantime, this peculiar mix of promiscuity and generosity had caused the large house at rue de Richelieu to evolve into the strangest ménage, where musicians, mistresses past and present, and members of the family all lived together in a rather poisonous atmosphere.

The doyenne of La Pouplinière's mistresses was Mme de Saint Aubin, a former singer and musician who ruled over the household "like an old sultana," as Giustiniana put it. La Pouplinière had long since ceased to love her, but he did not have the strength to send this crafty and rather domineering woman away. She had become an accomplished hostess, having taught herself how to organize a good concert and an elegant dinner, and the old man depended on her to run his crowded house. When she raised hell—which she often did—he simply raised her income.

Mme de Saint Aubin's major enemies in the house were M. and Mme de Courcelles, La Pouplinière's brother-in-law and his pretty young wife, who occupied a large apartment in the house with their daughter, Alexandrine. The Courcelles were allied with the Zimmermans—he a retired Swiss Guard, she the former Sophie Mocet, La Pouplinière's most recent mistress—and had the backing of La Pouplinière's scheming nephews. M. de Maisonneuve, on the other hand, was in the camp of Mme de Saint Aubin, together with the latest entry in the household, Emmanuel-Jean de La Coste, a seedy-looking former Celestine monk who had escaped from his monastery some years earlier and run off to Holland with a girl and a bag of stolen diamonds. He had returned to France and lived by doing small spying jobs for the government. In Paris he had crossed paths with Casanova and tried to swindle him for a thousand écus worth of lottery tickets. When that had failed, he had managed to worm his way into La Pouplinière's household and, through flattery and favors, had become his close adviser.

The challenge of seducing a rich old man who stubbornly refused to remarry and over whom so many Parisian women were fighting appealed to Giustiniana's vanity. She had done her homework, and she knew she was stepping onto a treacherous stage. But she also knew her strengths—her charm, her vivacity, her youth— and a part of her was eager to test them outside her usual circle of Russian and Venetian friends. "Who knows?" she gamely wrote to Andrea. "In the end, for the sake of doing you a favor, I might succeed in moving him more than all these other women have."

The long-sought-after invitation also made her deeply apprehensive. This was not entirely a game; it was a scheme that could change her life forever. She knew herself well enough to foresee that once she started, she would probably play her hand to the end. The seduction of Consul Smith had been a similar proposition, but then she had had Andrea to back her up. Now she was alone, on unfamiliar terrain, facing a cast of complete strangers.

She was also three years older—wiser, perhaps, but also a little more oppressed by the sense of time passing quickly by:

> *Ah, Memmo, tell me where those happy hours have gone? Where are you, my true heart? . . . When will your head and your heart be joined to mine? If only you knew how much I love you and how unhappy I am! Nothing moves in my heart anymore unless I think of you. I shall soon be twenty-two years old, and you know what it means for a woman to be twenty-two. . . . Half my life, or in any case half of the better part of life, has gone by.*

How have I lived it? . . . Only you know everything about my life, and I would be so happy if it could end with you. Farewell, my Memmo. I shall never be happy if I cannot join you some-where, somehow. Love me as hard as you can, and remember your truest and most unhappy friend. Farewell, I embrace you a thou-sand times.

It took Giustiniana less than a month to ensnare La Pouplinière. These are the accounts she gave Andrea of her success:

Paris, January 22

Mon cher frère,

. . . I went to La Pouplinière's on Monday. . . . There was quite a crowd, and the master of the house was very sweet with us. The concert he gave was in our honor, and I must say it was the best orchestra in the world. I have never heard a better cello or a better oboe. The hautbois des forêts *and the clarinets—wind instru-ments that are not much used in our parts—are admirable. I praised with honesty, I hope I praised with grace. I looked at him with great composure, and I never spoke excessively, though I could have spoken more. He in turn praised the precision with which I judged what I heard and what I saw; I am told he never pays this kind of compliment. With great courtesy he invited us to the regular Saturday concert. What do you say of my beginning? But enough of this. . . . It is too early to justify your hopes. . . . Farsetti came to see us on Tuesday and stayed all day. He brought me a book of French ariettas. . . . I spent a good deal of time learning a few of them well: if I want to please the old man, I will have to have him ask me to hum a few French songs.*

Paris, January 29

Mon cher frère,

. . . Saturday I went to the great concert at La Pouplinière's and there were lots of people. He was rude to everyone but very sweet with me and invited me for dinner on Wednesday. Let me handle this, but you must be patient. . . . Would you believe how many compliments I received at La Pouplinière's on Satur-day? Two ladies sent the ambassador of Naples here to tell

*me a thousand things. . . . I will wait for you here: we shall
live together whatever way we may. Do you have the courage for
that? . . . Come laugh with me about all these crazy people. . . .
And don't stop loving me, my heart.*

Paris, February 12

Mon cher frère,

    *Listen: I have many things to tell you. I see my luck approach-
ing; but since your insistence has brought me to where I am, I
want your advice to count. My dearest friend, my heart and my
soul are always with you. . . . I stayed home until Wednesday,
when I had dinner at La Pouplinière's. There I noticed that my
innocent efforts had touched his heart because his attentions
toward me were considerable. . . . Friday he paid us a visit, a
favor he never bestows, and Saturday we went out to Passy with a
huge crowd. It is a large house, beautiful and full of those com-
forts that are so scarce in Italy and that you are so fond of. It is
divided into small apartments, with a splendid* salon. *We walked
in the garden, which is even more beautiful than the house but not
very green. We left Passy, and we had lunch at his house in Paris
around one o'clock. So many attentions! . . . In short: he told me
he did not want me to go to London under any circumstances,
saying he would die at the thought that I should leave him; he
asked me to stay in his house, provided I was willing to live with
his sister-in-law here in Paris, and promised he would make me
happy. You can imagine how little I liked his proposition; but we
must see where it leads. . . . One must raise the stakes and then be
willing to take half. So I mentioned a few problems, but I did not
say no. . . . He is an extremely generous man. . . . What I fear,
though, is his passion for arranging marriages. He has a nephew
who looks like a* chaise *porter. . . . I'd rather marry the old man.
What do you think? Would I be fulfilling your project with
honor? Enough: you can trust me. . . . The next day his secretary
came to see me, and after lengthy preambles he said he was sure
his master would offer me a life annuity of between eight and ten
thousand francs and his house to live in if I stayed in Paris. You
can imagine my surprise! And my answer! I pretended I did not
believe the proposition came from his master, whose sensitive way*

*of thinking I went on to praise, even though I knew perfectly well
that it did. I pointed out to him in the most delicate manner that
perhaps he did not realize the kind of person I was or my station in
life, and at that I let the matter drop, though I did mention, in
passing, that if I wished to marry the way an honest girl like
myself should, I hoped that good and noble proposals would not
be lacking in my father's country. We'll see what effect these
words will have. . . . Meanwhile, I'm rather happy with myself,
and I hope you are as well. . . . I hope I'm being clear despite the
rush with which I'm writing you; but since you know my heart I'm
sure you understand me perfectly. . . . Farewell, love me. All the
handsome men I see are not worth your little finger.*

> *Paris, February 26*

Mon cher frère,

*I didn't write to you last week, my dearest friend . . . but it
wasn't my fault. Last Monday I was about to sit down to write
my letter when Mr. de La Pouplinière came to see me—for the
third time. After we had exchanged the greatest courtesies and I
had said a few words I thought would be to his liking, he asked
me to go with him to the new Opéra Comique. How could I
refuse? But you'll be surprised to hear the rest. . . . Not only has
La Pouplinière fallen in love with me: he will marry me. That's
what he said, and he promised he would give me an income worth
his reputation. Who would ever have thought a man in his sixties
could even think of marrying a foreigner whose character and station, so to speak, he hardly knows? Yet that is the way it is, my
Memmo. Your prayers, your advice, my own wisdom . . . and
above all the wish to see your project, about which we laughed so
much, succeed—all of these have made my good fortune.*

Everything was falling neatly into place, it seemed, but the deal
was not yet sealed. In the weeks ahead, indeed right up to the wedding ceremony itself, Giustiniana used all her charm and her
manipulative skills to make the marriage happen, even as a sharp
anxiety began to gnaw at her. Her first move had been to seek the
support of Mme de Saint Aubin. She had "worked on her" until
she had her "completely" on her side, she told Andrea rather

naively. The truth was that the old mistress was playing her own game: she saw Giustiniana as a useful if temporary ally in the drawn-out struggle against the other ladies of the house and gladly instructed her on how best "to please the sultan." More coaching came from the duplicitous runaway monk La Coste, who became Giustiniana's friend "by dint of his clever ways." Meanwhile, the Courcelles and the Zimmermans remained highly suspicious and treated her with deliberate coldness. Quietly, they started a denigration campaign against her. Anonymous letters began to circulate, accusing her of "the most infamous behavior." She received threats and was followed around by shady characters.

Well aware that members of his own household were trying to discredit Giustiniana, La Pouplinière nevertheless continued his assiduous courtship. He took her to the theater almost every night and had her over for dinner at his house after the shows. This was usually a relatively intimate affair—fifteen to twenty people, mostly members of the household. Mme de Saint Aubin made sure that even such small "family gatherings" were tastefully organized and the musical entertainment was of a superior standard. "When it's time for dessert," Giustiniana wrote to Andrea, "the horns and clarinets blend with other, gentler wind instruments and produce the sweetest symphony." Those celestial sounds helped her bear the strain of those evenings, during which she was "treated like a queen" but openly despised. It was a truly joyless home. "The sadness that lines the old man's face makes the gaiety of the younger members of the household look so affected. Everyone laughs to make *him* laugh. The place reminds me of the backstage at the Opera, with all the springs and the ropes of the set in full view."

Yet the more her own mood blackened, the more La Pouplinière was drawn to her. He saw the two of them as kindred spirits. "What interesting melancholy dwells in your soul?" he asked her one evening when she was particularly downcast. "For it stirs my own, it pokes at it. . . . All my happiness depends on whether I can make *you* happy. You'll find honesty and candor in my character. You'll see: I'll succeed in earning your respect, and that's really all I hope for." Giustiniana was touched by the sweetness of the old man's words, and she admitted as much to Andrea: "His eyes were veiled with tears as he said these things to me; he cried and was not afraid to show me all his tenderness. . . . He really moved me. I told him I was filled with feelings of gratitude toward him. He could see it was true, and he looked happy. . . . He gave me his hand and told me to swear I will be his."

Mme de Saint Aubin planned a surprise party for La PoupliniÈre's Saint's Day. She alerted Giustiniana, so she would not forget to bring a present, and purposely left Mme de Courcelles and Mme Zimmerman in the dark. The "old sultana" choreographed the event with exquisite taste. When all the guests had arrived, two singers who had pretended to be playing chess at one of the little tables in the first salon rose and sang a beautiful duet in praise of La PoupliniÈre. As soon as they finished, "the most heavenly" music started in the next salon and the guests moved along. In the middle of the room Mme de Saint Aubin herself was giving a virtuoso performance at the harpsichord of a piece she had written for the occasion. When the last notes of her composition had died, the guests were drawn by lively sounds further down the suite of glittering rooms, where a group of singers acted out scenes with a La PoupliniÈre theme—his wealth, his generosity, his love of the arts. The program ended with Mme de Saint Aubin reciting a musical poem in honor of the master of the house while she plucked skillfully at the strings of her harp.

"La PoupliniÈre was so moved he wept the whole evening," Giustiniana reported. "And in the end I did too, though I don't quite know why." The success of the soirÉe was also a reminder of the importance and the power of Mme de Saint Aubin's role in the house. "Everything was this woman's creation, and she was praised by all but the other ladies of the house, who had not been told a thing." When the musical entertainment was over, Giustiniana gave La PoupliniÈre his present, embellishing the moment with a bit of stagecraft of her own. Playfully, she drew the old man aside. "Come, now," she said. "I must give you something too." She was wearing a black braided string around her neck from which hung a little heart of gold "gently resting on my breast." She took out a pair of tiny scissors, and with one clean clip she cut the little heart loose. "This is for you, it will remind you of mine," she said to the old man, while to Andrea she wrote: "How happy he was! He adores me . . ."

La Pouplinière was now in a hurry. He realized that the embittered members of his extended family would go to any length to sabotage his marriage to Giustiniana—including Mme de Saint Aubin, who had never seriously thought he would actually take her young protégée for a wife. He acted with speed and secrecy. Before the end of February he instructed his lawyer, M. Brunet, to work on Giustiniana's naturalization papers. He made her sit in front of the portraitist "every morning until two hours past midday." He pressed the Wynnes to send immediately for the wedding authorization from the Venice Archdiocese (an official document signed by the archbishop stating that Giustiniana had no other ties and was free to marry). Finally, he presented Giustiniana with an engagement ring—two hearts elegantly entwined—and the promise of a generous income. "I think he has in mind something on the order of forty thousand francs," she told Andrea. "That would be ten thousand silver ducats a year. What do you say?"

It was nearly twice as large as the income of the entire Memmo family.

Andrea had finally returned to Venice, and from what we can infer from Giustiniana's letters he was following the developments very closely. Without his letters, it is impossible to know how he really felt about the situation. Still, the plan had been his idea from the beginning, and as far as one can tell, he seems to have been very interested in the details of the arrangements. He certainly said little to dissuade her from going ahead with the marriage. Indeed, when the Wynnes' request for an authorization from the archdiocese arrived in Venice, Andrea was quick to offer his assistance and even pulled a few strings to accelerate the matter.

By early March, on the other hand, Giustiniana was facing a serious crisis: the prospect of spending the rest of her life in that extravagant and poisonous household was making her very anxious. There was no way of telling how Andrea could ever fit into such an arrangement as long as the old man was alive. And after La Pouplinière's death, then what? The likeliest outcome would be total war between her and the mistresses, the relatives, and the various hangers-on. It was easy enough to see the material advantages the marriage would bring her. It was not so easy to imagine how she could live happily as the *maîtresse de maison* at rue de

Richelieu. "How important can those advantages be when they are measured against one's happiness?" she asked Andrea. "As rich as he is about to make me, it will never be worth what I am giving him. My happiness for money! But does my happiness have a price? It is all so different from the way we once thought we could live, always free, always together in boundless happiness. . . . I speak to you of things that truly sadden me, and I wonder if you feel what I say with the same power I feel in saying it."

Giustiniana still had time to stop the plan from being rushed through. As hard as it was, and as pressing as La Pouplinière could be, she could still say no and keep her reputation—and her future—intact. She often felt "the strongest desire to refuse the greatest fortune ever offered me." Yet despite her wavering she continued to let events unfold, reminding herself of the logic behind this improbable marriage: it would bring her and Andrea close again. "You will come to Paris shortly, won't you?" she asked Andrea uneasily. "Whatever I will be able to give you is yours, and I would resent you as much as I have admired you if you were moved [to refuse it] by a form of false sensitivity. . . . I want you to be my husband's best friend, and I want him to satisfy all your needs. Leave it to me."

On March 6, she wrote, "My good fortune is still moving forward steadily. The old man wishes to marry me in a month's time." The pace of events accelerated. The following week she wrote, "I don't have a minute to myself. . . . The man can be brutal. . . . He evicted a niece of his from the house by doing all sorts of impertinences because she occupied the best apartment—which as of today is being readied for me."

Inevitably, word about the impending marriage began to leak out. By the end of March the story about how the young and beautiful Venetian had hooked one of the wealthiest men in Paris was on everyone's lips. Mme de Pompadour herself, perhaps longing for distractions from the gloomy war bulletins, was said to be following the story with amusement from her chambers at Versailles. At the Hôtel de Hollande there was an atmosphere of celebration. The Wynnes were thrilled at Giustiniana's catch. Mrs. Anna in particular could not believe her daughter's luck and was furiously corresponding with the religious authorities in Venice. All the

Russians came to congratulate their friend. Prince Dolgorouki and the Muscovite were so caught up in the general excitement that they even stopped talking about their duel.

The wedding was to take place in mid-April, on the first Sunday after Easter. The Venetians felt especially proud. On April 1, Ambassador Erizzo informed his friends in Venice about Giustiniana's "spectacular good fortune."[8] Farsetti, the spurned suitor, now filled his days running errands and acting as Giustiniana's secretary at the Hôtel de Hollande. He consoled himself with the notion that he had been instrumental in arranging the excellent match. "Your Excellency must surely know," he wrote to Andrea, "that Signora Giustiniana Wynne is close to making a very advantageous matrimony, even though her husband-to-be is not young. What gives me pleasure is that I brought her into that house and introduced her to that person."[9]

He added, at the request of Giustiniana, that it would be nice if Andrea could make the journey to Paris on this "splendid occasion."

CHAPTER *Seven*

Early on April 4, as a new day was breaking over Paris, Giustiniana sneaked out of the Hôtel de Hollande wrapped in a cloak, the hood pulled over her head. She took a horse-drawn cab to a nearby church, paid the coachman, got into a second cab, and had herself driven to yet another church. From there she took a third cab and exited the city from the eastern Porte Saint-Antoine, leaving an erratic trail behind her to confound any pursuer. At full gallop, the coachman drove her out to a Benedictine convent in the small village of Conflans, some two leagues beyond the city limits.[1]

The abbess, Henriette de Mérinville, was expecting Giustiniana. She took her in under the pseudonym of Mlle de la Marne and assigned her to a small room in her own private apartment. The past few weeks had been especially hard, and Giustiniana immediately felt relieved in the company of this warm, generous woman who went by the religious name of Mother Eustachia. It was so peaceful. From her window Giustiniana looked down to the valley where the Marne flowed gently into the Seine. Angelic chants rose from the chapel and drifted to her quarters. Everything around her, even the crisp cleanliness of her simple room, had a soothing effect on her frayed nerves. At last she felt safe behind the thick convent walls.

The strain had started long before the marriage preparations. When Giustiniana had left Venice in September 1758, she had been keeping a secret she had not shared with anyone—not even Andrea. She continued to hide it day after day, in solitude, concealing her growing despair behind her infectious charm. She coped in silence with violent bouts of nausea during the long trip to France. In Paris, frequent spells of drowsiness forced her to seek refuge in the privacy of her small room. Yet she threw herself into the social mêlée with as much energy as she could muster, and she made her way into La Pouplinière's heart with the kind of recklessness that comes from sheer desperation. But she could not hide her condition indefinitely: by the end of January she was already five months pregnant. She decided to confide her secret to the one person who might spare her the sermonizing and help her find a practical way out of her trouble.

After his triumphant return from Holland, Casanova had moved out to Petite Pologne, a small community northwest of Paris, just beyond the city walls. He lived in style: he rented a large house called Cracovie en Bel Air, with two gardens, stables, several baths, a good cellar, and an excellent cook, Mme de Saint Jean, who went by the name of "La Perle." He kept two carriages and five very fast *enragés,* the mettlesome horses bred in the king's stables and known for their furious speed—one of Casanova's greatest pleasures, he tells us in his memoirs, was "driving fast"[2] through the streets of Paris.

Initially Giustiniana was somewhat dismissive of Casanova. She invited him over to the Hôtel de Hollande, but she did not encourage his advances. In fact, when she wrote to Andrea she was quite biting in her description of his general demeanor. Very quickly, though, she began to warm to him—and she stopped mentioning him in her letters. One night in late January she went to the Opera Ball wearing a black domino that covered her face completely. She cut herself loose from the rest of the company—Ambassador Erizzo, Farsetti, the Russians, her sisters—and sought out Casanova. He was thrilled by her attention, of course, and when they finally managed to be alone in a box, he smothered her with declarations of undying love. The next day he showed up for dinner at the Hôtel de Hollande, covered with snowflakes. Giustiniana was in bed writing a letter and received him in her small room. The two of them talked until dinner was called. Not feeling hungry, she stayed in bed. Casanova, smiling at the pleasant intimacy growing between them, bade her farewell, and went downstairs to sup with the rest of the family.

Two days later, a young footman came out to Cracovie en Bel Air and handed Casanova an envelope from Giustiniana. It contained a stunning letter, written in great haste, that was rambling, confused, and filled with desperation. In the interest of secrecy it was unsigned and bore no date:

You wish me to speak, to tell you the reason for my sadness. Well, then, I am ready to do so. I am putting my life, my reputation, my whole being in your hands and through you I hope to find my salvation. I beg you to assist an unhappy soul who will have no other recourse but to seek her own death if she cannot remedy her situation. Here it is, dear Casanova: I am pregnant, and I shall kill myself if I am found out. It is now five months since my weakness and someone else's deception caused me to hide in my breast the unhappy evidence of my ignorance and carelessness. No one knows about this, and the very author of my misery has been kept in the dark. I have managed to hide my secret so far, but I will not be able to deceive the world much longer. . . . My belly will begin to show. . . . And my mother, so proud and unreasonable, what will she do with me if she learns the truth? You think like a philosopher, you are an honest man. . . . Save me if it is still possible and if you know how. My whole being, and everything I possess, will be yours if you help me. I will be so grateful. . . . If I go back to my original state my fortune is assured. I will tell you everything: La Popinière [sic] is offering me his house, he loves me and will provide for me in one way or another if only I can keep the whole thing from collapsing. Farsetti too is offering me his hand, but I am sure I can get all I want from the former provided I free myself of the burden that dishonors me. Casanova dearest, please do your best to help me find a surgeon, a doctor . . . who will lift me out of my misery by delivering me with whatever remedy and if necessary by force. . . . I do not fear pain, and as for payment, promise [the surgeon] anything you like. I will sell diamonds; he will be amply rewarded. I trust you: I have only you in the whole world. You will be my

Redeemer. Ah Casanova, if only you knew how much I have wept! . . . I have never had anyone to confide in, and you are now my guardian angel. Go see some of the theater girls, ask them if they've ever found themselves in the need to deliver themselves the way I wish to do. . . . I didn't have the courage to speak to you in person about this. Oh God, if only you knew what I am going through! Let's do all we can to make me live. . . . Farewell. . . . Save me. I trust you. *

Stunned by Giustiniana's revelation, Casanova rushed over to the Hotel de Hollande. He was surprised that she was already five months pregnant because she was "slim" and her figure was "beyond suspicion."[3] She said she wanted to go ahead with the abortion as soon as possible. He warned her that it could endanger her life; besides, it was a crime. Giustiniana repeated that she would rather die than tell her mother the truth. "I have the poison ready,"[4] she blurted out. Casanova took pity on her and agreed, against his better judgment, to take her to a midwife who might suggest a remedy. They planned to meet again at the following Opera Ball and sneak out together.

The next ball was held in mid-February, at the height of Carnival. Giustiniana and Casanova arrived separately. Both wore a black domino, but Giustiniana could easily identify Casanova because he wore a white Venetian mask with a small rose painted under his left eye. After midnight, when the crowd was at its thickest, the two slipped away, found a hackney cab, and drove back across the Seine to the Left Bank, to meet the midwife in a rundown little apartment in rue des Cordeliers, near the Church of Saint-Sulpice.

Reine Demay, a louche, unkempt woman in her thirties, let them in. Her late-night visitors in their full Carnival attire impressed her. Giustiniana in particular struck her as "a young and pretty woman,

---

*This remarkable letter from Giustiniana to Casanova was sold at auction in Paris at Maison Drouot on October 12, 1999. The sale was brought to my attention by the dean of Casanova specialists, Helmut Watzlawick. The present owner of the letter, who has asked to remain anonymous, has kindly allowed me to print its contents.

magnificently dressed, wrapped in a pelisse of grey silk lined with sable; the skin of her face was very white, her hair and eyebrows dark brown; she was neither tall nor small . . . spoke French with difficulty."[5] She too noticed how Giustiniana was "very thin," considering the fact that she was by then into her sixth month.

According to Casanova, Reine Demay said she would prepare a potion that was certain to induce an abortion, adding that it would cost them the considerable sum of fifty louis—half the yearly rent he paid for Cracovie en Bel Air. And if perchance it did not work, she would teach them a surefire way to kill the fetus. The conversation turned uncomfortable. Abortion was a serious crime, punishable by death. It occurred to Casanova that he should have been more circumspect in the matter. It was certainly not prudent to bring Giustiniana to this shady midwife in the dead of night. Suddenly he was in a hurry to leave. He left two louis on the mantelpiece. Awkwardly, he pulled out two loaded pistols he had brought with him. Was he threatening the midwife? Was he trying to reassure Giustiniana? Whatever his intention—it may be he simply pulled them out in order to get dressed—the sight of the pistols sent a shiver down Giustiniana's spine. "Put those weapons away," she said. "They frighten me."[6]

It was after three in the morning when they stepped outside. Giustiniana complained that she was cold. They decided to drive out to Petite Pologne, warm up by the fire, and have a quick bite to eat before returning to the Opera Ball. The streets were empty. A cab took them flying across Paris. It did not take more than fifteen minutes to reach Cracovie en Bel Air. Casanova lit a fire, opened a bottle of champagne, and asked La Perle, grumpy and sleepy-eyed, to fix an omelette. The nasty aftertaste of their visit to rue des Cordeliers quickly faded, and the host was now in his most gallant mood. As they sat by the fire, talking and sipping champagne, Giustiniana's reticence also seemed to fade, as if she wished to forget for a while the reason that had brought them together. Casanova was quick to seize the moment. "And now we have finished the bottle"—this is how he describes the scene in his memoirs—"and we rise, and half-pleadingly half-using feeble force, I drop onto the bed, holding her in my arms; but she opposes my intention, first with honey-coated words, then by firm resistance, and finally by defending herself. That ends it. The mere idea of violence revolts me."[7]

Casanova drove Giustiniana back to the Opera Ball and soon lost her in the crowd. She found her friends, who asked her where she had been for so long. She waved to them mysteriously and headed for the dance floor. She danced hard until six in the morning while a thousand candles slowly burnt themselves out in the hall. The crowd gradually thinned. In the smoky predawn haze she wondered whether her movements had been sharp enough to damage the child growing inside her.

In her letter to Casanova, Giustiniana had not revealed who the father of the child was. It may have been Andrea: if she was into her sixth month when she went to visit Reine Demay, it meant the child had been conceived in the last days of August or the first days of September—in other words, during the month or so before the Wynnes' departure from Venice. And if Andrea was the father, one must presume she decided to keep him in the dark in order to protect him. But it is just as plausible that her pregnancy was the fruit of her brief and much-regretted affair with her nameless lover. The picture of what exactly transpired during Giustiniana's last few months in Venice is too blurred to provide a definitive answer. So blurred, in fact, that yet another possibility comes to mind: the day the child was conceived might have been so close to Giustiniana's reconciliation with Andrea that it could well be that she herself was not entirely sure whose child it was. Whatever the truth, Giustiniana, mindful of the price her mother had had to pay for secretly having her child, was determined not to keep the baby.

Casanova had been right to think he had made a mistake in taking Giustiniana to Reine Demay. Word of their visit quickly spread in the shady underworld around the *foire* in Saint-Germain-des-Prés. On February 26, less than two weeks after their unpleasant meeting with the midwife, a man appeared on Monsieur de La Pouplinière's doorstep claiming to have very damaging information on the young Englishwoman who frequented his house.

Louis de Castelbajac was an impoverished marquis and a well-known crook. Tall, gaunt, and somewhat sinister-looking, with devilish eyes and a pockmarked face, he had migrated to Paris from his estate near Toulouse and lived by extortion and larceny. Working the streets at the *foire,* he had picked up information about the nocturnal visit to the midwife and decided to profit by it. He teamed up with Reine Demay and called on La Pouplinière—possibly with the connivance of some of the *fermier général'*s embittered relatives. He told him that a young woman whom he identified as Giustiniana had gone to see Reine Demay two weeks earlier. The midwife had examined her, he said, and had found her to be in an advanced state of pregnancy. The young woman had asked for an abortion, and the midwife had refused. La Pouplinière showed Castelbajac the door, insisting that the person in question could not have been Giustiniana. On his way out, Castelbajac said he would send the midwife over to confirm the story. Sure enough, later that day, Reine Demay appeared at La Pouplinière's and repeated what Castelbajac had said. She too was promptly dismissed.

A few days later, La Pouplinière instructed his trusted secretary Maisonneuve to pay Giustiniana a visit, just to be on the safe side. Rumors about her pregnancy had been whirling around ever since La Pouplinière had begun to court her. Several anonymous letters had surfaced, one of which—apparently penned by the duplicitous Abbé de La Coste—accused Giustiniana of having already given birth to two children in Venice, besides being pregnant with a third. La Pouplinière had expected his family to undermine Giustiniana any way they could. For that very reason he was pressing ahead with the marriage as fast as possible. But he was not about to abandon all prudence.

The day after the strange visit by Castelbajac and Reine Demay, Maisonneuve called on Giustiniana at the Hôtel de Hollande. There was nothing unusual about his appearance, as he often came by on behalf of La Pouplinière, whether on business related to the marriage or simply to drop off a gift: theater tickets, a piece of jewelry, a basket of fruit for the family, a fresh catch of fish on a Friday. This time, however, he cut the civilities to a minimum and went straight to Giustiniana's room. "He told me of the slander being thrown at me," she wrote to Andrea. "Laughing a little, and using as much grace as he possibly could, he asked me if I would allow him to put his hand on my belly. I was happy to oblige him, and he begged to be forgiven a thousand times even as he cursed the slanderers."

Giustiniana said very little in her letters to Andrea about what was actually going on behind the scenes. She told him about the threats, the slanderous attacks, but she was never very specific; as she explained it, it was all part of a vague and mysterious plot set up against her by La Pouplinière's relatives. But she did tell Andrea about the bizarre Maisonneuve episode—indeed, she told other people as well, as if she had a particular interest in advertising both the motive and the outcome of his visit. How could she possibly have been in a state of advanced pregnancy, she seemed to be implying, if La Pouplinière's own secretary had put his hand to her belly and had pronounced it to be flat? But then it was probably a more cursory inspection than she was letting on, for even if her pregnancy was not very visible it is hard to imagine Maisonneuve taking a close look and still walking away convinced that everything was normal.

Whatever Castelbajac's objective was—a straightforward pay-off from La Pouplinière's relations, hush money from La Pouplinière himself, extortion money from Casanova, or perhaps all three—his nefarious scheme quickly backfired. After he and Reine Demay brought formal charges against Casanova and Giustiniana for demanding an abortion, La Pouplinière had Castelbajac followed and soon found out that he was indeed plotting with his relatives. The *fermier général* immediately brought a countercharge against the marquis and the midwife. Castelbajac, Demay, La Pouplinière, Casanova—all but Giustiniana—gave sworn testimony to the police during the legal proceedings in March, even as the wedding preparations moved rapidly forward. The three inquiring officers were inclined to believe that extortion was indeed the prime motive behind the initial charges brought by Castelbajac and Demay. "Threats, anonymous letters, paid agents: nothing was spared to give [La Pouplinière] the sorriest impression of me. Thank God they have failed and all their plots were uncovered,"

Giustiniana assured Andrea, who was finding the situation more and more confusing.

The case against Casanova and Giustiniana, however, was not closed. As a precautionary measure, La Pouplinière instructed his new confidant, the Abbé de La Coste, to write up a memorandum "on the whole Miss Wynne affair,"[8] a copy of which was sent to Choiseul, the increasingly powerful minister of foreign affairs who had granted the Wynnes an extension of their stay. Gossip about Giustiniana's pregnancy was still rife, and La Pouplinière evidently wanted to set the record straight so as not to jeopardize her application for naturalization.

The immediate threat of a trial had receded but there was little relief in sight for Giustiniana. By the end of March she was nearing the eighth month of her pregnancy. The quack brews Casanova was secretly administering to her were having no effect. And though she was still unusually thin, the daily task of hiding her condition was becoming more and more involved. She had to be alone when she dressed and undressed. She had to be careful not to raise suspicions with her secretive behavior. She had to choose with care the clothes best suited to camouflage her growing silhouette. Hardest of all was the constant, searing anxiety that her mother, who apparently was not aware of the rumor, might find out. Giustiniana became so desperate to dislodge the child inside her that she did not balk when Casanova came to her with a most outlandish proposition.

Casanova's principal benefactress at the time was the Marquise d'Urfé, a rich Parisian lady obsessed with the occult. He had managed to convince her he had special divining powers—he could read numbers, he was in touch with fundamental forces, he knew the secrets of the cabbala. He often dined alone with the marquise and cultivated her credulousness to his material advantage. It was said that she was at least partly responsible for his lavish lifestyle in Petite Pologne. One evening, in the penumbra of Mme d'Urfé's drawing room, he asked her whether she knew the alchemistical formula to induce an abortion. She answered that Paracelsus's *aroma philosophorum*, better known to his adepts by the contraction "aroph," was an infallible remedy.

Aroph was indeed a well-known medicament among alchemists

of the sixteenth and seventeenth century, and one finds several formulas for the potion in their writings. The basic ingredient was powdered saffron, which was believed to induce menstruation, and it was usually mixed with a paste of honey and myrrh. Casanova read all he could find on aroph in Paracelsus and in the *Elementa Chemiae* of the Dutch physician Herman Boerhaave. The special brew, he learned, was not only supposed to bring on menstruation but also to loosen the outer rim of the womb, thereby facilitating the discharge of the fetus. It was to be applied at the top end of a cylinder and inserted "into [the] vagina in such a way as to stimulate the round piece of flesh at the top of her such-and-such."[9] This was to be done three or four times a day for a week. Casanova burst out laughing when he read these careful instructions.

He went over to the Hôtel de Hollande and told Giustiniana of his latest discovery. In a typically Casanovian gesture, he supplied an addition of his own to the list of instructions: in order to make the potion more effective, it was necessary to mix it with freshly ejaculated semen. Giustiniana gave him a slanted look and asked if he was joking. Not at all: he would show her the manuscripts. She told him not to bother—she was hardly in the mood for reading the arcane theories of some alchemist she had never heard of.

Casanova writes that Giustiniana "was very intelligent [but] the candour of her soul prevented her from suspecting a fraud."[10] It seems more likely that she was simply at the end of her tether. They agreed to meet secretly in the garret of the Hôtel de Hollande when the rest of the lodgers had retired. In the meantime Casanova enlisted the help of the kitchen boy and Giustiniana's chambermaid, Magdeleine (he had discovered they had been using the garret for their private amusement and blackmailed them into becoming his accomplices). A mattress was taken upstairs as well as blankets and pillows. On the appointed night, Casanova let himself into the hotel through a back door and made his way up to the rudimentary bedchamber carrying his alchemist's paraphernalia. Shortly after eleven Giustiniana joined him upstairs. There were no preliminaries. The mood was very businesslike: "In our utter seriousness we appeared to be a surgeon getting ready to perform an operation and the patient who submits to it. [Giustiniana] was the operating surgeon. She sets the open box at her right then lies down on her back, and, spreading her thighs and raising her knees, arches her body; at the same time, by the light of the candle, which I am holding in my left hand, she puts a little crown of *aroph* on the head of the being who is to convey it to the orifice where the amalgamation is to be accomplished. . . . We neither laughed nor felt any desire to laugh, so engrossed were we in our roles. After the insertion was completed, the timid [Giustiniana] blew out the candle."[11]

Needless to say, the magic potion did not work, on that night or the few others in which they met in the garret. In fact, Casanova never even experimented with aroph: unbeknown to Giustiniana, he brought along whatever homemade concoction he could put together at Cracovie en Bel Air before coming into town for his nocturnal exercises—usually just plain honey. Faced with yet another failure, Giustiniana finally gave up the idea of ridding herself of the fetus and instead turned her attention to finding a suitable place where she could deliver the baby clandestinely. It was a common enough practice. She had heard there were convents where young pregnant women could go. It was a matter of finding a friendly place where she could feel comfortable and where her secret would be kept safe.

By the end of March the search had become frantic. The pressure from La Pouplinière was becoming unbearable. Giustiniana's naturalization papers, signed by Louis XV, had arrived from Versailles.[12] The Venetian documents were also ready and on their way to Paris. There was nothing to prevent the marriage from going ahead as planned in mid-April. Even the official portrait was near completion. And the impatient *fermier général* kept asking Giustiniana to set up an appointment with his dressmakers—which gave her a nightmarish vision of a busy band of seamstresses laying their searching hands all over her.

This time Casanova came through for her. He turned for advice to the Countess du Rumain, a well-connected Parisian *grande dame* "who was more beautiful than pretty . . . and was loved for the sweetness of her character."[13] The countess was intrigued by Casanova's divinatory powers (later on she too became an adept of the "abstruse sciences"), but she was also a practical woman and enjoyed using her influence to help others.

Casanova told the Countess du Rumain the whole story. At the end, he asked if she knew of a safe refuge where Giustiniana could deliver the baby. The countess wasted no time. She contacted another friend, Madame de Mérinville, who was evidently quite experienced in such matters, and begged her to receive Giustiniana as soon as possible as her pregnancy was already so advanced. The financial and logistical arrangements were worked out by the countess, Madame de Mérinville, and Casanova, who claimed he gave Giustiniana two hundred louis to pay for transportation and expenses during her stay at the convent. Within a few days everything was ready. La Pouplinière's dressmakers visited Giustiniana at the Hôtel de Hollande on April 3 and discussed various ideas for her wedding trousseau. It was a brief, preliminary meeting—no searching hands. Early the following morning she made her escape to the convent in Conflans.

Giustiniana left two letters behind—one for her mother and one for La Pouplinière. To both she wrote that she had been forced into hiding because of the constant threats she kept receiving by those who opposed the marriage. It was not just her reputation that was being sullied; she feared for her life. Under such circumstances she could not possibly go ahead with the marriage, and she would not reveal her hiding place until it had been called off. To mislead the police, she said she was staying within the city of Paris.

As Giustiniana settled into her spare room at the convent, fear and confusion took over at the Hôtel de Hollande. When Mrs. Anna finished reading Giustiniana's letter, she immediately suspected Casanova of kidnapping her daughter. Ambassador Erizzo, who had admonished the Wynnes against having anything to do with him, was also convinced of Casanova's involvement. Casanova, of course, feigned complete ignorance about Giustiniana's whereabouts. In fact, he even appeared for dinner at the Hôtel de Hollande the very day of her disappearance, asking with a perfectly straight face why everyone was wearing such a sullen expression and whether Giustiniana was upstairs in her room. The next day Mrs. Anna drove out to Petite Pologne with Farsetti and begged Casanova to tell her where her daughter was. Again he assured her he didn't have a clue and promised he would do all he could to help find her. A few days later Mrs. Anna, with the full blessing of Ambassador Erizzo, sued Casanova for conspiring to kidnap her daughter.

Soon Giustiniana was able to reassure her family. She befriended the uncle of Mother Eustachia's chambermaid, who worked at the convent, and paid him to take her letters into town and deliver them to another intermediary, a man she referred to as "the Savoyard," who posted the sealed envelopes at different mailboxes around Paris. Giustiniana assured Mrs. Anna and her siblings that she was well but insisted she would not reveal her hideout until she was sure she would not have to marry La Pouplinière. Communicating with Casanova was easier: she sent her letters for him directly to Countess du Rumain via Mother Eustachia. She was deeply grateful to him and to his lady friend, she wrote. She had found peace at the convent and the abbess was very kind. There were books to read and plenty of time to rest, though she complained that the absolute confinement imposed by Mother Eustachia weighed on her spirits at times.

In Paris, meanwhile, the inquiry into the ill-fated trip to Reine Demay's was slowly moving forward. Antoine Raymond de Sartine—a rising star in the city's judiciary, whom Louis XV would soon name chief of police—summoned Casanova for an informal talk at his private home. He told him he was going to have to answer the very serious charge of having solicited Demay to perform an abortion on Giustiniana. But if he was innocent, he should tell him the whole truth—tell him why Giustiniana had disappeared and where—and the entire matter would be quickly settled. Casanova assured Sartine that the charges were false. "Alas, Monsieur, there is no question of abortion; other reasons prevent her from returning to her family. But I cannot tell you more without a certain person's consent, which I shall try to obtain."[14]

Casanova realized that his vague explanations had not convinced the magistrate and he would soon find himself in very serious trouble unless he told him the truth about why Giustiniana had run away. But he needed to have Countess du Rumain's permission. He went to her the next day, and, pragmatist that she was, she called on Sartine and told him the whole story herself. Giustiniana was indeed pregnant, she explained, but no abortion had been performed; she was now waiting to deliver in a convent near Paris and would go back to her mother after the baby was born.

Sartine was an understanding man; he knew the ways of the world. He listened carefully to what the countess said. It was all he needed to know; they could count on his discretion. A few days later Casanova was summoned for a formal deposition before the presiding judge, who was none other than Sartine himself. He admitted going to the Opera Ball wearing a black domino on the night that was mentioned in the suit but denied ever paying a visit to Reine Demay. As for Giustiniana, he said, "neither I nor any member of her family ever thought she was pregnant."[15]

Sartine spared Casanova an arrest warrant but advised him not to leave Paris until the case was closed. For good measure, Casanova dropped a handsome bribe of three hundred louis into the lap of the court clerk. Shortly after his testimony, Castelbajac sidled up to Casanova with an offer: Demay was ready to retract her accusation—claiming she had mistaken his identity—in exchange for a hundred louis. The midwife appeared at his house in Petite Pologne a few days later in the company of a conniving witness and, after taking a look at Casanova, said loudly that he was not the man she was looking for: "I have made a mistake."[16] She was not the only one trying to make some quick money from the sordid episode. Mrs. Anna's lawyer, M. Vauversin, also stepped into the fray, secretly offering Casanova advice on how to counter his client's suit against him.

Delighted at the opportunity his enemies were handing him, Casanova sent a detailed report to Sartine on all the financial shenanigans. In short order, Demay was arrested and imprisoned at the Grand Châtelet for attempted extortion; Castelbajac was sent to the Bicêtre, a prison just south of Paris, for his complicity in the affair; and M. Vauversin was temporarily disbarred, much to Mrs. Anna's discomfiture.

Casanova could breathe again, but despite the arrest of two of the claimants he was still not cleared and the two cases that had been brought against him remained pending. Giustiniana's disappearance continued to be a topic of gossip in Paris throughout the spring of 1759. "You would not believe, sir, the noise this affair has made here," one of Andrea's correspondents wrote. Several weeks after her escape "she still remains the news of the day in a country that usually thrives only on novelty. If poor Miss Wynne had wanted people to know she was in town, I can assure you she would have been very satisfied, for I can't remember anyone being talked about so much."[17]

Inside the court, Casanova had testified that pregnancy was not the cause of Giustiniana's disappearance. But of course the talk outside the court was that she was indeed expecting a child. How else could one explain her sudden bolting and, even more so, her refusal to emerge from hiding? Her own explanation—that she was running away from threats and a marriage she couldn't face—simply did not make sense. The substance of Castelbajac and Reine Demay's depositions soon became general knowledge. An anonymous and very derogatory pamphlet on Giustiniana made the rounds. Andrea's name cropped up frequently in conversations around town as the presumed father. And La Pouplinière, of course, was made to look like a fool.

Inevitably, rumors about the causes of Giustiniana's disappearance reached Venice as well. Andrea did not quite know what to believe. He had stopped receiving letters from her after she had gone into hiding. His friends were asking whether what they heard was true. He did not know what to say. Her mysterious behavior had left him defenseless in the face of the most insidious attacks. Utterly confused, he resorted to reading excerpts of some of Giustiniana's earlier letters out loud to prove to others that she had harbored misgivings about the marriage and might well have fled out of sheer panic. But beyond defending Giustiniana's honor, what was he to believe? Could it be that she was really pregnant? If so, who was the father?

Andrea's attempts to get credible information from his friends in Paris were frustrated. "You must let me know once and for all precisely what has occurred," he urged Casanova, to no avail. Farsetti was not much help either. He wrote to Andrea about Giustiniana's "enemies" but never provided a convincing picture of what was actually going on, probably being in the dark himself.

Farsetti seemed more interested in denigrating Casanova at every opportunity: "If she had never met that man or if she had sent him away as I told her to do, she would be married by now."[18]

Even more disquieting than Casanova's prevarications and Farsetti's petulant letters was the short note Ambassador Erizzo sent Andrea in reply to his frantic queries. Erizzo was a respected statesman, a senior member of the Venetian ruling class. Even though Andrea belonged to a younger generation, the ambassador always addressed him as one of his own. His harsh words must have weighed heavily on Andrea's heart.

> *Esteemed Friend,*
>
> *I had the honor of receiving two letters in which you urge me to tell you what has happened to your beautiful Miss Wynne, who has not written to you for many days, and who, to your surprise, is beginning to be talked about in the most equivocal manner; and so you would like me to give you an accurate report on what has occurred. I very much wish I were in a position to oblige you; but the anecdotes are numerous and of such a nature that I would be compelled to write for two hours—and this after I have just finished writing a long dispatch. Suffice it to say that her conduct was ridiculous and imprudent in the extreme, and if she had sought advice from sensible people everything would have been settled. I believe it is entirely superfluous to say more since it would appear, if what I have been told is correct, that you are in a better position to inform me than I am to inform you. It is believed, among other things, that she has rushed to Venice or wherever you might have told her to go. Please forgive me.*[19]

April turned into May. The days grew longer and warmer. The countryside around Conflans teemed with new life. Spring showers washed over the lush green hills and the air was sweet with the scent of lilac. Inside the convent, Giustiniana waited peacefully for the birth of her child. She had grown close to Mother Eustachia despite their difference in age; the abbess was nearly thirty years her senior. During their long conversations, she had talked to her as if to an older sister about her love for Andrea, the hardships they had faced together, her uncertainty about the future. Little by little the spiritual quality of the place had affected Giustiniana. She was more at ease with herself despite a natural trepidation as her labor approached. Many hours passed in prayer, and the amiable Father Jollivet often took her confession. It was a difficult time, but Mother Eustachia and Father Jollivet made her feel a little less alone.

At the end of May, Mother Eustachia informed Countess du Rumain and Casanova that Giustiniana had given birth to a baby boy. The delivery had not presented special problems, and the mother was in good health. No official record of the birth has survived. The boy's destiny remains a mystery. Even his name is unknown. Mother Eustachia arranged for the child to be sent "to a place where he would be properly cared for"[20]—perhaps a local peasant family or else an orphan's home, as was the custom in such cases. Giustiniana never mentioned him in her correspondence. She certainly never spoke of him to Andrea. Only a handful of people knew what had happened at Conflans, and the secret would have died with them had Casanova not betrayed it in his memoirs some thirty years later.

Giustiniana could now reveal her whereabouts and go back to her family after a short period of recovery. But her return had to be negotiated with as much skill and diligence as had been used to organize her disappearance. As soon as she was fit to be seen in public again—albeit only behind the grille of the convent parlor— she wrote to her mother and told her where she was. Mother Eustachia also contacted Mrs. Anna, explaining that she had just discovered Giustiniana's real identity. The letter, dated May 27, is a little triumph in the art of deception:

Mlle Justiniana Wynne finally opened up to me yesterday evening. She told me, Madame, that you are presently living at the Hôtel de Hollande, rue Saint-André-des-Arts. Had I known this before, I could have spared you so many worries. She has been with us ever since coming here on April 4. You mustn't begrudge me my taking her in. I did not dare expose a young

woman of her age and station to the dangers of wandering alone
in search of other communities, certain as I was that someone
would soon come to claim her. Yet nobody came to ask for her....
She has seen no one in the parlor and has received no letters. She
has conducted herself with great piety here. She has a charming
character. I love her with all my heart, and I would be handing
her back with the greatest regret if I didn't know it was for her
greater happiness. I would be delighted, Madame, to give you a
token of my respect at any time, and I have the honor of being
your very humble and very obedient servant.

Sister de Mérinville, abbess of Conflans[21]

The letters drew a stream of people to Conflans. Mrs. Anna
arrived at the convent the very next day. She was accompanied
by M. de La Pouplinière, who had his personal train of followers:
M. de Maisonneuve; his confidant, the Abbé de La Coste; and his
notary, Maître Fortier, who had come to take a sworn deposition
from Mother Eustachia in order to establish the exact date of Giustiniana's arrival at the convent and the length of her stay. Father
Jollivet also gave testimony that he had "taken confession many
times" from Giustiniana.[22] Amidst the general confusion, La Pouplinière advised Mrs. Anna to have notarized copies made of
Mother Eustachia's letter to her and Father Jollivet's deposition as
soon as she got back to Paris. It was important, he explained, to
protect Giustiniana's reputation with official documents.

Once the formalities were out of the way, the little crowd gathered by the grille, behind which Giustiniana was smiling coyly.
There was a very emotional exchange. Giustiniana feigned surprise at what had been said about her in Paris during her absence.
She acted bewildered when she was told that criminal charges had
been brought against Casanova on her account. La Pouplinière led
the conversation, and Giustiniana was struck by "the expressions
and tears of the old man, who loves me to the extreme." Her
miraculous reappearance—the actual sight of her as she sat behind
the grille, looking "even more beautiful than before"[23]—so galva-
nized the *fermier général* that he saw no reason why the marriage
could not go forward after all. Mrs. Anna announced that she was
withdrawing her charges against Casanova now that her daughter

had reappeared and the matter had been cleared up (that wasn't enough for Casanova, who requested a written apology that he then had notarized). The other, more serious charge of attempted abortion was still in place, and the pending trial was a problem, of course. But La Pouplinière felt it was much simpler to clear Giustiniana's position now that the truth was out. The wedding, he proclaimed as he took leave and headed back to Paris, would take place "as soon as the trial is done away with."[24]

When her visitors had left, Giustiniana withdrew to her chamber to review the situation with Mother Eustachia. It had been a turbulent and confusing day. She was baffled by La Pouplinière's plan to go ahead with the wedding. Even though she was no longer pregnant and there was no practical obstacle to the marriage, she had had plenty of time during her long seclusion to reflect on the wisdom of that enterprise. The idea of being thrown back into the clutches of La Pouplinière's avaricious relations terrified her. Perhaps more important, her stay at Conflans had changed her: the extravagant notion of marrying the old *fermier général* seemed to belong to another life.

Giustiniana and Mother Eustachia agreed that there was no need to rush back to Paris. Besides, if she left the convent she might well be called to testify in the proceedings that were continuing against Casanova. Even worse was the possibility that Reine Demay—who had been released after spending three weeks in jail—might be asked to identify Giustiniana as the woman who had visited her in rue des Cordeliers on the infamous night of the Opera Ball in the company of Casanova. Better to allow La Pouplinière time to sort things out with the court officials and return once the proceedings were over.

In the following weeks Giustiniana gradually recovered her spirits as well as her slender silhouette. She was allowed out of the convent for short walks in the gardens, and she received regular visits at the grille from a doting La Pouplinière, as well as all the clamoring members of her family and her many friends. Toward the end of June her visitors planned a *fête* outside the convent to honor Mother Eustachia and the Benedictine nuns for looking after Giustiniana so well.

Andrea, meanwhile, was still very confused. Giustiniana was in a hurry to renew her correspondence with him in order to reassure him. As a gesture of goodwill, Mrs. Anna handed over to Giustiniana those of Andrea's letters that she had intercepted during the previous weeks—most of which she had opened and read anyway. But she forbade her daughter to write to Andrea because she still suspected him of having had a hand in Giustiniana's disappearance. Farsetti, terrified of incurring Mrs. Anna's wrath, at first resisted Giustiniana's pleas to act as her secret postman. Only at the end of June, during her final days at Conflans, did he finally agree to mail her first letter to Andrea since she had sneaked out of the Hôtel de Hollande nearly three months earlier.

Mon cher frère,

My dear Memmo, forgive me. I know you will forgive me in the end. But still I begin by asking you to forgive me; to make it easier for you to read my letter with a favorable attitude, I shall first accept some blame. But the only crime I have committed is not having written to you for so long; and if I prove to you, my dear friend, that it was impossible for me to do so before, I think you will want to forgive me. I love you, I am your friend; my Memmo will always mean the same to me; and your letter, which Farsetti showed me yesterday, which made me feel that despite my enemies' craftiness, despite all that was said about me, you always held me innocent, even though my silence with you suggested I might be guilty, would have convinced me more than ever of the excellence of your character—if I had needed any more convincing. You are well worth my breaking the prohibition to write to you. Let me rise to this renewed expression of respect and friendship I receive from my Memmo, even if it means that everything might go to hell. I begged Farsetti with so much fervor that he promised he would send you my letter; and so I write to you stealthily, even as I am being watched, and I want to tell all my story.

Here at last was the letter Andrea had been waiting for. Of course Giustiniana's narrative was skillfully edited. She told him that the warnings and threats she had received from anonymous writers

had compelled her to go into hiding. "All the necessary preparations have been made for your downfall," she quoted from
memory. "Go into hiding as soon as you can. This is a serious
affair." It had reached the point where she was seeing "poison
everywhere." La Pouplinière himself had told her their enemies
were "capable of anything." She had had no option but to escape
somewhere. "The day before I left," she added, recasting events in
such a way as to make her tale more credible, "the old man's dressmakers came by to take my measurements, and it was a good thing
they came because it eased the suspicions instilled in him after my
flight." She described her trip to Conflans and her meeting with the
"excellent and very amiable" Mother Eustachia—who, she added,
was related to some of the best houses of France. At first the
abbess had not wanted to take her in, Giustiniana told Andrea,
contradicting Casanova's version of the facts, but the sight of such
"a nicely dressed young woman with jewels" had moved her.
Mother Eustachia had questioned her intensely during the first few
days, and eventually she had relented. "She could see I was still
frightened, and since she cared for me, she stopped questioning me
so as not to agitate me further." Her identity would have remained
a secret, Giustiniana claimed, if on May 23 she had not heard
Father Jollivet speak in such a way as to force her to reveal who
she was:

> That day the confessor came to the abbess's parlor and unwit-
> tingly started to tell her what I recognized was my own story—by
> chance I was there keeping the abbess company—as if telling the
> latest gossip from Paris. He talked about the girl's flight just
> before her wedding to a rich financier, he mentioned all the equivo-
> cal things being said about her, including the fact that she had
> run away to give birth and that Monsieur de La Pouplinière was
> convinced about it. Such were my surprise and my confusion that
> without even realizing what I was saying I blurted out, "It is not
> true. Miss Wynne is a lady who belongs to one of the oldest and
> noblest families. Miss Wynne is an honorable young woman. I
> am that young woman . . ." You can well imagine their surprise.
> Both tried to explain to me how imprudent I had been in not hav-

*ing identified myself before, and they persuaded me to write to
my mother. Which I did.*

La Pouplinière now came regularly to the convent, the letter
went on. He was working hard to close down the Casanova trial.
"God only knows what happened . . . because I know nothing
about what Casanova is up to," she assured him. In any case things
looked promising on that front. "I believe I shall be cleared very
shortly." Of course there was again all this talk about the marriage, she wrote in conclusion. "The old man is waiting for everything to be over to marry me; but I am still unsure (and please
leave me free to decide for myself). I am not counting on it as
much as others are, even though it does appear to be so close."

In fact, it was not nearly as close as she thought.

Giustiniana left the convent sometime between the end of June
and the beginning of July. Her return to Paris came on the heels of
several weeks of behind-the-scenes negotiations involving La
Pouplinière, members of his family, and the office of Choiseul at
Versailles. The Wynne Affair, as it was known, had caused such a
commotion in Parisian society that the government was no longer
well disposed toward Giustiniana, and her position was not
improved by the fact that the British were pounding the French at
Le Havre. Louis XV had signed her naturalization papers only
three months before. But they had been intended to open the way
for her marriage to La Pouplinière before the scandal. In the wake
of her disappearance and the drama that had ensued, not to mention the fact that she still might be summoned as a codefendant
in the trial of Casanova, her position was quite different. La Pouplinière's relatives took advantage of this new mood of impatience
at Court. They used their strong connections with the Choiseul
camp to obtain nothing less than Giustiniana's banishment from
the country. There was no need for a dramatic announcement;
the Wynnes were simply informed that their papers, which were
expiring anyway, would not be renewed. Technically, of course,
Giustiniana was now a naturalized citizen. But there was little
point in challenging the powerful Choiseul. The time had clearly
come to continue their journey to England.

Choiseul's office convinced a reluctant La Pouplinière to go along with the decision by suggesting that Giustiniana might go abroad for a while, possibly no further than Brussels, and return to Paris once the situation had cooled down. To many it was clear that the old man had been fooled. "Monsieur de La Pouplinière flatters himself that the noise will die down as soon as she is out of the kingdom and that he will then manage to settle things more easily," one observer wrote to Andrea. "I wouldn't want him to be taken by surprise and led to rid himself, unwittingly, of Miss Wynne."[25]

Giustiniana was confined to the Hôtel de Hollande from the day she left the convent until her departure to Brussels, initially set for July 14. "It is my mother's idea, and you know one has to do things her way," she told Andrea. Mrs. Anna hardly spoke to her daughter. She had been on the brink of an exceptional marriage only four months earlier; now the family had to suffer the humiliation of being kicked out of the country on Giustiniana's account. The atmosphere in their apartment was tense. And the summer heat made packing their trunks all the more uncomfortable.

Mon cher frère,

We leave for Brussels having been dismissed by the minister, probably thanks to the work of the old man's relatives, who will have had no trouble in convincing the authorities that it was wrong for such a fortune to end up in the hands of an Englishwoman— especially in these times. As an excuse, we were told that our papers had expired and winter had been over for a long time. . . . I cannot tell you how disgusted I am with this country and with [La Pouplinière's] household. . . . Oh, why are you not here to advise me? Dear Memmo, how many woes I have suffered, how many scares, how many slanders! My story is so unlike me. Never mind . . . you will know all. . . . You have always been my best friend and always will be. I still love you, Memmo. You know that. I always wonder whether I shall ever find my Memmo again. Shush, I know I shall one day. . . . I'll write to you every week. . . . While I appreciate your intention in reading my early letters to many of your friends so they might see that what was being said about me was very unlikely, I must confess that I feel bad about the fact that what I wrote to you in private for only you to read should be judged by others. Farewell, my Memmo; love me and write me long letters.

The pressure on Giustiniana to testify at Casanova's trial evaporated once it became clear she would be leaving town. La Pouplinière insisted that it would be "indecent" to summon her before the judge, offensive to her *and* to him, since after all he still intended to marry her. His embittered relatives saw that there was no point in dragging out the fight. Choiseul himself probably let it be known that he would be happy to see the Wynne Affair come to a swift conclusion. In the end, Giustiniana was spared a humiliating trip to court and her name was officially cleared. "The sentence that establishes my innocence is all I really [wanted]," she wrote to Andrea, greatly relieved.

There was one last, pathetic scene at the Hôtel de Hollande. A few days before her departure for Brussels, Giustiniana sent a note over to La Pouplinière thanking him for all he had done to get her out of her legal troubles. She also told him with a clarity she had never used before that it was foolish to continue talking about marriage even as she was packing her trunks. But since he persisted in holding on to that illusion, she felt compelled to refuse his hand. It was a strong letter and unambiguous for once. "Imagine a well-thought-out, well-crafted piece of work," she proudly told Andrea.

The effect of her letter was not what she had expected: "The old man rushed over to see me, and his tears were the only answer I got from him." Not at all resigned, La Pouplinière sent the Abbé de La Coste and Mme de Saint Aubin to talk things over with Giustiniana and her mother. But it was much too late in the game. Even Mrs. Anna, who had been such a keen supporter of her daughter's marriage to the *fermier général,* could see through that shady, calculating couple. She gave them "a very rough dressing down" and accused them of giving the old man the runaround for their personal benefit. "She so treated them as scoundrels that they rushed off, saying 'Madame hears no reason. . . . It is impossible to come to terms with her.' "

The Wynnes left Paris for Brussels around mid-July. They had certainly made their mark since arriving from Lyon nine months earlier, and Giustiniana, of course, had been the talk of the town during much of their stay. Now they were the enemy on the run— a disgraced English family fleeing through the back door in the stifling midsummer heat. Giustiniana was glad to escape, to leave it all behind her—the deception, the intrigue, the lying, the sheer awfulness of what she had lived through. As far as she was concerned, it was already part of the past. "I look upon this story with such indifference I feel it never happened," she wrote to Andrea, who was apparently still somewhat "distressed" over the lost opportunity of a great marriage. She, on the other hand, was already looking ahead to their short stay in Brussels and their new life in London. After all she'd been through, she added with a bit of sarcasm, it shouldn't be too hard for her "to ensnare an English duke."

In her letters there was, of course, no mention of the baby she was leaving behind. Did she ever visit him before departing? Did she stay in touch with the people he had been entrusted to? One searches in vain for an answer in her correspondence: there is not even a hint as to what she was going through because of this separation. However intense her maternal feelings toward the child might have been, she forced herself to keep them secret. With Andrea so far away, she had no outlet for her pain. Casanova, to whom she had become so close in a short period of time, had already drifted out of her life by the time she left Paris. In his memoirs there is no mention of a final farewell between the two. He had simply moved on to his next adventure.

Meanwhile, the original traveling party had lost two of its members. Zandiri had returned to Venice, and Toinon, who had seemed destined for spinsterhood, announced to everyone's surprise that she was staying in Paris because she was about to become engaged. So there was going to be a marriage after all. "Plain as she is, she has nonetheless managed to find a lover who will marry her as long as she has a virginity to lose," a well-informed friend of the family wrote to Andrea. "She claims to be intact from that point of view, and so this happy wedding will take place shortly."[26]

The Wynnes ended up staying in Brussels more than a month. They took rooms at the elegant Hôtel de l'Impératrice and waited for instructions from Lord Holderness. Giustiniana was determined to make the most of their stay. "I have decided to enjoy myself . . . and to humor my temperament," she wrote, flaunting her brittle new gaiety. "I spend my time as best I can; I laugh at everything and often at myself." Brussels was the ideal place to have some fun. It had the insouciance of a provincial capital governed by a wise and popular ruler, Prince Charles of Lorraine. Giustiniana, Bettina, and Tonnina were soon regulars at the theater and the opera. They dressed up, they danced, they flirted. "We are the beauties of the land," she reported with a cheerfulness Andrea had not heard for months.

The dreary Farsetti quickly arrived to spoil the fun. Still obsessed with Giustiniana, he followed the Wynnes to Brussels convinced that the moment was finally his. He had stood by her during difficult times, he had lent her money, he had posted her love letters, he had tried to protect her from other suitors—as well as from her own imprudence. The time had come to claim Giustiniana for himself. But Giustiniana was tired of Farsetti's nosy, self-righteous manner. Her resentment toward him, long stifled out of self-interest, was ready to burst.

"Farsetti joined me here shortly after my arrival and immediately started to show off," she complained to Andrea. "He was full of claims, full of jealousy. . . . I dismissed him a thousand times so that he would return to Paris, and a few times I was rather sharp. . . . I owe him a lot because he was full of attention for me [in the past]; but I cannot forgive his doggedness in loving me." The poor man did not know what had hit him. Utterly stunned, he left Brussels the day after his arrival. As for Giustiniana, she continued to have fits of rancor even after his departure: "Ah, Memmo, that Signor Farsetti was deadly. . . . His envy, his designs. . . . No man has ever hurt me more. . . . The whole of Paris knew that he wanted to marry me and that I constantly had to refuse him. . . . [Ambassador Erizzo] always claimed it was Farsetti who messed up the deal with the old man. All I know is that he must have cried often for having taken me to him in the first place."

After Farsetti left town, Giustiniana threw herself into Brussels' festivities with a greater vengeance. Prince Charles, the attractive and amiable governor, was quick to notice her. "He looks at me, he laughs with me, he pays me a thousand compliments," she reported. She was flattered by the prince's attentions, but she knew a man of such lineage would always be beyond her reach. It was Charles's closest friend, the Count de Lanoy—"handsome, broad-shouldered and full of spirit"—who caught her fancy instead. The attraction was mutual. Soon the young count was openly court-ing her. She did not discourage him. Her coquettish self was back, and she savored anew the pleasure of being wooed by a dashing young man.

"There is someone here whom I believe I would rather come to like if I were staying in Brussels longer," she confessed to Andrea. "He's always with the prince, but he does his best to see me as much as he can. And I must say I find him very lovable." The count followed her everywhere. At the theater he always sat in a box next to hers, from which "he never ceases to look at me." She had enticed him with her new liveliness and the "attitude of *petite-maîtresse*" she had adopted "to amuse myself." Giustiniana's attrac-tion to him was easy to explain: "I found in him something which reminded me of my Memmo, and I liked him."

After much chasing around, she and the count met in the merry confusion of a *bal masqué:* "I went, and, holding my mask up as I approached him, I pretended not to know him, took his hand, called him some English name, and asked him to take off his mask. He laughed at what he thought was my mistake, followed me around, and teased me a thousand times. He told me he loved me all the while he pretended to be the Englishman. Prince Charles then came toward me, and the three of us started a conversation that turned out to be very lively because, pretending not to recog-nize the prince behind his mask, I said a thousand crazy things."

That night the count wore a cocked hat with a white feather, and a mask in the Venetian style. His resemblance to Andrea sent shivers down Giustiniana's spine: "Oh God, Memmo. . . . He is your size, and he moves his head exactly the way you do. . . . He makes a thousand movements similar to yours. . . . And, if I may say so, even his wit is similar in tone to yours." Despite the count's insistence, though, Giustiniana never asked him to visit her at the hotel. "What say you about my success? It cost me something, 'tis true; but I wanted to put myself to the test, and I now find one can manage anything."

As their stay in Brussels came to an end, the pleasant but somewhat futile flirtation with Count de Lanoy gave way to reveries of a deeper kind about Andrea. She was, she now realized, the victim of a well-known conundrum of the heart: drawn to men because they reminded her of her true love, she inevitably discarded them because they were not him. "Ah, dearest Memmo, where are you? In truth, I have little to thank you for: you have robbed me of any chance I might have had of loving someone else. . . . I love no one, and, by God, I have loved no one after my Memmo. And what is better still—and worse for them—is that I tell all my admirers: No, I shall never love anyone after my Memmo. One can love but once in a lifetime."

Strangely, there is no deep sadness in these letters to Andrea. It is as if Giustiniana were beginning to draw strength from the very notion that she would never love anyone again the way she had loved and still loved him. The endurance of her feelings gave her a sense of security, even of well-being. It was not entirely paradoxical, for the dream of a life together was always with her, seemingly irrepressible. "Oh, dear Memmo, will you be able to make the long trip to London one day? In that case, good-bye to all our lovers, good-bye to our friends, good-bye to the whole world. . . . Don't you think? I know: you don't have money. But don't worry, the day will come when we will both have some."

Giustiniana's spirits were up when the Wynnes left for London in mid-September. Apart from crossing the choppy Channel, the family was looking forward to the end of a very long and tumultuous journey. Lord Holderness had secured a temporary house for them in a pleasant part of London. He had also sent a French tutor, M. Verdun, over to Brussels to get acquainted with Giustiniana's young brothers. Lord Holderness intended to send Richard and William, who were now fifteen and fourteen, up to Cambridge to get a proper education. Mrs. Anna was of a different mind, but this was no time to quibble. As for the "three Graces"—Giustiniana, Bettina, and Tonnina—Lord Holderness was already looking around for suitable matches. "A viceroy for me, or maybe a governor in America," Giustiniana bantered. "Don't laugh, and be patient. Giustiniana was born to be someone, you'll see."

Nearly two months in Brussels had indeed invigorated her. Only a few days before she and her family left Brussels, however, the Parisian nightmare was suddenly brought back to her by the shocking news that La Pouplinière had married a young and pretty woman, Thérèse de Mondran, in a rushed ceremony in Paris. Giustiniana had never met her, but it turned out that the Abbé de La Coste and Mme Saint Aubin had been plotting in favor of this marriage even as they had been pleading with Giustiniana at the Hôtel de Hollande. Undoubtedly bruised, Giustiniana nevertheless maintained her sense of humor: "I heard, to my surprise, I must confess, about the marriage that was arranged for him in a flash. . . . I then remembered that the other old man, Smith, had done the same. . . . I haven't any luck with these old men."

CHAPTER Eight

The crossing from Calais to Dover took no more than a few hours, but the sea was rough and the passage seemed interminable. Giustiniana was hugely relieved when she stepped ashore and felt the firmness of the ground beneath her feet. She had sat belowdecks with the rest of the family and had been "sick to death" as the boat had pitched and crashed in the murky Channel waters. Now, as she stood safely on the windswept pier, in full view of the chalky white cliffs, the dizziness and nausea abated and her natural color returned. It felt strange to be back in England—the Wynnes' "other" home. But it felt good, too. Seven years had gone by since she had last come to her father's country. She had been a young girl then, and Sir Richard had died only a few months before. This time it was different: she was coming to find a husband. She was coming to stay.

A government coach sent by Lord Holderness met them at Canterbury. The family traveled to London in great comfort. They were dropped off at "one of the prettiest houses" near Saint James's Park, which was to serve as their temporary home. The Wynnes were not accustomed to such luxury. "We could not have come to London through a better door," Giustiniana exclaimed, beaming. Holderness at once sent his personal secretary to see them settle in, and in the evening he appeared at the house himself.

He was not a very handsome man. He had a large nose, a sagging jaw, and a skin condition over much of his face that made his appearance somewhat "offensive" to the more squeamish.[1] He carried himself with an air of such gravity that he came off as slightly pompous. Nevertheless, he welcomed Giustiniana and her siblings "like a father" (he was cooler toward Mrs. Anna) and announced

that his wife, Lady Mary, would be back from the country the following month and would introduce them to society. He would personally make sure they were soon presented to Court as well. Until
then, it would be good form if Giustiniana, Bettina, and Tonnina
stayed mostly around the house.

Holderness's directive must have sounded excessively rigid to
these cosmopolitan girls who had danced till dawn in Paris and
Brussels, but it was no time to show resistance: they were entirely
in his hands. Besides, he had explained that he was imposing this
temporary confinement for their benefit. That first night Giustiniana went to bed exhausted but reassured—even flattered—by the
solicitude of this important man.

Robert d'Arcy, Fourth Earl of Holderness, had indeed reached
a position of considerable power and influence, much to the surprise of some of his contemporaries. In the mid-forties, after he
returned to London from his diplomatic posting in Venice, he
joined the Society of Dilettanti and became a busy bachelor on
the London social and artistic scene—he cultivated a passion for
opera and masquerades that he had picked up in Venice. In 1749 he
was named ambassador to The Hague. There he married Mary
Doublet de Groeneveldt, the daughter of a prominent Dutch
businessman. He seemed destined for an honorable if not particularly brilliant diplomatic career in His Majesty's service. But the
Duke of Newcastle, then prime minister, "fetched"[2] him from his
post at The Hague in 1751, and, at the age of thirty-one, Holderness was appointed secretary of state alongside William Pitt the
Elder.

His meteoric rise caused many to shake their heads in disbelief.
Pitt himself considered Holderness a "futile"[3] young man. Horace
Walpole described him as a lightweight and a "blabberer"—though
he acidly acknowledged that the young secretary of state at least
"did justice to himself and his patrons, for he seemed ashamed of
being made so considerable for no reason but because he was so
inconsiderable."[4]

Holderness had enough ability to hold on to what was given to
him, and he remained a loyal protégé of the Duke of Newcastle for
most of the decade. But by the end of 1759, after three years of

war, he was looking over his mentor's shoulder to the growing "peace party" that was gathering at Leicester House around the Earl of Bute, the rising star in Parliament (and future prime minister under George III).

Bute knew all about the Wynnes through his mother-in-law, Lady Mary Wortley Montagu, who was still living in Venice. She had sent her daughter a warning about Mrs. Anna and her children just as they had set off on their journey across Europe the previous October:

> *My dear child,*
>
> *I am under a sort of necessity of troubling you with an impertinent letter. Three fine ladies (I should say four including the Signora Madre) set out for London a few days ago. . . . As they have no acquaintance there, I think it very possible (knowing their assurance) that some of them may try to make some by visiting you, perhaps in my name. Upon my word I never saw them except in public and at the Resident's, who, being one of their numerous passionate admirers, obliged his wife to receive them. . . . I have said enough to hinder your being deceived by them, but should have said much more if you had been in full leisure to read novels. The story deserves the pen of my dear Smollett.*[5]

By the time the Wynnes finally arrived in London, long preceded by this unflattering introduction, Holderness was in the thick of his political maneuvers aimed at endearing himself with the Bute camp. Clearly he did not want his guardianship to get in the way of his more important pursuits. Since leaving Venice the Wynnes had acquired a reputation as something of a traveling circus, and the recent gossip coming from Paris about Giustiniana's adventures there had done nothing to improve their reputation. While Holderness felt compelled to sponsor their presentation to Court, if only to honor Richard Wynne's memory, it was important to him that it be done judiciously. The last thing he wanted was for his Venetian charges to be running around London out of control.

Initially, the Wynne children took Holderness's orders in stride.

After all, their momentary seclusion gave them a little extra time to prepare for their appearance in the best houses of London. Giustiniana looked forward to reading "new English books in order to take my bearings in my country and not appear too much the foreigner." The picaresque tales of Lady Montagu's "dear" Tobias Smollett were probably a little old-fashioned for her. But after the dryness of the French *philosophes,* she was eager to immerse herself in the English novels she had heard so much about. Henry Fielding and Samuel Richardson had already produced their great works the previous decade. Now Laurence Sterne was the new author everyone in London was talking about—he had published the first two volumes of *Tristram Shandy* only a few months before the Wynnes arrived.

However, reading books was not enough to keep the family quietly occupied. After just a few weeks of Holderness's strict regime, a grumpy mood took over the household. "We're all bored in the extreme with London since we cannot go out or see anyone," Giustiniana complained. "We cannot even go to the park. . . . His lordship keeps us in perpetual servitude."

Holderness did make one concession: the Wynnes were allowed to visit the Venetian ambassador and his wife, over on Soho Square. This privilege hardly enlivened their social life. Count and Countess Colombo were a "charming couple," but they were not much fun. The Countess was "always amiable [but] practically always ill . . . and always alone." Giustiniana went to the embassy mostly to collect her mail and talk about Andrea with the ambassador, who, like other diplomats before him, was so titillated by their story that he offered to become their secret go-between.

The Wynnes were also allowed to receive a select list of visitors at home, but Giustiniana found the guests who crowded their small drawing room even duller than the ambassador and his wife. They were either old acquaintances of her mother's from their previous trip to London or part of the steady trickle of nondescript Wynne relations who came over out of curiosity about their Italian cousins. None of them earned an individual mention in Giustiniana's letters. "I do not enjoy myself with these people," she complained. "We are always onstage. And everyone stares at us and talks as if we were the most beautiful women in the whole kingdom."

The mood in London was very different from the one in Paris. England was winning the war; the Wynnes arrived in town as His Majesty's soldiers were taking Quebec and routing the French in Canada. Confidence was high, and a growing sense of predestination gave a purpose to the conflict that the French increasingly seemed to lack. Newspapers and periodicals led the patriotic fanfare:

> *Come on ye brave Britons, let no one complain*
> *Britannia, Britannia, once more rules the main.*[6]

It was turning out to be "the glorious fifty-nine," to use the expression in vogue that season.

After three long years, however, a feeling of lassitude was taking hold of the country, even as dispatches continued to bring good news from the battlefields. Whereas Parisians went from deep gloom to wild celebration depending on the latest war bulletin, the British seemed far more subdued in their reactions. "You must not imagine that victories are received here with loud cheers," Giustiniana explained to Andrea, who was eager to learn all he could about the war. "At the most, a few burning candles appear on the windowsills. . . . One hardly talks about the war. . . . There is more interest in it in Venice than here, where it truly matters. Maybe the English talk about it between themselves. Maybe they're just tired."

Admittedly, Giustiniana was catching only glimpses of London, but the little she saw was uninspiring. The ladies did not dress well. Their hairstyles were out of fashion. Conversations rarely went beyond polite formalities. There was no exciting intellectual dispute to follow—nothing like Rousseau and d'Alembert battling each other's ideas in the press or the polemics surrounding the publication of a new volume of the *Encyclopédie*. Indeed, aside from lengthy reports on the war and rousing calls to victory, the periodicals seemed mostly preoccupied with such mundane topics as the latest development of the ribbon loom or the newest method of collecting taxes. There were few public festivities and no *bals masqués* whatsoever, the Anglican bishops having recently managed to have them outlawed.

It is not surprising that Giustiniana thought the most interesting figure parading through this gray landscape was the flamboyant Kitty Fisher, courtesan extraordinaire, who had managed to set herself up quite extravagantly: "She lives in the greatest possible splendor, spends twelve thousand pounds a year, and she is the first of her social class to employ liveried servants—she even has liveried chaise porters. There are prints of her everywhere. She is small and I don't find her beautiful, but the English do and that is what matters."

The notorious rivalry between Kitty Fisher and Lady Coventry, the former Mary Gunning, was a favorite source of social chitchat. "The other day they ran into each other in the park," Giustiniana wrote to Andrea, trying to entertain him with some local color, "and Lady Coventry asked Kitty the name of the dressmaker who had made her dress. [Kitty Fisher] answered she had better ask Lord Coventry as he had given her that dress as a gift. Lady Coventry called her an impertinent woman; the other one answered that her marrying a nutty lord had put enough social difference between them that she would have to withstand the insult. But she was going to marry one herself just to be able to answer back to her."

Giustiniana had arrived in London in early autumn determined to charm her way into the best houses of London. By November her enthusiasm was already flagging. There was so little going on in her life that she had to spice her letters to Andrea with secondhand anecdotes. As she waited for Lady Holderness to return from the country and rescue her, a feeling of futility took hold of her. She became more introspective. Her life was so unsettled now, so uncertain; that she missed Andrea was one of the few certainties. She felt the emptiness every day. Brief trips to pick up his letters at the Venetian Embassy were her only joy. But each one of those journeys also brought more confusion. "You are still more precious to me than anything else in the world, and you always will be," she wrote tenderly. ". . . But I am so unsure about everything. And do you know why this is? Because I still love you horribly."

The prospect of another round of husband hunting was suddenly very dispiriting. During those long, rainy autumn days, she wondered for the first time whether a husband was necessary at all. How "convenient" could a marriage of convenience really be? Could she not find a better way to live? Perhaps it had to do with her character, she mused, perhaps with the way she had lived her life so far—but it occurred to her that she had come to value her independence more than the security that might come with a good marriage. Surely an income of her own, even a small one, would give her the freedom she needed to shape her life. "You want me to find a duke or an earl," she complained to Andrea. ". . . I believe I want none of that. . . . A husband is a nasty thing."

Holed up in Holderness's guest house, Giustiniana explored alternatives to marriage. One solution was to invest the small inheritance she had received from her father—fifteen hundred pounds—in order to generate an income she could live on instead of using that sum as a dowry. She admitted that such an arrangement might force her to live more modestly than was her taste: "I hate mediocrity . . . and I am not virtuous enough to live well in a lesser rank." But at least she would no longer feel hostage to the imperative of a "good" marriage. There was no doubt in her mind that her future would feel less uncertain. In that sense, she would certainly "improve her condition."

She pictured Andrea raising his eyebrows as he read her letter in the privacy of his room at Ca' Memmo. His protestations, she warned him, were not going to stop her: "You will scold me, of course, but I have already written to Paris to gather information. I understand that interest rates are much higher there. I will live here for the time being, and I shall have my seat at Court if I choose to wait long enough. And if I get bored I'll move back to France, unless of course you should ask me to rush back to Venice."

Perhaps she was getting a little ahead of herself, she admitted. These were still little more than "barely sketched and rather confused ideas." Andrea needn't worry: she wasn't giving up the plan "to ensnare" that English duke. Not yet, at least. But she was "disenchanted" with people of high rank and their society, and serious about wanting to take charge of her own life. She needed to keep her head clear, to weigh her options more realistically. Even though Mrs. Anna's friends downstairs kept blabbing away about what an excellent husband she would find, she knew that the more time passed the harder it would be to find a match that would suit her. And the more she thought about cutting herself loose from the obsession with marriage, the more she liked the feeling: "If I keep on thinking in this manner, maybe these ideas will take shape after all."

There were also physical changes that needed to be taken into account. Giustiniana was still a very pretty young woman—"the belle of the belles," as she said to Andrea with a lingering sense of entitlement. Now that her Parisian experiments in hairdressing were over her black curls again fell freely over her sweet, lively face, and her dark, beautiful eyes were as penetrating as ever. Yet the youthful glint that had warmed so many hearts in Venice and Paris and Brussels had lost some of its sparkle. Motherhood had left her a little rounder, too. "I'm becoming womanish," she observed with a touch of sadness as her birthday approached. "I'm nearly twenty-three. The best part of my youth is behind me. . . . What beauty I had is probably fading."

Her sister Bettina was four years younger and bursting into full bloom. It was her turn now. She would be the one attracting all the attention when the Wynne sisters were launched into society. "She's a beauty now, and she is kind and spirited without ever being affected," Giustiniana remarked proudly. "We'll see how she is received when we go out in public this winter. Her figure would certainly not be considered slight in Italy or France, but it is very much appreciated here." Right behind Bettina was Tonnina, who would soon turn eighteen. The youngest of the three sisters had much matured since the days when she had stood passively in the arms of Alvise Renier. Giustiniana assured Andrea that he would scarcely recognize her: "She's never been more beautiful or more charming. . . . If she doesn't put on more weight, she will please very much. If you could see her bosom now, her arms, her hands, her natural whiteness, and the self-assurance she has gained with the help of some graceful manners she acquired in France."

As for the unmarried older sister, she was apparently quite

ready to cede center stage: "I'm no longer tempted to please, and I really no longer wish to work hard to bring a man where I want him to be. I'm so tired of whimsical love, yet I feel I have lost the kind of sensibility one needs for a great passion. . . . Ah, you know me well enough. You know I'm meant for an unhappy life. The idea of marriage scares me more and more. I would never marry a man I admired so as not to make him unhappy. And I would never marry one I despised so as not to make us both unhappy."

This was Giustiniana's life in London as she depicted it—a solitary life of reading and writing, a life into which "not a single man" ever strayed. And what of Andrea? He went to the theater. He attended amusing dinners at their friends' palaces on the Grand Canal. And by his own admission he was enjoying a new season of gallantries. While she lived the life of a recluse, she complained, "you happily make love to the ladies." Her tone was often self-mocking, and one feels that despite the complaining, she derived real pleasure from writing to Andrea. Her letters to him were more and more an outlet for her powers of observation, her sense of irony, and her humor.

Andrea teased Giustiniana about his flirtations in Venice—had they not renewed their vow "to tell each other everything" after the Paris scandal? Yet he now confessed that there was one young woman in particular who was vying to become his *favorita*. The problem, he explained, was that the lady in question was very jealous of Giustiniana and could not stand to see her picture still hanging so prominently among Andrea's collection of portraits and miniatures. In fact, she had demanded its prompt removal. He sheepishly admitted that he had given in to her request. Giustiniana skewered him for this act of betrayal with a comic description that was all the more admirable given the circumstances:

> *Imagine making such a demand! And worse, having it fulfilled! I'm furious about this. It is too awful! Too horrendous! My heart is filled with rage. . . . What now? My portrait is no longer in the middle of all those pictures of gorgeous sultanas that enlivened that extraordinary cabinet? . . . My glory hath been crushed, and now I have been thrown into the chaotic throng of*

your old mistresses! . . . Oh, you unfortunate portrait! Your reign is over. . . . And so you are left to dangle from the victorious chariot of a rival. . . . My dear Memmo, as you can see. . . . I hold the destiny of my exiled portrait close to my heart. And the consequences of this shameful removal make me tremble, for I can gauge the power of the person who now occupies you by the quality of the sacrifice you have made (you will forgive my vanity).

Giustiniana took a guess. "Quick: tell me her name," she quizzed him nervously. "Admit the *belle coquette* is M.C." And indeed it turned out that it was Marietta Corner, the same young woman who had caused her so much grief in the early days of her relationship with Andrea. This time Giustiniana was not going to let her heart be torn apart by pangs of jealousy. She tried to laugh about it, to treat Andrea's dalliance with Marietta as lighthearted comedy. she wanted to show herself in command of her emotions. "I take pity on you, my dear Memmo," she went on, "for you are dealing with someone who has only her beauty to offer, and surely she will bore you very soon. I know you well. . . . I bet she'll use gentle violence on you by asking to read my letters so as to calm her anxiety, real or fake as it may be. . . . Well, if that's so I'll turn very mean and tell you that I love you with the greatest intensity. . . . I will also tell you freely that I'm sure I shall never be forgotten by my Memmo."

Her jocular tone did not entirely mask her sadness. A whole year had passed since she had last seen Andrea. So much had happened in both their lives, yet he was still at the center of hers. She loved him—"horribly" was the word she had used—and she was not ready to be pushed into the background by another woman. Did she seriously feel threatened by Marietta? Probably not. She knew Andrea too well to fear that he might attach himself to a woman who had, as she put it, "only her beauty to offer." But all his light talk about portraits being shifted around was hurtful. Even though she hid the pain so artfully, it still showed through her persiflage in the most touching ways. She could go on at length poking fun at her rival, making sarcastic remarks, ridiculing the whole affair; then, practically in the same breath, she would start writing about the two of them again. She would soon be presented to Court. What would he like her to wear? What colors did he have in mind? "I thought I might wear *pensée* or yellow, the color dark-haired women use in France. I could wear a satin dress lined with marten furs—I have some beautiful ones. . . . But tell me what you'd like. . . . See, I fret over these little things as if I were still there with you."

The distance between them, however, was real, and news traveled even more erratically than usual on account of the war. There were plenty of opportunities for delayed information to play havoc with their lives. It was autumn—Giustiniana had left Paris three months before—when Andrea first heard of a nasty anonymous pamphlet about her that had apparently made the rounds in the French capital at the time of the Castelbajac-Demay affair. Andrea never actually read the incriminating "brochure," but, from what he was told, he understood that it contained a description of Giustiniana's behavior that was very much at odds with the one she had given to him back in June. It was only hearsay, of course, but Andrea was assailed by unpleasant doubts all over again. He confronted Giustiniana with the rumors he was hearing. Coldly, he asked if he should be writing to her at all.

Giustiniana's heart sank. Why was Andrea needlessly digging up the past, throwing at her the sad debris of her Paris debacle? His cruelty wounded her: "Your friendship is so unpredictable, you give credence to the most horrible things so easily. . . . I shall only tell you this: no such brochure against me exists and the ill-informed people who are spreading this around with the object of hurting me are misleading you. Believe in your Giustiniana, who has never debased herself to the point of hiding the truth from you. She tells you she is innocent of all the accusations that have been made against her. . . . I will force you to be my friend in spite of yourself and your mistresses. . . . I have lost your heart, but I have not deserved all the rest."

There was no reply for nearly a month, and this silence broke her even more than the accusations. Then one day she found a clutch of three letters from Andrea waiting for her at the Venetian Embassy. She was overwhelmed with happiness:

So many riches to bring me joy! You remember me and I find you are still my friend, and maybe something more? My poor Memmo, you are still mine, then! How much we have lost, both of us, in robbing ourselves of our hopes and dreams! You seem to have lost your aptitude for refined pleasures; I have no true enjoyment left and cannot find a man I like as much as you, nor will I ever. In the passion I used to feel for you there were a thousand combinations that kept my mind and my soul perpetually excited. Oh, I loved you so! And by God, I do not feel my heart has yet been emptied of all that passion. I make this wager: that if I should ever come close to you again I will love you madly, if only you will allow me to.

In mid-November the Wynnes moved to a smaller house on Dean Street, near Soho Square. It had been "elegantly furnished" by the previous occupant, the paramour of "one of the richest men in England." But they felt a little cramped in their new home— something that was not likely to improve the atmosphere in the house very much. Dean Street itself was a busy commercial lane. The neighborhood was respectable but no longer as fashionable as it had once been—occasionally one even caught a whiff of the crowded taverns and seedy bathhouses of Drury Lane, just a couple of streets away. For some time, what was known as the "polite end of town" had been moving to the west of Soho, toward Grosvenor Square and Cavendish Square.

The two boys, Richard and William, were still living with the family in the house on Dean Street. Holderness had arranged for them to go up to Cambridge shortly after their arrival in London, but Mrs. Anna had resisted in the hope of providing them with a Catholic education (in this she was abetted by an Irish priest she had known during her first stay in London, who had now reappeared in their life). Holderness, of course, would hear nothing of it. Mrs. Anna made hysterical scenes and even threatened to follow the boys to Cambridge. Tensions in the house were always high.

Increasingly wrapped up in his political schemes, Holderness visited less and less often. "I fear his lordship will soon be disgusted with my mother," Giustiniana worried. "She is inconceivably mad."

The bad feelings between Holderness and Mrs. Anna were exacerbated by the difficulties he was facing in getting the papers for the Wynnes' formal presentation at Court. Mrs. Anna's ancestry was again an issue; her title of nobility seemed as dubious in London as it had in Venice. More paperwork was needed; dispatches had to travel to and from Venice across war-torn Europe. It was all terribly time-consuming. Again Giustiniana enlisted Andrea to help speed things up. "Imagine this to be one of your many projects," she said to encourage him, adding that her mother was especially "grateful" to him. "She sends her regards and begs you to continue to assist us. . . . How different from what she once was like! If only she had known you then the way she knows you now, she could have spared herself, and us, so much pain."

The Venetian authorities might also have been somewhat hesitant to vouch for Mrs. Anna's title of nobility lest Andrea and Giustiniana take advantage of their seal of approval and resuscitate their marriage plan. Giustiniana felt it was crucial to disabuse them on this point: "They must be absolutely certain that not only are we not planning to return to Venice . . . but we could not possibly be thinking of getting married because we have come to understand the permanent damage we would be inflicting upon ourselves. . . . We will never marry, not even if you came to London. Besides, I hate the idea of marriage too much even to think about it."

Their subtle diplomacy did not produce results. There was, briefly, some talk about a possible presentation in the future. "Presently all seats at Court are occupied, and not until the Prince of Wales's wedding might there be room for me."* But those vague hopes soon flagged. The Wynnes "could not have come to London through a better door," as Giustiniana had put it so enthusiastically, but a month and a half after their arrival, they still languished on the fringe of London society.

It was partly to relieve the tension in the house that Mrs. Anna

*The Prince of Wales did not marry Charlotte Sophia of Mecklenburg until September 8, 1761. By that time he had already succeeded his grandfather as George III.

accepted an invitation from a friend of the family to spend a few days in the country. It was hardly the sort of adventure to lift Giustiniana's spirits: she had no particular longing to be in the countryside, and she was tired of making polite conversation with Mrs. Anna's dreary little set. "They are of course very good people, with the best possible hearts, and so enchanted by us they would do for us anything we pleased. . . . But unlike what you might think, they are not to my taste." No doubt Giustiniana would have preferred to stay home rather than trundle out to the country with the rest of the family. In the end she went "to make Mother happy" and hoped "to alleviate the boredom" by reading more of those "new English books" she had told Andrea about.

The five-day visit to the country turned out to be even more dreadful than Giustiniana had anticipated: "I was bored to death. Imagine a crowd of pompous councillors and self-important English barristers. The horror!" The food was lousy and the company unspeakably dull. She was forced to escape to the garden so many times that she caught her first English cold.

In late November Lady Holderness finally came to town, to the immense relief of the three Wynne sisters. She immediately invited them over to take a good look at the young Venetian girls her busy husband had entrusted to her care. There followed a more formal invitation to her first "assembly" of the season.

Lady Holderness was an attractive woman of about forty, with a pleasant manner and a warm smile. Giustiniana was touched "by her ladyship's goodness." She found her "still beautiful and very charming"—the sort of woman only "a truly fickle man or else a husband could ever tire of." There was an advantage, she explained to Andrea, to being shown in society by such a fine lady: "I hear there is great impatience to see Bettina; and we are expected to make a charming impression." They had waited around the house for too long, but there was some compensation in hearing that "the country is curious in the extreme to see us, including the princesses, who have been asking about us."

There was a good deal of wishful thinking in all this. London society was terribly stuffy and exclusive—far more than Paris society—and it was not about to swing its doors wide open to the Wynne girls. True, there was some curiosity about them, especially Giustiniana. "There is a Miss Wynne coming forth, that is to be handsomer than my Lady Coventry," Horace Walpole wrote to a friend with anticipation. But it was the sort of curiosity reserved for the amusing and the vaguely exotic. Even Walpole was mindful that a different young beauty threatened Lady Coventry at the end of every summer "and they are always addled by winter."[7]

A year had passed since Lady Montagu had sent her acidulous missive to her daughter, Lady Bute, whose influence in society was rising in tandem with that of her husband in politics. Now it was Lady Bute's turn to regale her mother with unflattering reports on the Wynnes in action. And Lady Montagu, sitting in her rented *palazzo* in Venice, made it sound as if she could not wait for the next installment of her favorite saga: "I am very much diverted with the adventures of the Three Graces lately arrived in London. . . . I am heartily sorry their mother has not learning enough to write memoirs."[8]

Giustiniana's initial burst of excitement at the prospect of going out in the world soon exhausted itself as she attended a string of "boring dinners" and "unbearable assemblies." She spared Andrea the details of these tedious evenings for fear of "passing my distaste on to you." With one partial exception: her evening at the home of Lady Northumberland, the most celebrated London hostess. Thanks to Lady Holderness, the Wynne sisters had received the coveted invitation. This time Giustiniana was suitably impressed by the grandeur of the scene. "The house is very large, magnificent, richly lit up and one can see the most beautiful paintings," she conceded. But she went on to describe herself wandering among a tired and aimless crowd. There were at least a thousand people at Northumberland House that night: "Some of them played cards out of sheer duty, others ambled distractedly, and everyone was bored. I was certainly in that number. . . . What was the use of hearing people say how pretty we were or clap their hands at a curtsey only less clumsy than those one ordinarily sees here?"

The only episode worth mentioning at all occurred in the picture gallery, where she suddenly came face to face with a celebrated Titian painting depicting an illustrious Venetian family.* It produced something of a shock. The contrast between the vague familiarity of the scene on the large canvas and those unfriendly surroundings unleashed a rush of nostalgia for the world she had left behind. Still, even a very good painting was not enough to fill an evening. "By misfortune I was unable to have a carriage until midnight."

Giustiniana began to turn down invitations, something she had rarely done before, whether in London, Paris, or Venice. "I go out very little in public so as to preserve the applause for my sisters," she joked. As she had predicted, the "applause" was going mostly to Bettina, now the most admired of the three sisters. Lady Montagu, hardly a fan of the Wynnes, had conceded even before they had left Venice that Bettina was likely to blossom into a paragon of Hanoverian beauty. She was tall, she said, "and as red and white as any German alive. If she has sense enough to follow good instructions she will be irresistible."[9]

Occasionally, Giustiniana attended a *conversazione*—a rather large assembly where there was, in fact, very little conversation. As many as a hundred ladies would gather in one of the better houses of London, with the odd gentleman in attendance, invariably "old or blind or loud." Giustiniana was freer to move around than she had been in other more formal occasions, but even these events she found tedious and suffocating. Few ladies were interested in speaking to her, and those who deigned to address her were not particularly friendly. "One ends up speaking only to people one knows, and the people one knows tend to spend their time at the gambling tables like almost everyone else." Giustiniana felt more and more alienated: "One is made to feel so isolated in this grand society. What a life!" She was especially disappointed by the lack of warmth and solidarity between women: "You cannot imagine the degree to which [they] are malicious. Friendship does

*Giustiniana wrote to Andrea that she saw at Northumberland House "a famous painting by Titian of a Cornaro family." That is indeed how the family in the painting was identified at the time. Recent scholarship has revealed that it is actually a portrait of the Vendramin family.

not exist among them. . . . I could never become a friend of any of them, and so I treat everyone well and pay many compliments."

In her letters she went out of her way to make her London life sound dreary and wasteful: "I don't go to the park so as not to die of cold . . . I read . . . I eat . . . I sleep a lot." There was no point in fretting about what dress to wear at Court, she groused, because Holderness confirmed that there were still no seats available for them. The damp London weather did not help raise her spirits: she spent half her time in bed nursing head colds that never seemed to end: "I am so congested I cannot stand it anymore. . . . This damned climate is damaging my health. . . . It is more unpredictable than Giustiniana herself." But there was no use blaming the rain, she added wistfully. The ennui that was sapping her energy "has more to do with my nature than with the climate."

In fact, Giustiniana was not being entirely truthful when she depicted herself as a depressed stay-at-home who spent her time curled up in bed, writing to her long-lost lover in Venice and pining for his replies. She had met, through the Holdernesses, a handsome young man who came calling on her at Dean Street and found, to her own surprise, that his pleasing manner and his sensitive nature were beginning to warm her heart.

Giustiniana's new admirer was Baron Dodo Knyphausen, a brilliant Prussian diplomat who was thirty years old—the same age as Andrea.* George Townshend drew a couple of sketches of him that are now at the National Gallery; in them he appears as a smartly dressed young man with thin legs, a pointed nose, a broad forehead, and strands of curly hair combed straight back.

Knyphausen had been in London little more than a year but had immediately been very much at the center of things, with easy access to the highest reaches of government as well as the most elegant houses in London. Frederick the Great held him in very high regard: he had named him Prussian ambassador to Paris when he was only twenty-four. In France, Knyphausen had demonstrated his considerable skills in the complicated diplomatic game that had

*Giustiniana wrote that Knyphausen was twenty-eight when she met him, but according to the *Allgemeine Deutsche Biografie* he was born on August 3, 1729, and was therefore two years older.

preceded the outbreak of the Seven Years' War, and his dispatches had been instrumental in paving the way for the alliance between Prussia and Great Britain. When war broke out, Frederick saw him as the ideal man to nurture the relationship with the British ally. The baron arrived in London as Frederick's special envoy in 1758 and developed a close working relationship with William Pitt, the principal advocate of the war. By the time he met the Wynnes, he had already negotiated three contracts for British war subsidies to Prussia.

Giustiniana was flattered by the visits of such a coveted young man. "All the ladies want him," she assured Andrea when she told him about Knyphausen. "He is the only fashionable man in England." It was not just the sudden gratification of male attention that drew her to him. She was intrigued by this thoughtful, introspective man with whom she could carry on a conversation that ranged beyond the niceties of social chitchat. As the weeks passed she caught herself thinking about him more and more; waiting for him to appear and brighten up the day. He too reminded her of Andrea, though in a deeper way than had the frivolous Count de Lanoy in Brussels at the end of the summer: "I find myself busy thinking about a man who not only resembles you physically but also has a similar character. . . . That is why I find him so special and why I like him so. . . . Will you forgive me this new friendship? Oh, if only you knew how much he is worthy of it."

Giustiniana grappled with these new feelings without quite knowing what to make of them. This was very different from willfully seducing an old man; different, too, from flirting gaily behind a Carnival mask. There was no room for coquetry here. Part of her wanted to give in to the new stirrings she felt inside her, yet after all that she had been through in Venice, and then in Paris, she was wary of more emotional strain. She was also confused: "I don't even know if what I feel for him is love or respect. . . . I tremble at the idea of giving myself over to a passion. I fear passion. I try to convince myself that I should always preserve the will of reason. I already worry about the future, and I am fragile and I am anxious."

As she ventured out cautiously on this new journey, she realized she wanted to have Andrea by her side. She would describe her feelings to him. She would take him along step by step. "Do not reproach me for this new folly," she pleaded. "For heaven's sake, be indulgent and charitable in the face of a weakness that in the beginning came about because of you."

Soon Knyphausen was stopping by the Wynnes' "every evening at the hour of the *conversazione*." He showed Giustiniana "a thousand concerns, a thousand attentions," but he was careful not to raise suspicions in the house by expressing "too evident a preference" for her. His assiduity kept her enthralled, to the point that she once forgot to post her weekly letter to Andrea. "I know my Memmo will forgive me," she wrote apologetically the following week, "for an involuntary sin. The mail day was taken up with my new Memmo, whom I believe I love with a good heart and who gives me no reason to complain or wish for anything better. . . . If what keeps me so occupied is but a passing fancy, I would to heaven that all my previous ones had been grounded in such respectable foundations. Each day I find this man to be worthier of my esteem. I have for him the same kind of respect I have felt only for you in all my life."

Soon Giustiniana and Knyphausen were also seeing each other "in secret, one, two, three times a week." They talked for hours, confiding in each other, testing each other, stretching the bounds of their new friendship. They were drawn together by the ease, the subdued joy they felt in each other's company, more than by physical attraction. "Respect and compassion are what our friendship is built upon," she told Andrea.

Knyphausen had only recently recovered from his own painful love affair. For many years he had been secretly in love with a young and beautiful lady whose reputation had been sullied by "a thousand weaknesses"—most especially a severe gambling addiction. A young baronet had then come along and offered his hand, and she had accepted without telling him about her debts. Though not rich, Knyphausen had stepped in to pay them and thus save her reputation. He had also paid for the wedding, as the baronet had not yet come into his inheritance, and kept his grief to himself. "He wept, he was in great despair, but he no longer saw this woman."

Giustiniana felt that Knyphausen was a kindred spirit. He was curious about her life without being censorious. He showed understanding, he was sensitive, and above all, he listened. And she was grateful to have someone she could count on to talk to without fear of exposure. At last she had found a refuge in the frosty landscape of London society. Knyphausen gave her comfort and made her smile. She told him what she could about her life in Venice, her great journey across Europe, her adventures in Paris. Andrea loomed large over their long conversations. He had been the love of her life, she told Knyphausen. Now, she reassured him, he was a very close friend—her *cher ami*.

They continued their clandestine meetings. The only other person who was certain of their relationship was Andrea himself, the silent partner who, for all we can guess, seems to have been more curious than jealous. "Nobody knows anything about my involvement," Giustiniana assured him. ". . . There is barely a suspicion in my own house." She and Knyphausen had no compelling reason to behave so secretively. Neither was married, neither was officially involved with anyone else. Yet for all their intimacy they still circled around each other with a lingering hesitancy, still unsure of themselves as much as each other. Secrecy, one feels, suited both of them.

Giustiniana reverted quite naturally to some of her old Venetian ways in order to deceive her mother and meet Knyphausen on the sly. She told Andrea about her frequent escapades so she could, in a sense, share the thrill with her old accomplice. She boasted, for example, of the time she wangled an invitation to lunch at some friends' house a couple of miles outside London. As soon as she arrived at the house she promptly took leave of her hosts, explaining that pressing business called her back to town. But instead of going home to Dean Street, she went directly to see Knyphausen, who lived just a few streets away: "He was busy with a government minister, from whom he took his leave. He put on a coat and left the house on foot. I followed him from a distance until we reached a little house he had at his disposal, and we walked in. We lunched, and a bottle of champagne put us in such an intimate mood that we shared our secrets and commiserated with each other until we were both crying. What a happy state it would have been if that mutual trust, that familiarity, had lasted longer! But he doesn't trust me entirely, nor do I trust him."

Over the course of the winter Giustiniana's doubts about Knyphausen gradually dissolved. "I am still enchanted by my man," she wrote in mid-February. "He's the most charming and the most decent one there is. We see each other; we tell each other all sorts of tender things. But are we quite sure of ourselves?" In March she was already more hopeful: "I could be happy with this man, dear Memmo, if my anxious soul would only let me enjoy the moment without all the inner turmoil. . . . He believes in me; I'm very close to believing in him. He sympathizes with me; and I do respect him. His soul is so pure! Oh, do let me tell you: he's just like you, and God knows it's the truth. And you do look very much alike, though I promise you are more handsome." By early spring Giustiniana felt more confident about her feelings for Knyphausen than she ever had, and Andrea must have assumed by then that they were lovers: "My love life goes on, and it looks as if we really love each other. I have nothing much to say beyond that, except to mention that we do have our moments of scorn, our bouts of jealousy, our tantrums, our peacemaking; usual things, and of no great importance. . . . Do you think I love the Baron? I firmly believe I do."

How far should she go? How far did Andrea want her to go? "Give me your advice, help me keep a little mistrust alive; tell me his heart is not as good as it appears to be. You are my only friend, and you will be as long as you live. . . . Oh, if only I could see you now!"

To Andrea, this longing Giustiniana had to see him, so emphatically stated even as she was meeting secretly with her new lover, sounded disingenuous. He chided her, surmising that if he were to appear suddenly in London she would receive him with much less affection than her letters suggested. Giustiniana was hurt by his sarcasm: "Oh God, you can be so unfair. Come here and see for yourself what my feelings are for you. Then you will judge me. I have hardened out of necessity, but I have remained your loving friend."

In this Giustiniana was truthful. She could not let go of Andrea—did not want to let go of him. And her letters, while mostly about her new lover, were still filled with ambiguous references to their own relationship. Yes, she loved Knyphausen, "but not in the way I once loved you. Oh, what a difference! Oh, happy rapture! How many times I have wept over you!" And again: "You know you can always expect the most tender transport on my part."

In a world of fantasy, she said, she would have loved both men. Had Andrea come to London to see her, had money not been an obstacle, "I would have introduced you at once to the man I respect more than anyone else after you, and who is so dear to me." They would have been together, the three of them, in a strange and happy harmony. "I would no longer have made distinctions between my lovers, and you would have both been my friends. What happiness! What joy I would have felt to be between these two dear persons! I would have held no preference, for I would have omitted everything that might have caused it. Oh God! Why are you not here now to make me revel in this pure and perfect happiness?"

In the real world, however, Andrea was far away and not at all likely to make the journey to London. Giustiniana could tell from his letters, affectionate as they were, that he was busy building his own life in Venice, courting other women, working on his political career. In London, it was Knyphausen who kept her heart warm and her mind occupied. She noticed how her daily life seemed less tedious now. He gave her new zest. "I go out nearly every evening," she noted to her own surprise.

By the end of the winter Knyphausen was often by her side, even in public. Officially, their liaison was still a "secret." But rumors, as ever, had spread, thanks largely to the indiscretion of the Venetian ambassador. Giustiniana discovered with horror that "charming" Count Colombo had been reading her letters to Andrea. Including, she fumed, "the one in which I gave you a detailed summary of my love life." In revenge, she immediately sent off "a short but strong" letter to Andrea, blasting Colombo for "his shameful behavior." She knew it would circulate in Venice and dishonor the ambassador. "By God, he will get what he deserves," she quipped.

One outcome of Colombo's "shameful curiosity" was that it no longer made much sense to go to extremes in order to conceal her friendship with Knyphausen. So they went to the Opera together to hear the Italian singers, and they visited the London gambling houses—always rife with crazed addicts—to watch and comment on the crowd. Giustiniana was still untouched by the disease: "All my pleasure is in making remarks, in criticizing, in amusing myself . . . with the Baron always with me," she wrote to Andrea, recalling their own thrilling nights at the Ridotto in Venice. The dinners and assemblies were as "insufferable" as ever, but now she had someone to laugh with during those stuffy affairs. They whispered clever remarks to each other, smiled in wry amusement. Their favorite little game consisted of "discovering a caricature in all the people we run into."

Giustiniana was having a fine time with Knyphausen, but she was not growing any more comfortable with the English aristocracy. Quite to the contrary, she felt increasingly at odds with the people she had come to dazzle. She had lost her natural gaiety, she complained. She began to strike a pose and suffer from ennui. Her occasional pleasure in going out endured only because Knyphausen, an outsider like her, played along. Giustiniana was genuinely fond of him. She treasured his company and his camaraderie, although she never spoke of their relationship in hopeful terms, at least not in her letters to Andrea. Marriage, apparently, was never seriously discussed. If Knyphausen ever considered the possibility, he did not make a decisive move in that direction. There were the usual obstacles: the difference in religion (he was a Protestant), the difference in social standing. He also had pressing issues on his mind: he was in the middle of intense negotiations with Pitt in a frustrating and ultimately unsuccessful attempt to persuade him to send a British fleet to the Baltic Sea to protect the coast of Prussia. As for Giustiniana, her letters to Andrea consistently maintain that marriage was something she no longer wanted. In fact, her hostility to the idea of marrying anyone at all hardened during that winter despite her feelings for Knyphausen. If she talked about the subject at all, it was in the frivolous context of finding Knyphausen the best possible wife: "I've got it into my head to set him up, and I've already made my choice; but it'll be hard because this little person I have in mind is very sly. . . . If she won't fall in love with him it'll be my fault; and the amount of effort I put into making him agreeable to her is the most ridiculous thing in the world."

Even as she felt her bloom was fading, Giustiniana was determined to keep her independence, and she willfully relegated the issue of marriage to the background.

In early March Andrea sent word to Giustiniana that their old friend General Graeme was on his way to London and would call on her as soon as he got there. The news filled her with joy. It felt as though a warm, familiar breeze had suddenly blown into town, bringing back memories and stirring old yearnings.

Graeme, a prominent member of the English community in Venice, had been a good friend of the Wynnes before their departure, particularly Giustiniana. As commander in chief of the army he was also in close contact with all the ruling families of the Republic and was a coveted lunch and dinner guest at all the best Venetian houses. He had grown very fond of Andrea, and their friendship had deepened during Giustiniana's absence despite the considerable difference in their ages. Graeme had had to sit out the war due to Venice's neutrality. But at seventy, the energetic general still hankered for some action. He even hoped his visit to London might help him obtain a command in North America.

In any circumstances, the arrival of this old Venetian friend would have been cause for celebration. But Giustiniana still felt so unsettled in her London surroundings that the news jolted her into a state of feverish excitement. She waited for him like a sentinel standing guard. At the end of March, she heard that Graeme was at last in town. Just as she was getting ready to pay him a visit, the old soldier suddenly appeared at the Wynnes' and she rushed into his arms: "I truly felt as if I saw a part of myself in him as I knew he was coming from where you are. . . . I ran to embrace him and then I kissed him for you, and now it seems I cannot see enough of him. . . . I speak about you all the time. . . . I assailed him with so many questions all at once! So my Memmo still remembers me, and I hear this from someone who sees him and is with him nearly every day. . . . Graeme made me laugh by assuring me that you still love

all the ladies; which means you don't love any one of them. Giustiniana may still hope to be dear to you."

She and the general saw each other again the following evening
at Knyphausen's and spent all their time together, catching up on
Venetian gossip. They were not really free to talk there, particularly not about Andrea. Next morning, Easter Sunday, the general
came by the Wynnes' again. Giustiniana became so engrossed in
their conversation that she forgot to join her mother at Easter
mass. "He stayed with me from eleven until after two. . . . What a
good soul! Right now he is the only man I love. . . . I would be so
happy if I could have him with me at the theater tonight. And all
this rapture is because I talk about you. Because all I do is think
about you. I am beside myself, by God, I still love you too much."

Her agitated ramblings with Graeme had brought Andrea back
to her in such vivid colors that Knyphausen, by contrast, appeared
bland. "I am afraid I shall grow bored with the baron," she confided to Andrea. "I love him and he loves me. We see each other
quietly. Our pleasures are always quiet. But though I make up worries and cause little quarrels and disputes and bring up suspicions
to give us a little vivacity, I fear we are deluding ourselves."

The general stayed only a few weeks, enough to take care of
some family business and to realize that, much to his disappointment, he was unlikely ever to see any more action in the field. But
the impact of his short visit on Giustiniana was considerable. It
unleashed a torrent of emotions that was bound to crash into the
still waters of her placid romance with Knyphausen.

Their "quiet pleasure" lasted through the spring. They shared more
dinners, more assemblies, and more *conversazioni*. "I am certainly
not lacking invitations," Giustiniana said with more than a hint of
disaffection. They still met discreetly at Knyphausen's little annex
around the corner from his house "on account of his many servants." The weather improved and brought new distractions. A
boxing match between the Irish and English champions kept
tongues wagging for days. Military operations on the European
front and in North America had resumed after the winter lull,
bringing another string of victories for the Anglo-Prussian coali-

tion and more calls for peace. Lord Bute, backed by the Prince of Wales, continued to strengthen his hand at the expense of Pitt. Holderness, though still secretary of state, had thrown in his lot with the rising new leader, prompting Pitt to comment with sarcasm that he was likely to become "the vortex"[10] of a future Bute government. Knyphausen, on the other hand, probably realized that his own star was already dimming with that of the Great Commoner.

Giustiniana no doubt followed these developments simply by virtue of the fact that she knew so many of the participants. Yet she seldom described the political scene for Andrea even though he would surely have been very interested in it. She did not have a taste for politics. Her taste was more for observing society. In the spring of 1760 nothing captured her imagination as much as the trial of Laurence Shirley, Fourth Earl of Ferrers.

Back in January, Lord Ferrers, an eccentric old man who lived in seclusion on his vast estate in Leicestershire, had summoned his faithful steward, Mr. Johnson, ostensibly to complain about certain accounts. When the steward had entered the parlor, Lord Ferrers had locked the door behind him, ordered the poor man to his knees at gunpoint, and told him "to make his peace with God, for he never should rise again till he rose at the Resurrection." Mr. Johnson protested that all the accounts were in order. Lord Ferrers replied that "he did not doubt his accounts, but he'd been a tyrant and he was determined to punish him" and discharged his pistol at close range.[11]

Lord Ferrers was brought down to London, imprisoned in the Tower, and tried for murder by his peers in the House of Lords. Giustiniana was riveted by the case. All the major newspapers and periodicals printed detailed accounts of the inquiry and long features on the streak of madness than ran through this illustrious family. Lord Ferrers begged for mercy on the grounds of insanity, not an unreasonable plea on the part of a man who, according to *Gentleman's Magazine*, "was subject to causeless passions, . . . walked hastily about the room clenching his fists, grinning, biting his lips and talking to himself, . . . [was] frequently absent when spoken to, [and made] mouths in the looking glass."[12]

He was nevertheless found guilty in the course of a three-day trial that attracted "all of London," as Giustiniana put it to Andrea. She managed to get into two of the crowded sessions and came away with the sickening impression of having been to another of those elegant assemblies rather than to a murder trial. "The ladies were dressed for a gala, and the trial room, very large, was entirely draped in red and crammed with people. I have never seen such a grandiose spectacle. His lordship's predicament was terrible, but the sheer magnificence and diversity of the scene were such that the death of that poor man was the last thing people thought about."

Lord Ferrers, the last member of the House of Lords to be tried by his peers, was executed on the morning of May 5. It is said a silk noose was used in deference to his rank.

Now that summer was near, the evenings were warmer and Giustiniana was often invited to dine at Vauxhall, the fancy pleasure garden built on the other side of the Thames. The excursion always made her apprehensive. She did not like crossing the river on the unsteady little ferryboats. The Thames was not particularly wide at the crossing point—"no wider than the Giudecca Canal," she explained to Andrea, referring to the waterway separating Venice proper from the Giudecca. It scared her nonetheless: "Yesterday evening . . . the tiny size of the little boat, the fact the boatman only had one arm and was accompanied by his ten-year-old son, I think all of those things together increased my fear. Anyway, whatever the reason, everyone had a good laugh at my expense."

Knyphausen was a reassuring presence in such circumstances. He was always tender with her, always considerate. But there was no real spark between them, no strong physical attraction. There never had been. And no matter how much Giustiniana kept telling herself what a likable man he was, how really fond she was of him, she could not bury her feelings for Andrea. They kept coming to the surface, sapping the energy she needed to stop her relationship with Knyphausen from running out of steam.

On a hot morning in early June, Giustiniana was at home, still in her nightgown, writing her weekly letter to Andrea. It was a perfectly innocent letter. She mentioned a dinner at Vauxhall, said she was glad a rumor about Voltaire having died had turned out to be false, and, with evident annoyance, promised she would send the petulant Marietta Corner an English cloak if she insisted. "But I must warn her that the cloaks here are nothing special. In fact, everyone seems to like Italian ones very much." Only toward the end did her tone become more personal as she again touched on the vexing subject of marriage. Oh, she would find a husband, no doubt, if only she set her mind to the task: "Everyone predicts I will get myself one if I stay here." But she did not want to remain in London much longer, not with her social position still so uncertain. What was the point? She had not come all the way to England to marry a dreary solicitor. Marriage, she insisted, was no longer a necessary part of her plans. "I mostly wish to choose a place to live in that I will like and where I will feel free. If I manage to get an income of six to eight hundred pounds sterling a year, as I hear I may get, then I can live well anywhere. As soon as I have secured that sum I will share my plan with you and ask for your advice. You know I love you and that I have always looked up to you."

Just as she was finishing up her letter, Knyphausen was announced. Giustiniana rushed into the next-door room to put some clothes on "and in my usual absentmindedness I left the letter on the table." Knyphausen walked into the room and saw it lying there. The temptation was too strong: he picked it up and read it, and when Giustiniana returned to the drawing room he made a "horrible" scene. She was a "wicked" woman, he shouted at her, and "thoughtless" and "duplicitous." He could not contain himself. "For two hours I had to withstand the assault of a man who rarely gets angry at all." She had never seen him explode like that before.

Later in the day the tempest finally subsided, and Giustiniana and Knyphausen made peace. She held her ground, insisting she would not give up writing letters to Andrea. "You are my true friend, as he himself has accepted." The baron, in turn, laid down his conditions: henceforth Giustiniana was to show him all their correspondence—her letters to Andrea as well as Andrea's to her. "What can I do, dear Memmo? Will you forgive me for this too? He is such an upright man, and I owe him so much I had to give in. So please refrain from writing about him. Do not show him you know about us. . . . He would never forgive me if he knew that I had divulged this secret to you. . . . Keep our friendship alive since that is all we may count on; and forgive my weakness for a man who is really quite worthy of respect."

She could feel her relationship with Knyphausen growing hollow even as she wrote these words.

G iustiniana spent much of the summer in bed. The air was hot and sticky. The marshes around the city seethed with malevolent insects, and fevers spread easily. Bouts of high temperature kept her confined to her room. Outside her window, the bustle in Dean Street had quieted. The "polite end" of London was mostly empty, its inhabitants having migrated to their country homes after the King's birthday in June. Lady Holderness had left town as well. Word was that only poor Lady Coventry was still at home, slowly dying of lead poisoning from using too much whitening powder on her delicate skin.

It was a strange time. In late winter the end of the war had seemed so near. Then, in early spring, news had come that preliminary peace talks at The Hague had collapsed. William Pitt, still in charge of government policy, was bent on crushing France's fleet and dismantling its overseas possessions. So the war had to go on: at sea, in North America, and on the Continental battlefields, where the exhausted Prussian Army, supported by the English Treasury, fought strenuously against France, Austria, and Russia. In London pro-German sentiment continued to be high. A poetry collection by Frederick the Great was the season's best-seller. "Mostly odes and a poem on the art of war," Giustiniana wrote wearily. "They read it here as if it were a reliquary."

Some days she was worn out by fever and shifted uncomfortably under piles of damp, crumpled sheets; others she was suddenly better and enjoyed the long hours she had to herself. Propped up by a pile of cushions, she read, she wrote, she slept. During those long, sweltering days she felt her tenuous ties to London dissolve as her mind wandered dreamily back to Venice. She imagined Andrea's life from what he told her in his letters. She saw herself floating back into his arms. The thought of returning to Italy was often in her mind, and she did not resist it.

Knyphausen hovered around her, ever solicitous. "He certainly loves me," she told Andrea, as if registering a self-evident fact; but she added little about her own feelings. She was annoyed by his insistence that he read her correspondence and was not beyond writing a few fake letters in order to mislead him. Nor did she hand over to him everything she wrote. In a letter clearly intended to elude Knyphausen's eye, she confessed to Andrea, "I might as well tell you, for your own glory, that I love less and less the man I should be loving more and more."

In mid-July she was shaken out of her feverish reverie. For weeks Andrea had continued to write with the detached tone he had been asked to use in order to avoid exciting Knyphausen's suspiciousness. In fact, he had become so adept at playing the part of the old friend—never allowing himself the slightest slip—that his coolness often made Giustiniana uneasy. The letter she now received was far more disturbing than anything he had written to her before.

Andrea confessed that he was tired of "easy, everyday gallantries." His brief affair with Marietta was over. He wanted to organize his love life more efficiently and possibly settle down with a lover who would also be good company "during the intervals." A woman he could talk to. A woman he could enjoy and respect at the same time. He went on and on, filling the page with justifications of every kind.

Giustiniana understood what this unpleasant letter was all about. She knew Venetian society well enough to see that Andrea was adapting to the local custom. He needed to focus on his political career, and his distracting love life would not do anymore. It was fairly common practice for a young Venetian patrician to seek a stable relationship with a married lady. Andrea had just turned thirty-one and was still a bachelor. He felt that at this point in his life it made sense to find himself an "official" lover.

Giustiniana must have half expected that this would happen one day, but the abruptness of Andrea's announcement was the real shock—not to mention his manipulative desire to involve her in the whole process. At the end of the letter he informed her that he had already whittled down the list of candidates to three names: M., C., and B. All of them were married, he added, and all of them were more or less available. Giustiniana was overcome by a feeling of dread when she realized the preposterous nature of Andrea's request: he wanted her to help him decide which of the three ladies was best suited for him. In her reply she accused him of using all his "accursed skill" to avoid responsibility for her "eternal downfall."

Knyphausen laughed loudly when she explained Andrea's predicament to him. He laughed out of relief as much as amusement. "Most of all," she noted bitterly, "he was glad to learn from your letter that there are no more ties between us that might give him reason to be jealous." There were moments when she thought she recognized, behind the screen of Andrea's outrageous proposition, the smirk of the inveterate prankster. But after reading his letter several times she became "quite certain" that his intention "to seduce those three dames was not a practical joke at all."

She was hurt, and the insidious way in which he made it sound "as if I should be thankful to you for this great token of your friendship" made it even more painful. "I still don't understand you," she confessed in yet another letter clearly written behind Knyphausen's back. "Are you seeking revenge? Are you putting me to the test? . . . Why is it you can upset me so much even from so far away? Even when I am willing to love someone else? Alas, you are the only one in my heart now. And I feel you want me to renounce all my claims forever."

Something in Andrea had changed. He was looking beyond her, looking for an attachment that would suit his life in Venice. Giustiniana understood all that, yet she also felt she had not entirely lost her place in his heart. She was going to fight for it, knowing well that if she had any chance at all of succeeding she would have to match his "accursed skill" with her own. "Besides," she concluded dryly, "if I leave the choice to you, I run the risk that you will pick one not to my liking."

With gritted teeth, she delineated her recommendation:

So you want to live your life openly, you want to be able to visit their house, you want to be able to be seen in their company because you are tired of all the discomforts of secret lovemaking, and you wish to see your heart involved to some extent as well as satisfy your mind. In that case I'm afraid that C. will not give you what you want. She is pretty, possibly the prettiest of the three; but if my memory is correct you were not so sure about her spirit. She also happens to have an unbearable husband who actually lives with her, and the company she keeps is not the most suitable for someone with your intelligence. B., who cannot be said to be pretty but is worth more than a few pretty ones together and who probably would flatter your vanity and excite your spirit more than the other one, lives too much of a sheltered existence to fit into your new lifestyle. Besides, I don't know whether she keeps any company at all; whether she is free to live as she wants within the family; whether she may come and go at her pleasure; I happen to know that her parents would curse you; that her husband is not at all accommodating and would never leave you alone. As you can see, I am inclined to believe that both C. and B. would be better suited to your old lifestyle rather than the one you wish to adopt. As for M., I have other reservations. It seems to me you wish to love with a cold heart; but I can assure you that if you ever did make love to her you would fall prey to a most powerful and most inconvenient passion. She is too beautiful, has too much heart, too much grace, . . . too many devilish tricks not to get you involved little by little. The trust she has so blindly put in you for so long is another obstacle. . . . Still, I do not have the heart to criticize her and am inclined to favor her. Of these three pieces of advice, take the one that most satisfies you. If you choose the first or second, I think I will flatter myself into believing that I will not lose you forever. If you choose the last, I will pin my hopes on the strong objections you would find blocking the way. . . . I have good reason to believe that M. does not hold the best impression of you. You, however, become twice as strong when you stick obstinately to an idea. And if indeed you manage to make her succumb, you will win twice. I also happen to believe, from the portrait you draw of her and the circumstances she finds herself in, that you were inclined in her direction before asking me for my

*choice. . . . But do as you please, for I confess that I do not have it
in me to say more.*

Giustiniana felt so close to Andrea and knew him so well that
she could not stifle a generous impulse toward him even in a matter
so obviously painful for her. Besides, she knew she had no right to
ask Andrea to remain faithful to her—certainly not as long as she
lived in London and Knyphausen was lurking in the background.
In a way she was conceding this to him by stoically supplying the
advice on the three young ladies that he had requested. Yet she also
thought that circumstances might conceivably change and that,
from a purely rational perspective, it was a mistake to give Andrea
the impression that she actively approved his plan. London had
turned into quite a disappointment, and it was beginning to look as
if they might not stay on for long after all. Was he not thinking at
all of the possibility that they might be together again soon? "It's
true that for some time now I have stopped expecting tenderness
from you, but if I should come back to Venice one day—which is
not impossible—I will be coming to you as a new person, changed
in my ways as well as my physical appearance, and in that case I
might well expect some of that tenderness again. Who knows?"

This was the first time Giustiniana had mentioned to Andrea the
possibility she might soon return to Venice. In the past two years
she had often entreated him to join her—in Paris, in Brussels, and
lately even in London—but it had been little more than wishful
banter. She knew he didn't have the money for the journey and
was too proud to accept it from others. In any case, she had always
imagined Andrea traveling to her—wherever she happened to be
at that time. Now she said she might be coming back to him. This
was not just a ploy to distract him from pursuing M., C., and B.;
she was speaking in earnest.

In late spring, when Holderness's disaffection for the Wynnes
had reached a critical point and hopes for a presentation to Court
had all but vanished, Mrs. Anna had quietly contacted the Venetian
authorities through Ambassador Colombo, seeking permission to
return to Venice with her children. She did not feel at home in
London and was increasingly nostalgic for her familiar Venetian
life. Once financial arrangements related to the children's estate

were worked out (the matter was apparently settled, though Giustiniana does not spell out the details), there was no compelling reason for the family to stay in London as far as she was concerned. On the whole, the children did not disagree. The girls were growing bored of living in a social limbo, and the boys, having returned to Dean Street for the summer holidays after a short trial period at Cambridge, were knocking around the house in the heat with little to do. The truth was that all of them missed Italy.

If Giustiniana had not raised the possibility of her return with Andrea before, it was partly because she had been less than certain that her mother's petition to the Venetian authorities would be accepted. The Wynne imbroglio had not been forgotten in Venice, and, furthermore, unflattering news about Giustiniana's antics in Paris had continued to reach the authorities there long after she had left the city. Yet the Wynnes were not seeking to return so that Giustiniana could marry Andrea—that much was clear. So it was not unreasonable to hope the Republic might prove lenient toward a family that had always considered Venice its home and whose connections there still counted for something. Giustiniana would probably have preferred to remain silent on the topic while the papers went back and forth between London and Venice, but Andrea's letter had upset her enough that she broached the subject of her return to test his reaction and possibly to delay his plan to seduce a new lover.

As the summer advanced, Giustiniana's health did not improve. She was under strict orders not to tire herself excessively by writing letters, but this was not the time for a lull in their correspondence. "Despite having been told not to, I cannot resist sending you a tender farewell from my bed. I continue to sweat profusely, which is a good sign. My God! If you were here at my side, keeping me company, I would not feel my illness at all. In fact, your presence would make me fond of it. But it is best I leave you now in the hope that I will be able to give you better news of my health."

A week later she gave Andrea a more detailed description of her condition:

> *I write to you from my bed, where I have been confined for the*
> *past six weeks. My illness started with a violent fever for which I*

was bled several times. It then turned into scarlet fever, and my skin was covered with red spots and pustules. When that was over I developed tertian fever, with such seizures that for the first time I feared for my life. Imagine: I felt my heart freezing over, and then the same sensation moving to my bones. I was increasingly short of breath, my limbs were hot as coals, and my trembling body was covered with big drops of sweat. These fits happen in the evening and often last more than two hours. While they last, I imagine I am dying, for surely this must be what one feels when it happens. . . . If I get up from bed I am immediately seized by the illness, which doctors look upon with great fear. As for me, I can say that it is the worst ailment that has ever befallen me, and whenever I have an attack I feel like calling the confessor as well as the surgeon. Yesterday evening I had a seizure that lasted all night. I have not recovered even as I write, and the deep chill inside me has not subsided. I don't know what will happen.

As Giustiniana battled her fever, the worst possible news arrived from Venice—it was extraordinary how untimely the mail could be. Evidently, the possibility of her return was not going to deter Andrea from carrying out his plan. He had already made his choice: he was going to pay court to M., the very one Giustiniana had been partial to despite her misgivings. Now she was sorry she had played along. Andrea did not make things any easier by pressing the point that he was merely following her suggestion. "I am, as you say, the principal cause of your current commitment, and I cannot complain," Giustiniana accepted grudgingly. "But I would much rather think of you making love to all the ladies, as things were before. . . . I would much prefer you were unattached, even if it meant you would not be attached to me either. . . . Oh, how I wish that letter in which I chose your lover had gone astray."

In mid-August the Venetian Embassy informed the Wynnes that they had been granted permission to return to Venice. The permit was valid for only eighteen months, but Mrs. Anna hoped it might be extended once they had settled there. The plan was to start the trip in September in order to avoid the worst of the summer heat.

They would travel by the same route they had used on their outward journey to England: Calais, Brussels, Paris, Lyon, then eastward into Savoy, hoping to cross the Alps before the cold and arrive in northern Italy sometime in October. They would stop for eight to ten days in Padua while Mrs. Anna went on to Venice alone to find a suitable house for the family. In fact, Giustiniana added, marveling at how Andrea continued to be very much in Mrs. Anna's good graces, her mother wished to know whether he could possibly secure them a temporary lodging in Padua through his family connections there.

After months of lethargy, the Wynne household came alive again. Mrs. Anna took command of operations, issuing orders to children and servants. A boat passage to France was secured. Clothes and linens were packed. Relatives and friends were notified of the imminent departure. Last-minute arrangements were worked out with Holderness, who did not appear especially sad to see them leave. While the rest of the city dozed off in the August heat, the house on Dean Street buzzed with activity.

The boys too were going back to Venice. Richard and William had spent but a few weeks at Cambridge in the spring, and Holderness would have liked them to return in the autumn, but Mrs. Anna managed to prevail. A tutor would travel with them to Italy to ensure their continued education, receiving a stipend of two hundred pounds a year plus room and board, all taken care of by the Wynne estate. "I can't begin to tell you," Giustiniana commented admiringly, "how Mother pulled it off."

While the rest of the house was busy with preparations, Giustiniana remained under observation lest her poor health jeopardize the travel plans. "They've reached the point that they very nearly prescribe the exact number of words I may set down on paper," she griped. After the drenching sweats, the worst seemed to be over. On August 19 she got out of bed for the first time in nearly two months. She felt very weak and was short of breath: "There is nothing worse than not being able to breathe: you can feel the most minute gradations of dying." Still, she was confident she would recover in time for the journey. "Exercise and a breath of fresh air will bring relief," she predicted. The prospect of returning to Italy was already improving her spirits.

Andrea was taken aback by the swiftness with which plans in London were changing. During the two years he and Giustiniana had been apart, their relationship had lived on through their letters. Knyphausen had been jealous because he had rightly sensed that things were not entirely over between them. Even as they had carried on their separate lives, they had continued to write to each other more as lovers than as friends. Yet, like all long-distance relationships, a large part of it had become imaginary—a dream world disconnected from reality. Giustiniana's sudden return seemed disruptive to Andrea. It was not clear to him what she expected of him, and he was worried about how Giustiniana's presence in Venice would affect his new relationship with M. Did she not realize they would be the talk of the town again? How should they behave in public?

Andrea's fretting startled Giustiniana. She tried to reassure him. He need not worry so much about the two of them being in Venice together again: it was not her intention to settle there. The dazzling city of her youth—the Venice she had known with him—was part of her past. The memories were still there, of course; they were the best she had. But she wanted to put all that behind her. The gossip, the intrigue, the small-town pettiness: it was all too tiresome, too suffocating, too upsetting. As far as she was concerned, the fact that Mrs. Anna was going to rent a house there was merely incidental. "I am returning to Venice, but Venice is not for me. . . . If I thought I would have to live in Venice, I would not come. . . . Let it suffice for now, and don't speak of this to any other living soul."

What did she have in mind? "I have a project, and I will tell you everything," she said. "But I cannot speak now. . . . Allow me to remain silent for a while more. . . . I will tell you in person." She never spelled out what her mysterious project was. From what she had told Andrea in the previous months about her desire for independence and a large enough income to get by on, it is plausible that she wanted to set up house on her own, cultivate the people she liked, and continue to travel at leisure. Where would she eventually live? Not in Venice, if she could avoid it. There were many small cities on the mainland territories of the Venetian Republic where it was possible to lead a pleasant life in the company of interesting, lively friends: Padua, of course, and Vicenza, Treviso and many others.

Part of the difficulty in imagining such a future was due to the fact that she was exploring a little-tested terrain. Other women in her social class were pioneering a similar lifestyle in the Venetian Republic, but they were either wealthy or divorced or both. It would be substantially harder for Giustiniana to manage on her small income. One also gets the feeling that she deliberately kept her project vague because she wanted Andrea to fit into it in some way. As a lover? As a friend? As her *cher frère*? Those questions she left unanswered.

Giustiniana was equally vague about her relationship with Knyphausen, which she had successfully kept hidden from Mrs. Anna. Andrea asked how his "rival" was taking the news of her sudden departure from London—an unsubtle way of shifting some of the burden of guilt onto Giustiniana by reminding her that she too had her own relationship to tend. She gave him little satisfaction on that count. "He loves me," she wrote hurriedly, "of that I am certain. You will know everything upon my arrival." Not a word about her own feelings.

The date of departure was fixed for the second week in September. Soon the rush was on: "I don't have a free moment because we have so many visits and my duties take up all my time during these last days here." Her letters became increasingly hasty and confused. Last-minute instructions were mixed with bursts of anxiety. She asked Andrea to call on Consul Smith to tell him they were arriving—she had never forgotten that "he was always a friend to me"—and also on her dear aunt Fiorina, whom she promised to buy a dress when they stopped in Paris; and on "all those whom you believe to be my friends." The passage across the Channel was constantly on her mind: "You cannot imagine how scared I am of it and how ill it makes me feel." Could he also remember to make arrangements for the house in Padua? "One must try to please [my mother], for after all she is still the same woman she once was. But now I believe she cannot get in the way of a pure and decent friendship [between us], nor does she plan to. Not after all the tokens of friendship you have given me."

Giustiniana knew that the difficulties in her relationship with Andrea would not come from her mother anymore but from what she called, with evident annoyance, his own new "lifestyle." "I regret more and more the advice I gave you to attach yourself to Signora M.," she confessed, "because I respect her too much and because she is the only one who is capable of kidnapping a friend away from me. . . . But we'll talk about all that." Andrea had never been very clear about his feelings for M. Did he love her? Giustiniana made a show of backing off, assuring Andrea she felt she had no claim on him anymore: "I want only friendship and sound advice from you, and I believe I deserve these." But her hope ran much deeper than that, and Andrea's lukewarm response to the news of her return made her departure all the more unsettling: "Will you be glad to see me after all? Will you still look fondly upon the woman you have been treating as a sister and a friend?" In her last letter to Andrea from London, dated September 5, she wrote, "You will see how much weight I have put on. But even if I had grown more beautiful, would it have made a difference? . . . I long to know whether you'll be happy to see me arrive. I am your friend, you know, and I would be so disappointed if, given such faint expectations on my part, I were to find you cold or little satisfied. . . . In the meantime, you may reassure your lady friends that I am not in a position to be feared. Farewell."

The Wynne caravan set off from Dean Street in mid-September. Mrs. Anna squeezed into the coach with her five children. The tutor hired by Lord Holderness would join them later on in Italy. But they had a new traveling companion, Miss Tabitha Mendez, an unmarried lady they had met shortly after arriving in London who had become a friend of the family. She intended to spend a year traveling in Italy and was happy to hitch a ride with the Wynnes. "She is thirty-two years old, ugly, comes from a Christian family, has assets worth twenty thousand lire," Giustiniana noted rather unkindly. She could be a little clinging "but is well read and rather witty," and it would be nice if Andrea could "pay her some attention" as she planned to stay in Venice for a month.

The passage to France was delayed for several days due to a mix-up in the booking arrangements. A vessel was eventually found, and this time the crossing went smoothly despite Giustiniana's fear of the sea. They arrived in Calais on September 22. *"Le plus dangereux est achevé,"* she wrote to Andrea, switching to French as soon as she was on French soil. "The worst is over." She also shifted to the formal mode of address, *vous,* as if a strange new reserve impelled her to put some distance between them at the start of the journey that would reunite them.

The original plan had entailed traveling to Brussels first, but the Wynnes changed their itinerary to make up for lost time and headed straight for Paris instead. Giustiniana feared the change might cause her to lose some precious letters from Andrea: "I have written to Brussels to request they be forwarded to me in Paris—in case you have sent me a few, as I asked you to."

A year had gone by since the Wynnes had left Paris under a cloud. On the surface not much had changed. France was still losing the war. The king was increasingly unpopular. Mme de Pompadour was losing her power and her health. There was growing disarray in Versailles, but the sprawling city was as restless and vibrant as ever. After four years of war, it was still the world capital of entertainment and fashion.

To Giustiniana, however, Paris seemed very different. She felt disconnected—an intruder in familiar surroundings. Ambassador Erizzo had returned to Venice. Casanova was in Genoa after having spent most of the year in Germany. Farsetti was still in town, but Giustiniana had no desire to see him. She knew, of course, that La Pouplinière had married. Now she learned that the new young wife, Thérèse de Mondran, had ousted the "old sultana," Mme de Saint Aubin, as well as most of her husband's extended family, from the house. The Abbé de La Coste had been paid off and sent packing too. In fact, of all the actors embroiled in the sordid Wynne affair, he was probably the one who had suffered the worst ending. In January of that year he had been jailed at the Bastille for forging lottery tickets and had been sentenced to "imprisonment in perpetuity." One of La Pouplinière's nephews saw La Coste "chained in public squares, an iron collar around his neck, and a sign over his stomach exposing him as a counterfeiter, his hat on the ground in front of him so that passersby might throw in a coin."[1]

The Wynnes were in Paris for a week. It gave them just enough time to organize the long trip to Italy and make a few purchases. Giustiniana was not in good shape. She had not fully recovered from her summer illnesses. Also, she was disturbed by the ghosts of her recent past, which still lingered in the city. She tried to distract herself by taking short walks and doing some shopping. She bought the dress for Fiorina and also looked, in vain, for a special pair of long muffs Andrea had asked her to buy him, which were still fashionable in Venice but had already gone out of style in Paris. "You can blame [the French]," she wrote irritably. "They have decreed that such muffs are no longer *à la mode* and have made them impossible to find."

Shortly before leaving Paris, Giustiniana received a letter that caused a pang of anxiety to rip through her. Andrea declared he could not wait to see her. He offered to come out to meet her, possibly somewhere in northern Italy. This was so unexpected. And what did it really mean? She was tempted to send him a detailed itinerary of their trip. "I will trace the road we will follow and the time it will take before I will see you again," she wrote, suddenly overcome with excitement. By the time the Wynnes left Paris, though, she had given up on the idea. She was afraid of building up her expectations. She never sent him the details.

Nevertheless, the fantasy of Andrea appearing along the road smiling sweetly and beckoning her into his arms stayed with Giustiniana throughout the several-day trip to Lyon. Her heart was full of him when she arrived in the city. She went looking for his muffs during their brief stopover, and this time she found them. She packed them in her trunk with the idea of buying a nice gift box when she got to Italy. As she put them away, she felt the strangeness of holding in her hands something that would soon belong to him. "I hope you will be happy with them," she wrote.

Her desire for Andrea now became overwhelming. During the long, difficult passage over the Alps, she dreamed he would be waiting for her in Turin. They would take walks together in the

Valentino Park. They would look at the pictures in the Palazzo Reale. They would go to the theater together. The theater! Did he remember the sweet hours they had spent together in their favorite Venetian theaters?

Andrea was not in Turin; how could he have known when she would be there? Giustiniana hoped he would be in Milan, where they arrived at the end of October. Instead, she found two letters waiting at the house of the Resident. In one letter Andrea told her he had found a house for them in Padua. It belonged to the family of Niccolò Erizzo, the former Venetian ambassador to Paris. They would be able to stay there while her mother sought a house in Venice. He offered to help Mrs. Anna look for one as soon as she arrived. In the second letter he apologized for not being in Milan. But she had not written him the details of the trip as she had promised. He could not understand why she had been so mysterious. Did she imagine he would have gone looking for her, clueless, in the taverns of Piedmont and Lombardy? Besides, the gossipmongers were already feasting on the news of her return.

Giustiniana did not hide her disappointment. She wrote to him in Italian now, but she still used the formal *voi:*

> *I did not write to you from either Paris or Turin because, with-out my realizing it, a fantasy took hold of me that you would come to me. Forgive me for thinking it; I have since come to appreciate your not having acted so foolishly. . . . I thank you for your nice thoughts and for your friendship; but I fear you, and I do not wish to appear so very weak. Let people say what they want about me in Venice; it is not in Venice I must or even want to live. I have entirely lost the pleasure I once felt in being there, and I know I will not regain it. During the time I spend there, it is likely that I shall live a withdrawn life. I am only trying to find some peace of mind, and I am sure you will not make my life dif-ficult. I want you to know that while I shall always be grateful for your company I am determined not to see you too often, even if you should insist. I respect your new ties. You have made me believe that I am responsible because I was the one to recommend them. Now I say you may even strengthen those ties since I must*

live happily with them. In fact, I beseech you to do just that, for without them God only knows what the two of us would be vulnerable to. I leave tomorrow morning. I will be in Padua within six days at the most, and I don't expect to see you there either. . . . Farewell. . . . Do not meet me there; I forbid you to. We shall see each other eventually, I will embrace you, and I will always be your friend. Will this not satisfy you? Have you ever expected anything different—or will you ever? Leave me to my peace and quiet; and let this be my biggest debt to you. . . . Farewell again.

Giustiniana had arrived in Italy with her dream of a life with Andrea still alive, but the signals coming from Venice were not what she had hoped for. She sensed the danger ahead, and she was looking to protect herself. If the end of their love story were indeed nearing, she would need "peace and quiet" to manage her emotions with dignity. But even as she prepared herself to let go, she could not extinguish all hope.

The following morning the Wynnes left Milan headed for Padua. They stopped in Brescia. They spent two days in Verona, where they visited the Venetian *rappresentante*, Alvise Contarini, "who treated us with the greatest kindness." Giustiniana took advantage of their stay in that city to buy an elegant box for Andrea's French muffs. They continued on to Vicenza, and the landscape became more and more familiar. The Wynnes had traveled the same road two years earlier at exactly the same time of year. As they coasted along the same fields, passed through the same villages, stopped at the same taverns, it felt to Giustiniana as if her life were winding back in time. Memories came flooding back as the coach sped along the road. Her longing for Andrea grew sharper.

Giustiniana had specifically asked him not to come to Padua. *"Ve'l proibisco,"* she had commanded. "I forbid you." Yet she must have hoped he would not listen to her and would read her words for what they really meant.

The dusty carriage splattered its way into the courtyard of Ca' Erizzo around lunchtime on November 5. The servants came out looking surprised. It appeared they had not been informed about the Wynnes' arrival after all. Giustiniana showed the letter in which Andrea told her that Chevalier Erizzo would let them stay in the house. The housekeeper grudgingly allowed them in upon the promise that a notice from the master of the house was on its way. The six Wynnes plus Miss Mendez stepped out of the carriage one by one, horses were led to drink, trunks were unloaded, servants raced about getting the house ready. In the general confusion, Giustiniana tried to keep at bay the sadness she knew would otherwise engulf her completely.

There was a letter from Andrea waiting for her inside. She tore it open. He sent his greetings. He hoped the trip had gone well and that the house was adequate. He also complained about Giustiniana's "style" of writing. Why was she sending such confusing messages to him? Why did she forbid him to come to Padua?

The pain was searing. She wrote back that same night:

> *Why, dearest Memmo, why humiliate me so the very first moment of my arrival? Why not see me before passing judgment on me? Do you know why I forbade you to come meet me? Because I'm still fearful of my mother; because one day she says one thing and the next day she says another. . . . You deplore my "style"? But my dear Memmo, would you have obeyed me if I had written to you more tenderly? Forgive me. Come see me anytime you want. But be easy on me. My only wish is to be your friend. Help me keep my resolution. . . . Farewell, dear Memmo. Forgive me for my brevity. I long to see you. You are and always will be my best friend. I will be here for a few days: take your bearings calmly. Try to understand what I'm saying to you. Know my heart. Do you really think I can be any different from what I am? Oh God, I have so many things to tell you! . . . Please tell Signora M. I send my most respectful greetings. . . . Farewell.*

She hoped Andrea would show up the following day or the day after that—it was only a half-day trip up from Venice. But he didn't. Nor did he send a word of explanation. Meanwhile, Mrs. Anna had slipped into one of her foul moods. She was tired, she said, and the family was such a burden. She threatened to stay in Padua instead of going on to Venice to secure a house. At the end

of a difficult day Giustiniana sent off a bitter note to Andrea—in
French again:

Mon cher frère,

*I hoped to receive news from you today, but you have not writ-
ten to me. I am delighted to find you at fault! I hope you will now
agree we are even. . . . I shan't write to you. . . . I will pay a little
price for it, no doubt, but I also hope to profit by your indifference.*

In the morning she received a surprisingly tender letter. There
was little in it to justify new hope: Andrea did not put into question
his relationship with M. But he admitted that he had not come to
Padua yet because he was unsure how he might react when he saw
her. His words suggested that he too was confused, a vulnerability
that touched her. She seized this chance to regain some emotional
balance of her own.

Mon cher frère,

*I take comfort in the fact that you seem calmer and more cer-
tain about my friendship. I have always treasured your sincerity,
and, believe me, I treasure it even more when it springs from such
delicate feelings. And to hear that you still fear me is no small
glory. What is more, I am your true friend. I have proved it to you
so far, I believe. I swear I will remain so until I die. . . . Should
this friendship please you, rest assured it will be yours forever.*

*When you say you want to protect me, I feel the power of your
gentleness. I'm also grateful for the effort you are making in not
coming out to see me. It's your decision, and I respect it. However, I can't but laugh when I hear that so many people are closely
watching every move you make, and it will be wonderful to tell
them all at last how wrong they were to think that you would
leave Signora M. and attach yourself to me again. I know the
country too; but I swear I never intended to defy its customs upon
my return or to expose you to slander, disapproval, or embarrassment. I will stay but a short while, and during that time I will
only seek peace and quiet. So I don't really care if people know
me for who I am now—an enemy of falseness, of seduction, of*

*things contrived, and above all of things that can cause damage
by hurting the souls of delicate people. . . . How you wrong me,
dear Memmo, in not treating me as a true friend! . . . I praise, I
admire your gratitude, your friendship, your commitment to the
gracious M., and I must be the first to applaud them. You needn't
fear I will come looking for you or force you to deceive her. She
can be at ease and trustful—and who, more than she, deserves to
be so? . . . Of course the sacrifice you made for her in not coming
out to see me displeased me. But now I swear I feel my soul is
large enough to make her a gift of my own displeasure. You are
worthy of her, she of you, and the more so for your mutual commitment. . . . But more to the point, Memmo, . . . give yourself
some credit for my feelings for you. Make sure she understands
the full value of your sacrifice. She is safe; of this you can be sure.
. . . Farewell now. And be glad I treat you as a friend.*

Giustiniana made it clear, however, that being his friend did
not mean she would assist him in his amorous intrigues. "If I
can help you in any way, I shall, with all my soul. But I'll be truthful: I'm simply not up to attracting [M.'s] husband's attention
for your sake." Had Andrea actually made such an indelicate proposal, or was she merely trying to forestall a request she saw coming? Whatever the case, she really didn't have the heart for that
sort of thing anymore. "I'm afraid that since leaving Italy I no
longer see the point of these games. . . . I will do whatever else
you ask."

Andrea expressed the hope that Giustiniana and M. could be
"good friends." She replied without a shred of irony, "It goes
without saying that I'm with you. You can imagine my strong
desire for such a thing to happen. [M.] is a lovely person." Giustiniana's offer of friendship showed remarkable self-control. It
also gave her the moral high ground. Andrea again brought up the
subject of Knyphausen to add some ballast to his side of this difficult correspondence. She replied with less ambiguity than in the
past. Marriage was not a likely outcome, she explained, on account
of her own disinclination: "I do not believe I will make a commitment so easily. Whatever my feelings are for the baron, I will work
to arrange my life in such a way that he will always be pleased to

regard me as his good friend. As for me, I value that man's friendship immensely."

Mrs. Anna traveled to Venice on November 8, leaving Giustiniana in charge of the family. "May God protect you," she quipped in
a note of encouragement to Andrea. "My mother is very wicked."
But time and circumstances had blunted the old animosity. When
he went to pay his respects and offer his help in finding a house, his
erstwhile enemy appeared genuinely glad to see him; she certainly
was grateful for his practical assistance. Giustiniana was happy to
learn that the two were getting along so well: "Do continue in the
same way. To make her less wild if nothing else."

Encouraged by so much cordiality, Andrea wondered whether
he might ask Mrs. Anna's permission to visit her daughter secretly
in Padua, conjuring up an excuse for the sake of M.'s peace of
mind. Giustiniana put her foot down. A visit by Andrea would have
put her in an awkward position vis-à-vis M., when she wanted to
make as smooth a return to city life as possible. "I absolutely insist
that you remain in Venice. No matter what excuse you might con-
trive in order to come here, your friend will not approve of it . . . ;
and you would risk losing moments of happiness I would not be
able to pay back. . . . You can easily see how the danger would be
far greater than the gain. . . . What difference does it make if we
see each other in Venice or Noventa*? The distance between us is
always the same, whether we are separated by a mile or by the
thickest wall."

M. was indeed growing wary of Andrea's solicitude toward
Mrs. Anna and the Wynne family. She suspected him, quite rightly,
of being in touch with Giustiniana. The messages traveling
between Venice and Padua became increasingly garbled: "Mon
cher frère, I . . . believe we don't understand each other much; but
since I am willing to believe anything I can assure you that you will
have little trouble in persuading me of anything. I do not doubt
your sincerity. In fact, I sometimes feel you are too sincere. It's
consoling to hear that the mere mention of my name creates such
an impression on your friend, not to mention the glory gained by
my self-esteem."

*A small town in the Veneto.

M.'s flare-ups reminded Giustiniana of her own "agitation" when she had first fallen in love with Andrea nearly seven years before and the pain and the pleasure she had felt at the time. "Do you remember, Memmo, the old, fleeting jealousies in the early days of our love? Oh, the sweet and blessed moments we enjoyed when peace would break out again! . . . Rejoice in what you have."

It was Miss Mendez's turn to make the half-day trip to Venice. Giustiniana reminded Andrea to take care of her: "Be so generous as to give her all the enlightenment a newcomer to the country will need in order to see all the major points of interest, get some learning, and have fun at the same time. . . . I shall be as grateful to you as if the kindnesses I ask of you were addressed to me." She tried to press Andrea's large muffs into the box she had purchased in Verona, but they wouldn't fit. So she asked Miss Mendez to pack them with her own clothes and give them to him in Venice. "Don't ask me what the price was," she wrote to him in an accompanying note. "I had money in Lyon, and I always meant for them to be a gift."

Each day Giustiniana felt lonelier. She was tired of being stranded in the dank and inhospitable house of the Erizzos. The late autumn cold chilled her bones. The wet weather sapped her spirit. She was saddened to learn about the death of King George II (he had died October 25). The rumors about Frederick of Prussia's health affected her even more. But it was not the news from abroad that depressed her so much as the ambiguous, hopeless notes she kept receiving from Andrea. He seemed so defensive—always asking forgiveness, always making excuses: M. forbade him to see her . . . M. forbade him to write to her. . . . How was she supposed to react? How was she supposed to feel?

A deep sadness was taking over. Nearly two weeks had gone by since she had arrived in Padua exhausted but also exhilarated at the thought of finally setting eyes on Andrea. The fantasy she had fed during the long trip home dissolved little by little. The remaining ambiguity in Andrea's letters only hurt her more. She could not bear the confusion anymore. She yearned for some final clarity—even as she dreaded it.

Mon cher frère,

   . . . I haven't written to you. Why I haven't written to you I don't really know, and I hardly know what I should be writing now. There are times I understand you, and there are times I don't. There are times I think you despise me, and there are times I think you are my friend. Now you treat me as your confidante, now it looks as if you are in love with me. I know the circumstances you find yourself in, and you know mine. Why all the intrigue? If your good friend forbids you to write to me, give her satisfaction. . . . A friend must be sympathetic, and I would be quite an ungrateful one if I expected you to sacrifice the slightest pleasure for my sake. I was so struck by this idea yesterday that I didn't want to write to you anymore. Believe me: let us speak the truth. If we meet, I will behave with the grace that my immutable friendship as well as the memory of my gratitude will inspire. But you have to live in Venice, and I don't. You have to cultivate the Venetian spirit, its genius, its weaknesses, and I don't—though I can accept all these attitudes and prejudices in you. So write to me about the king of England, write to me about the war or other news. I shall be happy. But don't write to me about other things, I beg you. And let us stop deceiving or hurting each other. Farewell.

During the next several days Giustiniana did her best to contain her anger for fear of making things worse between them. "I read and I keep myself busy trying not to get too bored," she wrote with a heavy dose of sarcasm. "Nothing much happens here, but I find that if I keep my expectations low time goes by just the same." On November 17 she received another rambling letter from Andrea. As usual, he was full of tenderness but also vague, evasive, inconclusive. This time she let him have it:

Mon cher frère,

   Such a long letter! So many justifications! And such sweet expressions! But Memmo, shouldn't I find it offensive that you should think such a letter necessary? Do you doubt my friendship to such a degree? Do you really think I would fail you? You force me to speak! You want me to explain the situation of my heart?

Well, then, I should adore the baron, yet I love him less than he deserves. But I am his friend and I will remain so for eternity. You want me to speak about you? All right, I'll give myself away. Your words, the letters I received from you during the last period in London and during the journey back, led me to believe that your commitment to me only involved your head. So I nourished the sweet illusion that I would find you again, not as my lover—for that was no longer suitable for either of us—but as my friend. . . . To do you a favor, I forbade you to come meet me as you had promised; but still I flattered myself that at least in Padua the first man I set eyes on would have been Memmo. It seemed to me I had a thousand things to tell you and a thousand things to hear from you. I thought about it a lot. I liked the idea. It often troubled me as well. I arrive; and I do not find you. Instead I hear a lot of talk about responsibilities, affections, feelings apparently stronger than those I thought you harbored. I must fight my first impressions. You force me to do so every day. I humiliate my vanity. I destroy my expectations. I vanquish my self-esteem. I even sympathize with you when you do not fly here to see me because love is apparently stronger than our very tender friendship. I make an effort and I gain control over myself. But I remain in a terrible mood, and my courage fails me. This is why I have been so erratic. This is the reason for my slights, for my nonsensical letters. But I'll put an end to it, I swear. You have sympathized with me a thousand times, and I sympathize with you and I forgive you. Perhaps I should even thank you since God only knows where all that excitement I felt when I arrived in Padua might have led if it had been encouraged in any way; whereas you know we must love each other only as friends. I have done a thousand crazy things. You had to take on a new commitment, for which you asked my advice and my approval. I too have a commitment, and I would be desperate if I could not keep it. Venice is not the country for me. I cannot live there with the freedom to which I am now accustomed; and then I cannot see myself living in a place where people affect superior airs with me or feel they have to extend their protection to me. I'm not sure yet where I'll go, but I have plans and I won't tell you about them because there is nothing more ridiculous than plans that are divulged too soon. A passion between us would be a real curse, and I know it might be rekindled in me. So again I thank you for having put me in a position to renounce such a passion forever.

I'll stop writing now because I don't feel at all well. . . . Farewell, and forgive me for not matching all your kind words. Today I have been sincere with you, and my sincerity cannot but tell you things which prove my fondest affection and friendship for you.

Giustiniana felt her strength failing after sending off her letter, and she retired to her room. "I've become melancholic, and this malady is affecting my mood and my spirits. I am not the same person anymore, and every pleasure has become dull and burdensome." The next day she felt worse, and after another difficult night she called for help. "I'm really not well," she wrote, switching back to French. "My health is very weak, and last night I really thought it was the end. I was forced to call Dr. Berci in at four o'clock in the morning. I've decided to put myself in his hands to cure what he calls my 'attacks of melancholic hysteria.' " She asked Andrea not to mention any of this to her mother in Venice. There was no point: "Apart from the fact that my suffering is great and my anxiety even greater, these illnesses are not dangerous."

Andrea wrote several times a day now—affectionate letters in which he wished her well. But Giustiniana no longer had the energy to write much at all. She asked him to forgive her "for not replying to all your letters." Andrea thanked her for the muffs. He and Miss Mendez had not taken to each other, he was sorry to report. Giustiniana asked him to make an effort despite what she now realized was a "silly" idea to get them together: "Try to appease her; she can be mean, and it is an advantage to have such people on one's side. You will tell me you don't much care. But my vanity is sensitive to compliments paid to you, and so I beg you to do this for me—even if it is but a whim on my part. . . . I'll stop now. I'm weak and this evening I'll take a cure. Again, I forbid you to say anything about this to my mother."

She spent the next few days drifting about the house, awaiting news from Mrs. Anna. Her tone with Andrea became more distant. On November 23: "I haven't written in two days. I really haven't had time. . . . A thousand necessary chores have robbed me of all my time. I have not had an hour to myself." And later: "Mon cher frère, forgive me, I have written little or nothing. I'm not well. I'm melancholic. The saddest curse has fallen upon me, and everything has become unbearable. I have received your letters regularly, and if I were sensitive to anything it would be to your kindness. . . . I'm sorry to hear about the difficulties you're facing in your love life. But Memmo, if you're sure of her, does anything else matter?"

The Wynnes had meant to stay no more than ten days in Padua. Three weeks had now gone by, and they were still camping out at Ca' Erizzo. There was apparently a bureaucratic hitch. Mrs. Anna had found a house, but she was hesitating because it was available for only six months. The city authorities, meanwhile, were waiting for Mrs. Anna to sign the lease before issuing an entry permit for the family, which was needed in addition to the residency permit they had already received when they were still in London. The delay was making Giustiniana irritable: "Why doesn't my mother take the house? And why haven't you persuaded her yet? Meanwhile, I'm stuck here; I'm not well, and I'm bored. . . . Since my mother can take the house for only six months, why all the fuss about the entry permits? We'll be there such a short period of time. . . . Come, Memmo, free us from this hindrance."

Giustiniana would think about the future later on. Right now she just wanted to rest; she wanted her room and fresh linen and a little peace. "Allow me to come to Venice and trust me, as you should, for I have forsaken all claims."

Finally, on November 26, word came that Mrs. Anna had secured the house and the entry permits had been granted. It would be another couple of days before their trunks were ready, and there were still a few errands to do before the trip to Venice. But the news cleared the air, and Giustiniana's spirits lifted for the first time since arriving in Padua. "It seems I am happy today, or at least not as sad as I usually feel. . . . I am much obliged for your sweet words in your last letter. But Memmo, you know we must not believe in them. And poor us if we should still listen to our hearts. I don't know what mine tells me about you; but even if it spoke out it would gain nothing, for I have sworn to be deaf. For pity's sake, let us remain friends.

"So I'll see you at Mira? I feel pleasure in imagining this reunion. . . . I don't drive the idea away from me. . . . *Basta.* Enough now. . . . Farewell, Memmo."

Did Giustiniana and Andrea ever meet at Mira? This is the last fragment of their correspondence to have come down to us, so we are left without an answer. One day, perhaps, other letters will reveal to us what happened that morning. But it is hard to escape the feeling that the little river town ten miles up the road from Padua was indeed where the final act of their love affair took place—whether or not Andrea ever made it to their appointment. Giustiniana's last letters are filled with so much foreboding that we, the prying readers, understand it is over perhaps even before she does. Yet in the tone of those letters we recognize a new resoluteness as well. It is the clearheaded determination of someone who has weathered a storm and is leaving it behind. Giustiniana was now ready to complete her journey, even as she made it clear that Venice was not her final destination and she was going to live her life beyond its stifling confines. And so we picture her boarding the *burchiello* at Mira with a steady foot and traveling confidently down the gentle waters of the Brenta, past fishing villages and elegant villas, then out into the lagoon, toward the shimmering city across the horizon.

Epilogue

G iustiniana's return to Venice after more than two years
abroad was not a festive homecoming. Amid all the fuss
over the Wynnes' staggered arrival in the city, with Mrs. Anna's
fastidious search for an apartment and the bureaucratic difficulties
over the entry permit, not to mention Andrea's panicky state and
M.'s suspiciousness, one can easily imagine the chattering men at
the Listone indulging in snide little jokes about the return of the
inglesine while the ladies chuckled behind their embroidered fans.

Even the small English community, which had always been a
haven for Mrs. Anna and her children, received them with a certain
reserve. Joseph Smith, now well into his eighties, was in the process
of resigning his consulship. He had settled into his new marriage
and was obsessively taken up with the sale of his large art and book
collection to the new English monarch, George III. The aging
Lady Montagu was her usual mordant self; according to a shocked
young English visitor by the name of Thomas Robinson, she had
also become "scurrilous in the highest degree."[1] Ambassador Murray, who had been quite happy in the company of the Wynnes in
the past, casting his interested gaze on the girls, now plainly made
fun of them in his dispatches to London. Mrs. Anna and her daughters were contributing "not a little" to the city's "amusements," he
wrote to Lord Holderness. "Their manner of going on has been so
very outré that I have no thoughts at present of visiting them, as I
don't care to be an eye-witness to the ruin of a family when there is
no possibility of saving them."[2]

It was not just the atmosphere in the English community that
felt different. The city as a whole had changed while the Wynnes
had been away. The long war combined with Venice's isolation
had dampened spirits and accentuated a general feeling of stagna-

tion. The more enlightened Venetians had lost their earlier enthusiasm for modernizing the state. Father Lodoli, the charismatic
Franciscan monk, had left Venice in semiexile and was living out
his last days in a state of destitution on the mainland. Little if anything remained of the hopeful band of reformists whom he had nur-
tured in the years before the war. The Tribunal of the Inquisitors
had strengthened its oppressive presence in everyday life, and the
secretive Council of Ten—the executive branch of government—
ruled with a growing disregard for the Maggior Consiglio, the
assembly of patricians that for centuries had been the very heart of
the Republic.

A few months after her return, Giustiniana witnessed at first
hand a turning point in the drift of the Venetian Republic toward an
increasingly authoritarian government in the hands of the Council
of Ten. Her friend Angelo Querini, a decent, civic-minded young
senator who had been (with Andrea) among Lodoli's most ardent
followers, was charged with conspiring against the Republic and
thrown into jail. Querini was hardly a revolutionary: his ambition
was to give back to the Maggior Consiglio some of the authority
that had been usurped by the Council of Ten. His arrest came as a
stern warning to the reformers of his circle, and it helps to explain
the more prudent approach Andrea would adopt in his political
career.

In her letters from Padua, Giustiniana had told Andrea she
intended to live as quietly as possible while she stayed in Venice.
But as Murray's disobliging remarks remind us, it was not long
before she was causing a certain commotion in town. Thomas
Robinson, the twenty-two-year-old son of Lord Grantham who
had been so surprised by Lady Montagu's loose tongue, was quite
taken with Giustiniana when he met her in the fall of 1760—to the
point that he apparently wanted to marry her. From the very
beginning, however, the fact that he was a Protestant and Giustiniana a Catholic was seen as an insurmountable obstacle. The young
Englishman was soon out of the picture: in early spring he left
Venice—the last stop on his Italian tour—and made his way back
to London.

Shortly after Robinson's departure, however, Giustiniana startled everyone by accepting the hand of Count Philip Orsini-Rosenberg, the imperial ambassador of Austria to the Venetian Republic. It was a remarkable coup; certainly that is how everyone around her perceived it. The count, a seventy-year-old widower, came from a very aristocratic Austrian family that claimed to descend from the Roman clan of the Ursini. He was ending his long diplomatic career with a luxurious posting, housed in the magnificent embassy on the Grand Canal.

His wife, Maria von Kaunitz, had died in 1755, a year after their arrival in Venice. After a brief period of mourning, the count had given himself over to a fairly dissolute life and was to be found gambling with his friends at the Ridotto when he was not chasing young actresses at the theater or visiting his favorite courtesans. Giustiniana's reappearance on the scene changed all that. The count must have known her from the old days he had probably met her at Consul Smith's early on, when her love affair with Andrea had been the talk of the town. But now he saw her in a new light: She was a mature young lady of twenty-four, with experience quite beyond her age. Her lively spirit enchanted him, and those "womanish" features she had complained so much about undoubtedly did as well. He fell in love with her, as other older men had before him.

Giustiniana must have been a little stunned to receive a proposal from a man of such exalted station. Of course, she had said that marriage "was not for her," that she prized her independence more than the security provided by a husband. But she had expressed those thoughts when she was still trying to make room in her life for Andrea, groping for an unconventional solution to an unconventional situation. Now her long affair was over, and she was doing her best to put it behind her. She needed to be practical, and she might well have concluded that her quest for independence required a detour through a few years of married life.

Ambassador Murray, so quick to dismiss the Wynnes when they had returned to Venice, deemed the news of such importance as to warrant a diplomatic notice to William Pitt himself. "The conversation of the town is taken up about a marriage which is shortly expected between Count Rosenberg and the eldest Miss Wynne,"[3] he wrote to the Great Commoner, treating the information as a matter of official significance, as indeed it was: Giustiniana, after all, was marrying an important minister of a Great Power with which Britain was still at war.

Andrea, still entangled in his complicated affair with M., must have appreciated the logic behind Giustiniana's snap decision: after all, he had always encouraged her to marry an old man and the *cher frère* in him surely saw the practical benefits of her situation. But it is hard to imagine that the news did not set off a certain amount of inner turmoil in the old lover.

The count and Giustiniana were married on November 4, 1761. The ceremony probably took place at the embassy. There was no fanfare, not even a public notice: it was a rushed, hushed affair in the presence of a priest, a few intimate friends, and her family (one imagines Mrs. Anna smiling, happy at last). Still, everyone in town knew about it. Lady Montagu was no longer on hand to deliver a pointed remark on the event, having finally returned home to England upon her husband's death, but her Venetian friend Chiara Michiel made sure she was kept informed: "Monsieur de Rosenberg married Giustiniana without declaring her either wife or ambassadress. . . . Such a marriage is well below his rank . . . but is worthy of his heart."[4] Lady Montagu replied rather philosophically, "Your words are subtle and just and noble, and I understand all that."[5]

Giustiniana, now Countess Rosenberg, settled into the elegant *palazzo* the Austrian government had leased from the Loredan family. As long as her husband was alive, she was guaranteed a very comfortable life. After his death, she would not inherit his possessions, which were already destined to her stepson, but the count set up a small trust that would give her an income of 2,000 Austrian florins a year for as long as she kept his name. That would be enough for her to live decorously, though not in luxury.

Her social rank, however, remained ambiguous. She was Countess Rosenberg in the eyes of her husband, but she was not—as Chiara Michiel had been quick to underline—the "ambassadress." Nor had the marriage put an end to all the talk about her questionable titles of nobility. The snobbery and condescension were depressing and terribly familiar to Giustiniana.

The Court in Vienna, not officially informed of the marriage, expressed deep misgivings. Prime Minister Anthon von Kaunitz, a cousin of Rosenberg's deceased first wife, involved himself personally in the matter and begged the ambassador to tell him exactly how things stood. Here is the count's reply—an extraordinary "confession," at once poignant and pathetic, by an old libertine in love with a much younger woman:

> *Sir, the trust and very special esteem I have always had for your Excellency make me seize with joy the opportunity I am offered to open my heart to you and make the disclosure you ask of me. It is true that I have married Miss Giustiniana Wynne in secret,* and the marriage will remain such as long as I shall be ambassador. But it is not true that she is the daughter of an English merchant. Chevalier Wynne, who died a Catholic some ten years ago in Venice, was a gentleman and belonged to one of the oldest houses of Wales. He was traveling in Italy when he married the daughter of Count Gazzini. After his death Lord Holderness was appointed governor of the family—just fifteen days ago the two Wynne [brothers], who are still minors, received written orders to return to England, where the eldest has an income of 6,000 pounds sterling from his estate. I say all this so Your Excellency may see that the family is very noble and I hold indisputable proof.*[6]

The count added that if this were still deemed insufficient, the Austrian Court should consider the following information as final proof of Giustiniana's aristocratic lineage: "Andrea Memmo, a Venetian nobleman belonging to one of the oldest families, was ready to marry her with the full consent of his entire family, but Mme Wynne did not grant her consent because he was a very disturbed young man. Similarly, Lord Grantham's son wished to

*In the register of secret marriages at the Patriarchal Chancery there is indeed a dusty old folder with the names of Giustiniana and Count Rosenberg scribbled on it. Unfortunately, as in the case of the folder related to Giustiniana and Andrea, the papers are missing.

marry her last year, but the young lady refused him as he was a Protestant."

The count "implored" the prime minister to grant his "protection" to Giustiniana, but Kaunitz was not impressed by the clarifications he received—he probably had less biased information to rely on than the one his old ambassador provided him. He left Count and Countess Orsini-Rosenberg hanging.

It cannot have been an easy period for Giustiniana, no matter how used she had become to this type of social ostracism. Was her disappointment lessened by the joys of marriage? It is difficult to imagine Giustiniana falling deeply in love with the count, but she might well have felt a growing affection and respect for this distinguished old man who was willing to put himself on the line for love of her. Despite the difference in age, people certainly assumed that the marriage was consummated and the relationship was physical, not only because of Rosenberg's reputation as a sexually active septuagenarian but because his young wife quickly became pregnant. "One hears the beautiful Giustiniana will soon give a new fruit to the world,"[7] Lady Montagu chuckled from London, eager to stay abreast of things in Venice. If it is true she became pregnant after marrying Count Rosenberg, then she must have lost the child—presumably to Vienna's great relief.

As the new Countess Rosenberg, Giustiniana was isolated on all sides. Not only was she not accepted by her husband's government, she was also cut off from Venetian society, for if Vienna did not recognize her as the wife of the Austrian ambassador, the Venetian authorities certainly did. As a foreign dignitary she was not allowed to come into direct contact with local patricians. The law was a residue of a past age. Yet it had lived on, much to the distress and irritation of the ambassadorial corps, and was being enforced with even greater severity than usual since the beginning of the war. If she and Andrea communicated at all at this point, it had to be in secret, as so often in the past.

In early 1763, however, they did see each other publicly at the house of a mutual friend, and the inquisitors deemed the episode "very serious in all its circumstances."[8] Andrea had just been elected to the position of savio di terraferma, with administrative duties on the mainland territory. One of his first and most delicate assignments was the resolution of a dispute with the Austrian government over the postal system. Giustiniana suggested she might be able to help, using her husband's connections, and they discussed the issue in front of other guests that evening. She then sent him a note on the matter. He was imprudent enough to reply.

Andrea realized his mistake, or perhaps he was tipped off that a government informer was about to denounce him for having communicated with the wife of a foreign ambassador. In any event, he went directly to the Tribunal of the Inquisitors and confessed his crime. The Tribunal stated that his action deserved "the sternest and most solemn punishment" but spared him in the end on account of his "spontaneous confession." There was a final warning, however: "In the future you will refrain from any contact whatsoever with the wife of [the] ambassador and with the family of that wife as well . . . and you are prohibited from going near her at public functions and celebrations. . . . You are hereby also informed that an attentive eye will always be watching you."[9]

The reprimand was so severe—and so reminiscent of his "fateful banishment" a decade earlier—that one has to wonder whether Andrea and Giustiniana were again seeing each other on the quiet and the information had reached the inquisitors. Alternatively, it is possible that the count himself tipped off the authorities preemptively, to make sure that Andrea would stay away from his young wife. Whatever the case, Andrea must have taken the rebuke seriously. His career was on track by then—he was moving ahead under the aegis of Andrea Tron, the powerful procuratore di San Marco who had been the Wynnes' neighbor back in the summer of 1756—and he certainly wouldn't have wanted to tarnish his reputation by breaking a law of the Republic, no matter how obsolete he may have considered it.

So after all that had passed between them, this is how matters stood between Andrea and Giustiniana in 1763, the year the war ended with the treaties of Paris and Hubertusburg and peace finally returned to Europe.

In 1764 the Austrian Court recalled its ambassador to Venice and sent him into retirement. Count Rosenberg had made no headway in his painful dealings with his government over his new spouse. He and Giustiniana left Palazzo Loredan and moved to Klagenfurt in the Austrian province of Carinthia, where the Orsini-Rosenbergs had their family seat. Despite his declining health, the count continued to press Prime Minister Kaunitz to grant protection to his wife. Once they were back in Austria, the possibility that they would not be received at Court in Vienna loomed as the worst possible nightmare. Giustiniana decided to take matters into her own hands. She enlisted the help of Lord Stormont, the British ambassador to Vienna, who asked the secretary of state, Lord Sandwich, to sign a declaration reaffirming that the Wynnes were indeed from a "very noble and very ancient Family."[10]

The statement was signed and sealed within a matter of days. Surely the irony was not lost on Giustiniana that the British, so maddeningly rigid when she had wanted to be presented to Court in London, were now so ready to help. Nonetheless, the Austrian government remained unimpressed. That summer Giustiniana wrote directly to Kaunitz:

> *Sir, it is with the greatest pain that I have learned of the deadly grief my husband has had to suffer on my account. I thought that such an authentic and honorable statement by the King of England* about my family as the one you received would have sufficed as proof of its antiquity. . . . I have no fear that once Her Majesty the Empress is informed of the truth she will not want to take away from me what I have been given by God, who wished me born a lady in a great nation and in a very old family. Your Highness, you know the ways of the world so well—could you not explain to Her Majesty the righteousness of my cause and the fatal consequences that might otherwise occur? Sir, your sense of justice is too well known for me to think that you might refuse your powerful help to a Lady who implores it.*[11]

The letter was sent at the end of July 1764 and was signed "Your humble and very obedient servant Countess de Rosenberg née Wynne." Kaunitz, well aware that her husband was not well,

---

*She is referring to the document signed by Lord Sandwich.

was clearly buying time. His tactic was soon rewarded. Count Rosenberg died the following winter, and the vexing issue of their presentation to the Court disappeared.

Her husband now dead, Giustiniana was free to leave Austria. But where should she go? There was no compelling reason for her to rush back to Venice. She had no house to return to. She was not particularly eager to live with her mother and her sisters again, and her brothers were studying in England. So she remained in Klagenfurt, staying on for another five years. Little is known about her Austrian period. It seems she overcame the initial hostility of the local nobility and managed to establish cordial relations with the Rosenberg family. Her character would have led her to make the best of her stay and to gather as many interesting people around her as she could. Still, she must have remained an outsider in the eyes of the provincial Klagenfurt society: it is hard to imagine Giustiniana turning into a German-speaking Austrian countess. In the end, one suspects she stayed in Austria in no small part because she wanted to set her financial affairs in order and ensure for herself an income from her former husband's estate that would give her the independence and the security she needed before she went back to Italy.

She returned to Venice around 1770. She was still only in her early thirties, and after six quiet years in Austria she was eager to lead a more engaging existence. However, she found that life in Venice had deteriorated greatly. Society had become stale. Cultural life was dead. Corruption was rife. Prostitution and gambling were out of control. These were all symptoms of a much deeper crisis. The Venetian ruling class seemed incapable of providing a sense of direction, of lifting its eyes beyond the lagoon that surrounded it. To Giustiniana, who had spent so much time abroad, the Republic must have appeared very old and tired—a wrinkled *grande dame* gazing out over the backwaters of Europe.

She took a house near Piazza San Marco and tried to build herself a new life as the widowed Countess Rosenberg. She called on old friends, and now that she was no longer the wife of the Austrian ambassador she was free to see Andrea again. She gathered a small *salon* around her and did what she could to interest herself in the life of the city. But her heart was not in it; the city no longer felt like home. Again one hears the echo of that earlier cry: "Venice is not for me!" She escaped when she could, often traveling to Paris and London. Each trip meant a tiring journey across Europe, but it gave her the oxygen she lacked in the stagnant atmosphere of the lagoon.

This was more than mere estrangement. Giustiniana felt increasingly vulnerable in Venice's vice-ridden atmosphere. She started to gamble and, like many of her friends, soon lost control over her habit. By 1774 gaming was ravaging so many lives that the government decided to close down the Ridotto, where she and Andrea had spent so many memorable nights stealing kisses and watching others play cards. Illegal gambling houses sprang up overnight in private homes and the streets around Piazza San Marco. Giustiniana dragged herself from one seedy hovel to another in the worst company, spending her limited money and amassing enormous debts. In a single night of madness she lost more than three thousand florins—one and a half times her yearly income. Her life was rapidly falling apart.

To extricate herself from this downward spiral, she decided to spend more time in Padua, where life was not as decadent and had a gentler rhythm. Although it was a provincial town, it was strangely more cosmopolitan than Venice. Perhaps it had to do with the old university, which was going through one of its better moments, or maybe it was due to the proximity of the countryside and the pleasant life that revolved around some of the elegant villas nearby. The environment was certainly more stimulating for Giustiniana. She rented an apartment in a *palazzo* by the Duomo. With the help of loyal friends and her own determination, she gradually pulled herself together—and out of debt.

She retained the house in Venice and followed closely what went on in the city, even though it was increasingly with the eye of an observer one step removed from the action. Her connections abroad and her knowledge of languages made her the ideal chaperon for foreign travelers, especially the English. The writer William Beckford, who became a close friend, describes how happy he was to have been recommended to "the fascinating" Giustiniana.[12]

When Archduke Paul and Archduchess Maria of Russia made a "private" visit to Venice in 1782 to honor the new commercial ties between the two states, she wrote a vivid account of what was possibly the last big extravaganza staged by the Republic. She wrote it in French, in the form of a long letter to her brother Richard, and it was published as a short book first in London and then in Venice. It was very well received in literary circles, and it remains immensely enjoyable to read today. Her old friend Casanova, who was back in Venice—now, ironically, working as a government informer and living in reduced circumstances—wrote her a fan letter praising her "easy and unpretentious style."[13] She replied with a very formal thank-you note. Neither made the slightest reference to the past, nor did they renew their close friendship.

Writing was Giustiniana's true calling. Her letters to Andrea bear testimony to her growing talent, of course, but now she devoted herself to the craft with more discipline and method. Her second book, also in French and published in London in 1785, was a collection of essays and reminiscences on a variety of topics, from education to the devastating effects of gambling. In one delightful chapter on the art of smiling there is a revealing passage that has its share of sorrow for the passing of time—she was then approaching fifty—but ends on a note of good-natured resignation:

> *Laugh heartily, charming and innocent youth! The age of smiling will soon be upon you. That will be followed in turn by the years of the expertly contrived smile: an air of peace and serenity will often hide the truly agitated state of your soul. And in your old age, when the book of passions is over, it will be too late even to smile. Your face will have lost all of that soft elasticity that allowed your expressions to change with so much ease. The Scissor of Time will have deepened those furrows drawn by the passions of your life: they will have become wrinkles that will never be erased. So what purpose could an awkward smile possibly have? It would only suggest ridiculous claims. An air of thoughtfulness and kindness will be all you really need. That is the natural order of things in the revolution that takes place on the face of a woman.*[14]

Giustiniana established a pleasant, productive routine for herself. She wintered in Padua, making frequent forays into Venice.

In the summer she moved to Alticchiero, a delightful villa on the southern bank of the Brenta, just a couple of miles from Padua, that belonged to her old friend Senator Angelo Querini. After his release from jail in 1763, the senator, disillusioned with Venetian politics, had retired to this "rustic house with no view."[15] Over the years, he had transformed it into an elegant country retreat devoted to classicism and the art of the "philosophical garden."

Giustiniana's friendship with Querini went back to the 1750s, but in those days her heart had belonged entirely to Andrea. She had kept in touch with Querini over the years—they shared many of the same friends, Andrea certainly being the first among them—but their paths had seldom crossed again until she left Venice for Padua. When finally they had the opportunity to spend time in each other's company it was perhaps too late for a full-blown romance between them. Yet their friendship acquired a romantic tinge it never lost. At Alticchiero, Giustiniana was always more than a guest: she was the lady of the house.

In homage to her beloved senator she composed a lovely guide-book to the villa and the garden—an enlightened and highly entertaining tour of the Querini estate. It was published in Padua in 1787 with excellent prints of the sculptures that adorned the property.

There was another man in Giustiniana's life at that time, very different from the senator. Count Bartolomeo Benincasa was an impoverished adventurer running away from a failed marriage in his native Modena when he arrived in the Venetian Republic some-time around 1780 and found his way into Giustiniana's circle of friends. He was a restless soul with literary ambitions, which she admired, and he was also ten years younger than she. In little time he joined her household and became her secretary and administra-tor, and perhaps her lover as well.

Benincasa was the opposite of Querini: verbose, affected, and shady, he made pocket money passing information to the inquisi-tors about the senator and his guests at Alticchiero. Yet despite his duplicity, he remained devoted to Giustiniana until the end. In 1788, with his help, she published her only novel, *Les Morlacques*, a romantic tale of love and death set in the rugged mountains of Dalmatia. The book is imbued with social commentary inspired by Rousseau on the evils of the city and the essential goodness of man in nature, but the pathos she brought to the story—not to mention the vampires and fairies that populate its pages—are the product of an imagination that in many ways already belonged to the nineteenth century.

Les Morlacques was her greatest literary success. By 1790, at the age of fifty-three, Giustiniana was at the top of her game: beloved hostess, respected intellectual, accomplished writer. She had not remarried but seemed content with the affection of Querini and the devotion of Benincasa and her many friends. Describing her small salon in Padua, where men of sciences, writers, and artists mingled with foreign travelers, Casanova, who had moved on to Dux, in Bohemia, and was at last scribbling away at his memoirs, wrote that Giustiniana, though sadly not rich, nevertheless "shines for her wisdom and all the social virtues she possesses."[16]

She would not enjoy her triumph for long. The illness that took her to her grave the following year—most likely cancer of the uterus—was already spreading inside her. She battled with it for nine months and suffered excruciating pain. An anguished Benincasa dutifully related the progress of the illness in letters to family and friends. Giustiniana's twelve-year-old niece, Betsey, who was summering in the countryside north of Padua with her family, the Richard Wynnes, wrote in her diary: "The poor Countess is to die. There is no remedy for her. Papa says they are all in a very great distress about it."[17]

As death neared Andrea too arrived in Padua—an old friend drawn to his first love. He was "distraught" by the sight of her ravaged body and the pain she was suffering, and he grieved quietly at her bedside. During the night "she started hemorrhaging again"; a priest was called in and "she was given extreme unction."[18] In the diaphanous early morning light Andrea bid her his final farewell.

Giustiniana died on August 22, 1791, in the house she had rented for the summer: a small, elegant *palazzo* with a pretty garden. Benincasa wrote a long, tearful report on her death for the inquisitors. Querini nursed "the bitter wound"[19] in his heart and placed a marble bust of Giustiniana in the garden at Alticchiero. She was buried in the Church of San Benedetto in Padua. Her brother Richard, who was with her at the time of her death, had a small memorial tablet placed in the church, high above the entrance portal.

Giustiniana was greatly mourned. Her virtues were praised in every form available, from the elaborate Latin inscription on the memorial's marble plaque to a long panegyric printed by her friends. But to my mind the simple words of an obscure Paduan chronicler by the name of Abbé Gennari evoke her best. "She was very beautiful in her youth," he wrote in his diary on the day of her death. "And always lively and full of spirit."[20]

I like to think this is how Andrea remembered Giustiniana in the darkening rooms at Ca' Memmo, where his own death was now casting its shadow. As he grew older, he revisited more frequently those hopeful days of his youth, when his heart had been filled with love and the end of the Republic had not loomed so near. No doubt he sometimes traveled as far back as the day he had first seen Giustiniana, so starkly beautiful, in the house of Consul Smith. Were those memories ever tinged with regret? Andrea was never one to dwell morosely on the past, but surely the irony was not lost on him that he had sacrificed the great love of his life for the sake of a dying Republic. He had served with great distinction. He had traveled widely. He had become a statesman, respected at home and admired abroad. He had accomplished what had been expected of him—and more. Yet each year he had grown more disgusted with the lethargic ruling class to which he belonged and more disillusioned about the future of Venice. Like so many patricians of his generation, he had become a deeply cynical man. And he had tempered the bitterness in his soul by giving himself over to the earthly pleasures life still had to offer a man with appetite and, as he put it, "good teeth."[21]

Andrea's political beginnings had coincided with the end of the Seven Years' War in 1763. Europe was at peace again, and he still believed that the strength and prestige of the Republic could be restored to a degree with the right mix of policies. He also felt that any radical approach to change would be counterproductive; in this he was far more pragmatic than his friend Querini, who spent two years in jail for openly challenging the status quo. Instead, Andrea focused his considerable intellectual energies on learning the inner workings of Venice's venerable but outdated machinery of government. He learned fast and got himself elected to a succession of important administrative posts, blending into the bureaucracy as he waited for the most propitious moment to step forward and effect some real change.

On the personal side, his dalliance with M. failed to produce the stable relationship he had been looking for. But in 1763, at the age of thirty-four, he met a stunning girl some fifteen years younger than he with whom he began an affair that was to last, on and off, for more than two decades. Contarina Barbarigo was the beautiful daughter of her famously beautiful mother, Caterina Sagredo Barbarigo.* She had wit, flair, and glamour. Eighteenth-century miniatures depict her with sharp, striking features, her hair piled up in a very tall beehive. Like her mother, she grew up to become the most celebrated Venetian beauty of her generation.

Did Giustiniana unwittingly plant the idea of seducing Contarina in Andrea's head? In a letter she wrote to him during her depressing stay in Padua, back in the fall of 1760, Giustiniana mentioned paying a courtesy visit to Contarina's famous mother, Caterina: "Mon cher frère . . . I can assure you that I was impressed by how cultivated and pleasant a lady she was. Her daughters are absolute wonders, and the one called Contarina is so gracious and well mannered—as well as being a real beauty and therefore very similar to her mother—that she is seen as a true marvel here. . . . In fact, she would be considered a sheer delight anywhere."

Contarina, however, was destined for another member of the patriciate. In 1765 she married Marino Zorzi, but the marriage was soon dissolved because he was impotent. Her affair with Andrea resumed—if it had ever stopped. But the politics of marriage among the ruling class were inexorable. In 1769, the year before Giustiniana's return to Venice from Austria, it was Andrea's turn

*See p. 49.

to marry. His bride was Elisabetta Piovene, a pretty girl of twenty who came from a good family in Vicenza. He does not appear to have been deeply in love with her, but there was no reason to believe they could not have a decent marriage and raise a good family. They had two daughters, Lucietta and Paolina, upon whom Andrea doted.

Andrea's career, meanwhile, had reached an important crossroads. In 1771, after a decade-long apprenticeship, he made his first important political move: a bold attempt to free Venetian industry and commerce from the suffocating control of the guilds. The reforms he advocated were intelligent and well thought out, but he found himself face to face with the "obtuse indolence"[22] of the Senate. Ultimately defeated by the conservatives, he was nevertheless rewarded with the powerful post of governor of Padua.

He ran the city during much of the 1770s and became a popular governor. He devoted a great deal of his energies to an ambitious and somewhat extravagant architectural project—the creation of a vast oval plaza on the southern rim of the city, known as Prato della Valle—in which he tried to put into practice some of the principles of rational architecture advocated by his teacher Father Lodoli. His stewardship of one of the largest cities in the Venetian State was deemed a success. In 1787 he was appointed ambassador to Constantinople, a prestigious post and, for Andrea, a highly symbolic one: his uncle Andrea Memmo, his role model and mentor, had been ambassador there half a century earlier.

From the point of view of his career, the 1770s were productive and rewarding. "Four men like Senator Memmo would be enough to govern Europe without difficulty,"[23] Emperor Joseph II of Austria is said to have declared after meeting Andrea. The statement might be apocryphal, but the currency it gained over the years reflected Andrea's growing reputation as a wise and effective statesman.

His marriage to Elisabetta, on the other hand, was not a success despite a fairly hopeful start. Andrea's continuous affair with Contarina cannot have helped. But family and friends mostly blamed Elisabetta's "bilious" character and poor health—not to mention her habit of drinking vinegar in the morning to stay thin. With time she grew weaker and became more withdrawn. When she died of "gastro-rheumatic fever"* in Venice in 1780, Andrea was not by her side but away in Constantinople, still serving as ambassador to the Porte.

During his five-year stint there—his first real time abroad—he began to see Venice's decline in sharper, more dramatic terms. Still, he did not give up looking for new opportunities that might give the Republic another lease on life. Like Giustiniana, he was an admirer of Empress Catherine the Great of Russia, and he worked tirelessly while in Constantinople to establish official relations with Moscow and build a powerful new commercial alliance with the emerging European power.

Upon his return to Venice in 1782, however, Andrea's confidence collapsed. The passivity and resignation of his peers depressed him profoundly. He accepted the ambassadorship to Rome, once an important post but by then little more than a sinecure. "I decided not to stay in Venice for a while," he explained to a friend, "because I knew it would have saddened me. I needed to distract myself for the sake of my health."[24]

He was fifty-four and a single parent with two daughters in tow when he arrived in the lazy and decadent Rome of Pope Pius VI. He had come to "distract" himself, as he had put it, and that is what he did. He cultivated the pleasures of a good table and threw himself into a whirlwind of sexual intrigue, becoming a favorite with Roman women—aging princesses as well as their shapely young maids. "Anything pleases these lovable sluts," he confided to a

---

*It was Giuseppe Perlasca, a well-known physician in Venice, who wrote that Elisabetta had "a bilious temperament" and was "frail on account of her abuse of vinegar, which she had taken in large quantities for a very long time early in the morning and on an empty stomach for fear of growing fat." She had developed "a yellowish mucus, itchy patches all over her body, insomnia, yellow blemishes." In addition, "her uterus was severely damaged, she had splitting headaches and gastro-rheumatic fevers." Perlasca ordered her to drink lemon juice and linseed oil, but she apparently drank only wine. Much to his frustration, she refused to be bled. A chronicler of those times, the Abbé Carlo Zilli, claims (see his manuscript memoirs quoted in Brunelli, *Un'amica del Casanova*, p. 260) that Perlasca attributed the actual cause of death "to the excessive amounts of mercury" his chief rival, the physician Fantuzzi, had prescribed to Elisabetta to remedy the consequences of a sexual indiscretion. Needless to say, this bit of information did not find its way into Perlasca's ten-page report to Andrea on Elisabetta's death, though it was apparently on everyone's lips in Venice.[25]

Florentine friend, "as long as they can possess a man who was never possessed by any woman for more than a few minutes." Tenderly, he added, "apart from la Rosenberg."[26]

Andrea took his job as a father very seriously—possibly more so than his position as ambassador. Despite his numerous gallant affairs, he made a point of spending time every day with Lucietta and Paolina, "my only true loves." He planned their education with the help of an able tutor and a French governess. "My girls will be beautiful and well educated. They're still a little rough around the edges, but far less than they would be if they had stayed in Venice."[27]

During his Roman days Andrea decided to rescue the memory of Father Lodoli from oblivion. The inquisitors had seized Lodoli's papers after his death in 1761, leaving them to rot in a damp cell in the prisons at the Ducal Palace. Two decades later, during one of his regular trips up to Venice, Andrea went rummaging there. All he found were piles of sodden and illegible paper. The discovery filled him with sadness. It also encouraged him to press on. He plumbed his own memory and used every scrap of information he could find—notes, letters, and above all the recollections of the monk's many devoted former students—to put together an extraordinary tribute to his teacher.

The first book of his two-volume work was published in 1786; the complete edition came out posthumously some fifty years later. *Elementi dell'architettura Lodoliana* was more than a book on Lodoli. The spirit of the 1740s and 1750s, when so many of the most promising sons of the Republic had "shaped their minds and improved their souls" at the school of the Franciscan monk, came to life again in its pages. In Andrea's eyes, Giustiniana had been an important part of that bygone world, so that the memories of the period became entwined with memories of "the one to whom I was entirely dedicated." In a whimsical, affectionate digression, he praised "her original mind" and those "rare qualities that made her soul sublime."[28]

Andrea's book was so rich in autobiographical references to his own youth that one has to wonder if the daily exercise of writing it, during those otherwise dissolute Roman days, was not also an attempt to redeem himself from the failure to live up to his own expectations.

His career, however, was not yet over. Just as he was distancing himself from the depressing political scene in Venice, the Maggior Consiglio, the supreme assembly of the Republic, elected him to succeed Andrea Tron, his political mentor, in the prestigious office of procuratore di San Marco. All at once he was catapulted back into the fray. His initial displeasure at having to leave behind his leisurely if somewhat futile Roman life quickly vanished. This unexpected tribute on the part of his peers renewed his vigor. He returned to Venice in 1787 and took up his new position amid great pomp, decking out the palace on the Grand Canal with banners and family crests and hosting the customary balls and receptions.

That same year, at the end of a long and difficult negotiation, Andrea married off his daughter Lucietta to Alvise Mocenigo, a member of one of the richest and most powerful Venetian families. (It was thanks to this marriage that Andrea's letters ended up at Palazzo Mocenigo, where my father found them two centuries later.) Andrea was doubly pleased: the match made sense from a practical point of view, and he was overjoyed because Lucietta and Alvise were genuinely in love with each other: "My Lucietta makes her husband happy, and he makes her happy. They are in love for their essential qualities, and they respect each other as much as they adore each other. They have become the paradigm of the enviable marriage. There are no displays of jealousy on either part nor the slightest appearance of infidelity."[29]

As was the custom, a stream of celebratory poems and miscellanies was printed at the time of the wedding. One slim publication, beautifully bound and illustrated, stood out among them. Giustiniana, by then living mostly in Padua, had come into town for the occasion and presented the bride and groom with a sweet allegorical composition in which Curiosity and Love conspired to join two lovers and then left the field to Perseverance—the only one who could make their happiness endure. She had written it in honor of Alvise and Lucietta, but it was, in fact, dedicated, in large, bold letters, to her own first great love—the father of the bride. She added these few lines, adapted from Lucretius, in which she invoked the aid of "nurturing Venus":

> *Thee I crave as partner in writing these verses*
> *I essay to fashion for my good Memmo,*
> *whom thou, goddess, hast willed at all times*
> *to excel, endowed with all gifts.*[30]

Andrea entered new negotiations to marry his second daughter, Paolina, to Luigi Martinengo, heir to another big fortune. The talks proceeded laboriously and then stalled altogether when the inquisitors put the future groom under house arrest for his licentious behavior (Andrea complained that Luigi had "taken on a Roman slut" while declaring his love for Paolina). They eventually resumed, and the wedding took place in 1789. The price, however, was high: Andrea's financial resources were so depleted that he was forced to cede Ca' Memmo to the Martinengos as part of Paolina's dowry.

Now that he faced the prospect of living out his old age in solitude, Andrea seriously considered marrying again. He broached the idea with his old flame, Contarina, who was not against it. But the conversation apparently soured over practical arrangements and led, unexpectedly, to the end of their long affair. "After twenty-five years of gallantry, love, and friendship," he wrote to Casanova bitterly, ". . . my relationship with Signora Contarina has suddenly ended on account of a trifling matter—and will not resume ever again."[31] He did not say what the trifling matter was.

Casanova frowned at the lost opportunity. He reminded his old friend that Contarina was rich and could have helped finance Andrea's renascent political career. Andrea was piqued: "You are wrong if you think she could have assisted me. . . . She is not as rich as she was. . . . I was going to marry her out of friendship, not out of material interest. . . . Naturally she would not have been a burden on me in any way, not even in bed—she would have had a separate apartment. I was not very keen on all that flabby flesh. . . . Good company, mutual assistance in our approaching old age, and nothing more. With time, the assurance of a comfortable life and good . . . food on the table—since you ask, I will tell you I am still a glutton, and though I eat less I still eat a lot since all my teeth are still healthy."[32]

Like an aging Don Juan, Andrea enjoyed gabbing about his active sex life with Casanova. "You cannot imagine what I have had to go through to cut off a useless correspondence with twenty ladies from different countries, all of whom wish me to believe they are endlessly in love with me," he bragged. Venice, he added, offered more than enough distractions: "I spend my time with my lovable old lady friends, and with even more lovable young ones. They are beautiful and crazy, and they might not give me everything I ask, but they still give me plenty."[33]

When he turned sixty he explained the logic of his frantic womanizing to his old companion: "I need the release, and since I do not gamble and there is nothing I want to buy for myself and I cannot stand trying to reason with our politicians and having nothing more to read . . . I spend my time with the ladies. Oh, you should see, Casanova, how many gorgeous girls have suddenly appeared in our little world here since you left! Surely you understand me if I tell you I try with every one in the hope of succeeding with a few. Without ever losing my sleep or my appetite over them."[34] In truth, he was not always up to par. To a less promiscuous friend than Casanova he once admitted offering a lady friend "a cock that was not as hard as she deserved."[35]

As the powerful procuratore di San Marco, Andrea seemed a strong candidate for the supreme office of doge. The old reformers—the friends of his youth—rallied around him in a futile burst of political activism. Andrea's vanity was certainly flattered by this belated support, but he quickly saw the drawbacks of a candidacy. They were financial, to begin with: it would be a very costly political campaign, and he simply didn't have the money to run. Furthermore, the Memmo family was on the way to extinction—neither Andrea nor his brothers had a male heir. Why bother to enter the race, he asked, if there would be no more Memmo descendents "to enjoy the glory" a *corno,* or ducal cap, would bring to the house? Finally, and perhaps most important, why give up the good life to spend his last years sequestered in the Ducal Palace? "Once elected doge," he explained to Casanova, "if I should chance to see a countess or a marchionness with beautiful eyes and pretty tits, light-hearted and lively, how do you suppose I could have her without being able to seduce her with the tools that I, as procuratore, am still allowed to use? For pity's sake, don't take the pleasure of women away from me, for it will lighten my spirit when I am a hundred years old. . . . Doges cannot indulge in such divine treatment."[36]

For all his genuine misgivings, Andrea's political ambition won the day. When the old doge, Paolo Renier, died in February 1789, he entered the race. For a moment, it looked as if he had a real chance of being elected by a reformist alliance. But it was much too late in the game. The dominant conservative forces in the old Venetian oligarchy coalesced to neutralize his candidacy. Andrea was outsmarted. On March 9, 1789—four months before the storming of the Bastille—the Maggior Consiglio elected a man so timorous of the weight that had been thrust onto his shoulders that he tearfully begged to be spared the honor. His name was Ludovico Manin, and he made history as Venice's last doge.

After his electoral defeat, Andrea threw himself back into work. Interestingly, he focused his efforts on Dalmatia—the very same region that had inspired Giustiniana to publish her novel, *Les Morlacques,* only the year before. The backwardness of this Venetian territory just across the Adriatic had become a vexing problem for the Republic and a real embarrassment. Andrea worked tirelessly on a plan to improve living conditions in those poor, disease-ridden provinces. After much prodding and cajoling, he was finally able to get a package of agricultural and administrative reforms approved by the Senate in 1791, around the time Giustiniana died.

Andrea's own health had already started to deteriorate. Gangrene was slowly spreading in one of his legs, and before the year was out he was confined to his rooms at Ca' Memmo. It was not just the atrocious pain that made the ensuing months so hard to bear; he was dying a poor man. There was very little left of the Memmo possessions; many of them had been wasted on an expensive political career. Even the family *palazzo* in which he was dying was no longer his. "Memmo is destitute," wrote a friend sadly. "He has had to give up his gondola too."[37]

It took Andrea another year to die. An endless stream of friends and former lovers came to see him as he lay slowly rotting in his bed, surrounded by medicines and surgical instruments and confabulating doctors. Among the well-wishers was a French artist and traveler by the name of Dominique-Vivant Denon, who later went to Egypt with Napoleon Bonaparte and became the founding director of the new Musée du Louvre. The man who would one day be known as "the Eye of Napoleon" kept a detailed record of Andrea's last days. "I went over to see poor Memmo this evening," he wrote to a friend on October 15, 1792. "It looks quite bad, and he knows it." Two days later: "His old lovers insist his blood is excellent. . . . But the disease keeps gaining ground." On October 26 Denon ran into Memmo's doctor, who said nothing "but lifted his eyes to the sky." He went back to see Andrea on November 1: "They amputated his big toe. . . . It is what I call uselessly tormenting the victim. At this point one must either amputate the leg or let him die as peacefully as possible."[38]

Andrea's ordeal lasted another two months. He died on January 27, 1793.

Four years later Bonaparte invaded northern Italy. With the French Army fast approaching, the Venetian Senate voted hurriedly for surrender and the Republic died a swift and inglorious death.

Postscript

A t least Andrea and Giustiniana did not live to see the end of their beloved Republic!" my father scribbled wistfully at the end of his notes to the letters. It was a typical thing for him to say: two centuries after Bonaparte's victorious invasion, the old Venetian in him still ached at the Republic's ignominious end. As I read those words I was also reminded of how much he had identified with Andrea, not to mention the terrible crush he had developed on Giustiniana and his disappointment at how things had turned out between his two lovers.

In September 2001, nearly five years after my father's death, I went to Venice with my family to write the book he had wanted to write. We found a small house on the Campiello agli Incurabili, just off the Zattere. It was right on the water and had a small enclosed garden filled with oleanders and laurels and roving wisteria. In daytime the reflections of the sun danced on the walls and created a sense of perpetual movement. At night, when the city was silent, the rhythmic sloshing in the canal signaled the ebb and flow of the tide.

I had never lived in Venice before. To me it had always been the city of my father's childhood. I saw it as I imagine most people do: as a museum full of tourists, a dead city. But as Venetians well know, it is much more than that. In Venice the past has remained alive in a vivid, disorienting way. It is with you all the time. It blends with the present. And sometimes, walking around the city, my head filled with Andrea and Giustiniana, I found myself slipping back in time so effortlessly that I didn't know what century I was living in anymore.

I passed by Ca' Memmo every week on my way to my youngest son's music class. It stands imposingly to the east of the vaporetto stop of San Marcuola, on the north shore of the Grand Canal. Consul Smith's *palazzo* is a little further along, on the same side of the Grand Canal, before the bend of the Rialto Bridge. It was recently converted into a luxury condominium for wealthy foreigners, yet the outward appearance of the building is the same as when Andrea and Giustiniana exchanged their first furtive kisses there two and a half centuries ago. Whenever I went by the very grand Palazzo Tiepolo, now Palazzo Papadopoli, I scratched my head trying to figure out which was the window on the mezzanine floor from which Andrea used to woo Giustiniana when the Wynnes lived next door.

The buildings are the same. The streets haven't changed. Even the names on the doorbells are familiar. Gradually, I came to see how much the love story my father had dug up in the dusty attic of Palazzo Mocenigo had taken him back not just to the city of his childhood, but to a place of the imagination where the great Venetian Republic lived on. And how the unraveling of Andrea and Giustiniana's long affair had evoked in him—in a way that was still somewhat mysterious to me but that I was beginning to understand—the much vaster demise that was taking place all around them.

On the other hand, I am sure my father took comfort in learning, as he progressed in his research, that his two heroes went on to have full and fascinating lives. Each went his own way: Giustiniana became an accomplished author; Andrea became Venice's last great statesman. But over the years they remained very close. Their world—the vanishing world of the Venetian Republic— was small enough that they were never very far apart. And when their paths did cross, they always met with that tenderness a first great love can create to last a lifetime.

Would Andrea and Giustiniana have been as distraught by the passing of the Venetian Republic as my father assumed? Probably not. Andrea always knew his life was tied to the fate of the city. But as much as he revered the Venice of the past, one has to wonder whether he would have shed a single tear for the passing of the inglorious Republic he had known in his lifetime. True, he was spared the final demise because his own death came sooner, but he was too intelligent a man not to see that Venice could not continue to survive by small concessions to change. By the time the gangrene began to spread in his own body, he knew the Republic was also doomed. As for Giustiniana, she died at a time when her life was no longer rooted in Venice. She lived mostly on the mainland. Her horizon had widened considerably. She traveled often. She wrote in French. She published her books in London. She was self-sufficient, independent, and worldly. In many ways she had become the woman she had tentatively begun to sketch in her letters to Andrea many years before, when she had so accurately predicted their separate fates: "You have to live in Venice, I don't."

NOTES

A Note on Sources

The letters on which I have based *A Venetian Affair* do not make a complete set. In Chapters 1 to 4 I have relied on Andrea's original letters to Giustiniana, which are still in my family's possession. Those letters are undated, and their exact chronological order is unknown. I have used them in the order that seemed to me most logical, but it is quite possible that certain events—minor ones, I hope—occurred either before or after the time in which I have set them. This section also contains several letters from Giustiniana to Andrea from the period 1756–1757. Chapters 5 to 9, on the other hand, are based entirely on Giustiniana's letters to Andrea. These are not the original manuscripts but handwritten copies that I suspect date back to the end of the eighteenth century. Of these, two incomplete and overlapping sets are available to the public. One is in the Biblioteca Civica di Padova (Bruno Brunelli used this set to write *Un'amica del Casanova*, his book about Giustiniana, published in 1924). The other was purchased in Venice by James Rives Childs in the early fifties and is now at Mr. Childs's alma mater, Randolph Macon College, in Ashland, Virginia. There exists at least one other set, identical to the one in Ashland, which is the property of Giuseppe Bignami, a Genoese collector.

It is unclear who transcribed the original letters from Giustiniana to Andrea and why he or she did so. I am inclined to believe that Andrea returned the letters to Giustiniana and someone in her entourage—possibly Bartolomeo Benincasa—transcribed them later on, perhaps with the idea of publishing them as an epistolary novel when the two protagonists were no longer alive. But until the original letters by Giustiniana surface, we will not know how faithful the copies really are. Of course, historians have by now corroborated most of the events in this extraordinary tale. But it is quite possible that the mysterious transcriber of the original letters indulged in a little editing for the sake of convenience.

Prologue

1. Gustav Gugitz, "Eine Geliebte Casanovas," *Zeitschrift für Bucherfreunde* (1910), 151–171; and *Giacomo Casanova und sein Lebensroman* (Vienna: Strache, 1921), pp. 228–261. Gugitz does not explain why Casanova chose to call Giustiniana's mother Madame XCV and Giustiniana Miss XCV. James Rives Childs suggests that the initials stood for "Xè'l Cavalier Vinne," Venetian for "It is Chevalier Wynne"; see Francis L. Mars, "Pour le dossier de Miss XCV," *Casanova Gleanings* 5 (1962): 21. More simply, the X could stand for the Latin

preposition "ex"; in this case the initials could mean "formerly of Chevalier Wynne." The letter "w" does not exist in the Italian alphabet and in the eighteenth century was often transcribed as "v."

2. Bruno Brunelli, *Un'amica del Casanova* (Naples: Remo Sandron, 1924), 21.

3. "L'epistolario, ultimo giallo," *La Nazione*, January 22, 1997, iii.

4. Jean Georgelin, *Venise au siècle des lumières* (Paris: Ecole des Hautes Etudes en Sciences Sociales, 1978), 18.

5. Giustiniana Wynne, *Pièces morales et sentimentales* (London: J. Robson, 1785), 36.

6. Luca De Biase, "Vincoli nuziali ed extramatrimoniali nel patriziato veneto in epoca goldoniana: i sentimenti, gli interessi," *Studi Trentini di Scienze Storiche*, vol. LXI, no. 4 (1982): 363. On the topic of clandestine marriages, see Gaetano Cozzi, "Padri, figli e matrimoni clandestini," *La Cultura*, no. 2–3 (1976): 169–213; and "Causarum matrimoniorum clandestinorum," Archivio di Stato di Venezia, Inquisitori di Stato, envelopes 528–534.

Chapter One

1. Gianfranco Torcellan, *Una figura della Venezia settecentesca: Andrea Memmo* (Venice: 1963), 23 and n. 2. In 1740 the Memmos' income had been 10,000 ducats a year, according to the official census of that year. See Georgelin, *Venise au siècle des lumières*, 521.

2. Marco Foscarini, *Della letteratura veneziana*, vol. 1 (Padua: 1752), 258, n. 99.

3. *Elogio di Andrea Memmo Cavalier Procuratore di S. Marco* (Venice: 1793), 5–6.

4. Andrea Memmo, *Elementi dell'architettura Lodoliana* (Zara: Battara, 1833), 77–78.

5. Pierre Jean Grosley, *Nouveaux Mémoires ou observations sur l'Italie et sur les italiens*, vol. 2 (London: Jean Nourse, 1764), 10.

6. Carlo Goldoni, *Il filosofo inglese*, in *Opere*, vol. 5 (Milan: Mondadori, 1959), 261.

7. Smith entered into negotiations with the Crown during the last years of King George II's reign. But it was not until after King George III's accession to the throne in 1760 that the talks accelerated. The deal was finally sealed in 1763. Smith's paintings and drawings became the cornerstone of the Windsor collection, and the Bibliotheca Smithiana is part of the Royal Library at the British Museum. On the sale of Consul Smith's collection to George III, see in particular Frances Vivian, *Il Console Smith, mercante e collezionista* (Vicenza: Neri Pozza, 1971), 69–93; Francis Haskell, *Patrons and Painters, Art and Society in Baroque Italy* (New Haven, Conn.: Yale University Press, 1980), 310; Anthony Blunt and Edward Croft-Murray, *Venetian Drawings of the XVII and XVIII Centuries in the Collection of Her Majesty the Queen at Windsor Castle* (London: Phaidon Press, 1957).

8. Quoted in Torcellan, *Una figura*, p. 42. For a more detailed description of Andrea's ideas about the theater and his admiration for French culture and language, see his report "Storia della Deputazione Straordinaria alle Arti" in the

Archivio di Stato di Venezia, "Inquisitorato alle arti," envelope 2, bundle 4, 33–36.

9. From Goldoni's dedication to Andrea in *L'Uomo di mondo,* previously published in *Opere,* vol. 1, 777–778.

10. "Appunti sul Giovan Battista Mannuzzi (1750–59)," in Archivio di Stato di Venezia, Inquisitori di Stato, referta del 22 marzo 1755. On the general topic of secret informers see Giovanni Comisso, *Agenti segreti veneziani nel '700* (Milan: Bompiani, 1945). Giovan Battista Mannuzzi was the best-known spy operating in Venice at the time, and he kept a close eye on Casanova. In an earlier report he described him as "a man with a tendency to hyperbole who manages to live at the expense of this or that person on the strength of his lies and his ability to cheat." Another insightful report by a lesser-known informer stated that Andrea's brother Bernardo was somewhat torn by his relationship with Casanova: "he is often with him, and he alternatively loves him and thrashes him." In general the government's once formidable system of informers suffered a steady decline in the eighteenth century. By 1760 the budget had dwindled to 4,000 ducats and only three spies were receiving full pay. One official deplored the fact that they were "so few and so mediocre."

11. De Biase, *"Vincoli nunziali,"* 319–367.

12. Lady Mary Wortley Montagu to her daughter, Lady Bute, October 3, 1758, *The Complete Letters of Lady Mary Wortley Montagu,* vol. 3, ed. Robert Halsband (Oxford: Clarendon Press, 1967), 179.

13. Quoted in Brunelli, *Un'amica del Casanova,* 4.

14. Wynne, *Pièces morales,* 195.

15. Ibid., 34.

16. Giacomo Casanova, *History of My Life,* vol. 3 (Baltimore: Johns Hopkins University Press, 1997), 172.

17. Wynne, *Pièces morales,* 35.

18. Letters of Andrea Memmo to Giustiniana Wynne (author's collection).

19. Casanova, *History of My Life,* vol. 5 (Baltimore: Johns Hopkins University Press, 1997), 171–172.

20. Wynne, *Pièces morales,* 35–36.

21. Ibid., 36.

22. Letters of Andrea Memmo to Giustiniana Wynne (author's collection).

Chapter Two

1. Pompeo Molmenti, *La storia di Venezia nella vita privata,* vol. 3 (Bergamo: Istituto italiano di artigrafiche, 1908), 175.

2. Giacoma Casanova, *History of My Life,* vol. 4 (Baltimore: Johns Hopkins University Press, 1997), 75.

3. Ibid., 191, 249.

Chapter Three

1. From the diary of Johannes Heinzelmann (December 10, 1755), quoted in Vivian, *Il console Smith*, 52.
2. Lady Montagu to Lady Bute, *Complete Letters*, vol. 3, 127.
3. Casanova, *History of My Life*, vol. 4, 136.
4. Murray to Holderness, August 15, 1755, British Museum, Egerton Papers, 3464, f. 272.
5. Lady Montagu to Lady Bute, May 13, 1758, *Complete Letters*, vol. 3, 145.
6. John Fleming, *Robert Adam and His Circle* (London: John Murray, 1962), 171.
7. Murray to Holderness, October 1, 1756, British Museum, Egerton Papers, 3464, f. 274.

Chapter Four

1. "Matrimoni Segreti," Anno 1757, n. 47, Archivio della Curia Patriarcale di Venezia.
2. John Eglin, *Venice Transfigured: The Myth of Venice in British Culture 1660–1797* (New York: Palgrave, 2001), 57.
3. Vivian, *Il console Smith*, 55.
4. "Atti di morte," Archivio di San Marcuola, Curia Patriarcale. Curiously, Andrea Memmo's biographer, Gianfranco Torcellan, states that Pietro "died prematurely" and was therefore unable to exert on his son an influence comparable to that of his older brother Andrea, the family patriarch. Torcellan, *Una figura della Venezia settecentesca*, 27. In reality Pietro died long after his older brother, so it appears his lesser influence on young Andrea was related more to character than to age.
5. For Antonio Maria Zanetti's dealings with Smith, see in particular Vivian, *Il console Smith*, and Haskell, *Patrons and Painters*.

Chapter Five

1. Vivian, *Il console Smith*, 210. The painting was eventually sold to George III. As for *The Woman with Dropsy*, it was taken to Paris by French troops in 1798 after Napoleon's invasion of northern Italy. Today it hangs in the Musée du Louvre, where it is registered as "the first gift to the Louvre."
2. Ralph Woodford was secretary to the British delegation in Turin. When Giustiniana met him, he was acting chargé d'affaires as Lord Bristol, the outgoing ambassador, had left in August, and the new ambassador, John Stuart MacKenzie, would not arrive until November 14, 1758. See John Ingamells, *A Dictionary of English and Irish Travellers in Italy 1701–1800* (New Haven, Conn.: Yale University Press, 1997), 1017.

Chapter Six

1. The Duc de Luynes died on November 2, 1758; *Gazette de France*, November 1758.
2. *Gazette de France*, December 1758.

3. *Mercure de France*, February 1759.
4. Casanova, *History of My Life*, vol. 5, 170.
5. Ibid., 172.
6. Ibid., 196.
7. Jean-François Marmontel, *Mémoires*, ed. John Renwick (Paris: Clermont-Ferrand, G. de Bussac, 1972), 104.
8. Niccolò Erizzo to Antonio Grimani, April 1, 1759, James Rives Childs Collection, Randolph Macon College, Ashland, Va.
9. Tommaso Farsetti to Andrea Memmo, March 26, 1759, James Rives Childs Collection.

Chapter Seven

1. In describing Giustiniana's escape from Paris I have used the information contained in her letter to Andrea dated June 24, 1759. The facts coincide roughly with those provided by Casanova in his *History of My Life* (see vol. 5, p. 212). Giustiniana wrote to Andrea that she had left Paris for Conflans on the morning of April 5. However, Mother Eustachia declared in a notarized statement that Giustiniana arrived at the convent on April 4 (see Francis L. Mars, "Pour le dossier de Miss XCV," *Casanova Gleanings* 5 [1962]: 25), and I have used that date.
2. Casanova, *History of My Life*, vol. 5, 182.
3. Casanova, *History of My Life*, vol. 5, 188.
4. Ibid., 187.
5. *Déposition de Reine Demay au commissaire Thiéron*. Archives Nationales (Châtelet), 10873, liasse 154. First quoted in Charles Henry, "Jacques Casanove de Seingalt et la critique historique," *Revue Historique* 41 (novembre–décembre 1889), 314.
6. Ibid., 315.
7. Casanova, *History of My Life*, vol. 5, 192.
8. "Mémoire de Emmanuel Jean de la Coste à Monsieur de Sartine, maître des requêtes et lieutenant général de la police de la Ville de Paris," May 2, 1760, Archives de la Bastille, Ravaisson-Mollien, 12099.
9. Casanova, *History of My Life*, vol. 5, 196.
10. Ibid., vol. 5, 198.
11. Ibid., 206.
12. "Naturalité à Justine Françoise Antoine Wynne . . . , Par le Roy, Versailles, 13 mars, 1759." The document, which also spells out in detail all of Giustiniana's rights as a French citizen, was published in its entirety in Mars, "Pour le dossier de Miss XCV," 27.
13. Casanova, *History of My Life*, vol. 5, 185.
14. Ibid., 238.
15. Ibid., 240.
16. Ibid., 242.
17. Anonymous letter to Andrea Memmo, July 10, 1759, James Rives Childs Collection.
18. Tommaso Farsetti to Andrea Memmo, September 3, 1759, James Rives Childs Collection.

19. Niccolò Erizzo to Andrea Memmo, May 27, 1759, James Rives Childs Collection.
20. Casanova, *History of My Life*, vol. 5, 242.
21. "Alexandre Fortier, notaire au coin de la rue de Richelieu et de la rue Neuve des Petits Champs," Archives Nationales, Minutier Central, Etude XXXI. Quoted in Mars, *"Pour le dossier de Miss XCV,"* 24.
22. Mars, *"Pour le dossier de Miss XCV,"* 25.
23. Anonymous letter to Andrea Memmo, July 10, 1759, James Rives Childs Collection.
24. Giustiniana Wynne to Andrea Memmo, Conflans, June 24, 1759, James Rives Childs Collection.
25. Anonymous letter to Andrea Memmo, July 10, 1759, James Rives Childs Collection.
26. Ibid.

Chapter Eight

1. Horace Walpole, *Memoirs of the Reign of King George II*, vol. 1, ed. John Brooke, (New Haven, Conn.: Yale University Press, 1985) 132.
2. Ibid.
3. Lord Newcastle to the Earl of Hardwick, January 2, 1760, British Library, Manuscripts, Additionals 35406.
4. Walpole, *Memoirs*, vol. 1, 132.
5. Lady Montagu to Lady Bute, October 3, 1758, *Complete Letters*, vol. 3, 179.
6. "The Year Fifty-Nine. A New Song," *The Gentleman's Magazine* XXIX (December 1759), 595.
7. Horace Walpole, *The Letters of Horace Walpole*, vol. 3, ed. Peter Cunningham (London: Richard Bentley, 1857), 263.
8. Lady Montagu to Lady Bute, November 9, 1759, *Complete Letters*, vol. 3, 227.
9. Ibid.
10. Lord Newcastle to the Earl of Hardwick, January 2, 1760, British Library, Manuscripts, Additionals 35406.
11. *The Gentleman's Magazine* XXX (February 1760), 44.
12. "Account of Lord Ferrers," *The Gentleman's Magazine* XXX (May 1760), 230–236.

Chapter Nine

1. Georges Cucuel, *La Pouplinière et la musique de chambre au XVIIIème siècle* (Paris: Fishbacher, 1913), 242.

Epilogue

1. Ingamells, *A Dictionary of English and Irish Travellers*, 672.
2. John Murray to Lord Holderness, December 1760, British Library, Manuscripts, Egremont 3464, ff. 272–286.

3. John Murray to William Pitt, July 10, 1761, British Library, Manuscripts, SP 99/68, ff., 184–185.

4. Chiara Michiel to Lady Montagu, March 10, 1762, *Complete Letters*, vol. 3, 288, n. 2.

5. Lady Montagu to Chiara Michiel, April 1762, *Complete Letters*, vol. 3, 288.

6. Count de Rosenberg to Prince von Kaunitz, Venice, March 21, 1762, quoted in Gugitz, *Giacomo Casanova*, 250.

7. Lady Montagu to Chiara Michiel, London, May 8, 1762, *Complete Letters*, vol. 3, 292.

8. Annotazioni n. 537, January 9, 1763, Inquisitori di Stato, Archivio di Stato di Venezia.

9. Ibid.

10. Statement by Lord Sandwich, London, May 21, 1764; quoted in Gugitz, *Giacomo Casanova*, 252.

11. Giustiniana Wynne to Prince Von Kaunitz, Klagenfurt, July 30, 1764; quoted in Gugitz, *Giacomo Casanova*, 254.

12. William Beckford, *Dreams, Waking Thoughts and Incidents*, ed. Robert Gemmett (Rutherford, 1971), 118.

13. Casanova's letter and Giustiniana's reply, dated March 18, 1782, appear in Aldo Ravà, *Lettere di donne a Casanova* (Milan: Treves, 1912), 227–228.

14. Wynne, *Pièces morales et sentimentales*, pp. 112–113.

15. Giustiniana Wynne, *Alticchiero* (Padua: 1787), 2.

16. Casanova, *History of My Life*, vol. 3, 172.

17. Elizabeth Wynne, diary entry June 23, 1791, *The Wynne Diaries*, ed. Anne Fremantle, vol. 1 (Oxford: Oxford University Press, 1935), 67.

18. The description of Andrea at Giustiniana's deathbed is in a letter by his daughter Lucietta to her husband, Alvise Mocenigo, dated June 17, 1791. The author's private collection.

19. Angelo Querini to Clemente Sibiliato, August 24, 1791, in *Alcune lettere inedite di illustri veneziani a Clemente Sibiliato* (Padua: 1839).

20. Abate Gennari, "Notizie giornaliere," ms. in the Biblioteca del Seminario, Padua, cod. 551.

21. Andrea Memmo to Giacomo Casanova, July 9, 1788, *Epistolari veneziani del secolo XVIII*, ed. Pompeo Molmenti (Milan: Remo Sandron, 1914).

22. Gianfranco Torcellan, "Andrea Memmo," in *Illuministi italiani*, vol. 7. (Milan: Ricciardi, 1965).

23. Brunelli, *Un'amica del Casanova*, 277.

24. Andrea Memmo to Giulio Perini, September 17, 1783, Archivio di Stato di Firenze, Acquisti e Doni, 94, bundle 146.

25. Biblioteca civica, Correr Manuscripts, Misc. IX, 1138.

26. Andrea Memmo to Giulio Perini, November 2, 1784, Archivio di Stato di Firenze, Acquisti e Doni 94, bundle 146.

27. Andrea Memmo to Giulio Perini, April 30, 1785, Archivio di Stato di Firenze, Acquisti e Doni 94, bundle 146.

28. Andrea Memmo, *Elementi dell' architettura Lodoliana*, 166.

29. Andrea Memmo to Giacomo Casanova, July 26, 1788, *Carteggi casanoviani* (Florence: Archivio Storico Italiano, 1911), 330.

30. Giustiniana Wynne, Countess Rosenberg, *À André Memmo Chevalier de l'Étole d'Or et procurateur de Saint Marc, à l'occasion du mariage de sa fille aînée avec Louis Mocenigo* (Venice: Rosa, 1787).

31. Andrea Memmo to Giacomo Casanova, July 9, 1788, *Epistolari veneziani del secolo XVIII*, ed. Pompeo Molmenti, 192.

32. Ibid.

33. Ibid.

34. Ibid.

35. Andrea Memmo to Giulio Perini, Archivio di Stato di Firenze, Acquisti e Doni, 94, bundle 146.

36. Andrea Memmo to Giacomo Casanova, March 29, 1787, *Epistolari veneziani del secolo XVIII*, 185.

37. Pietro Zaguri to Giacomo Casanova, January 15, 1791, *Epistolari veneziani del secolo XVIII*, 119.

38. Dominique-Vivant Denon, *Lettres à Bettine*, ed. Piergiorgio Brigliadori et al., (Arles: Actes Sud, 1999), 126, 129, 137, 142.

SELECT BIBLIOGRAPHY

Archives

Archives de la Bastille, Paris
Archives Nationales (Châtelet), Paris
Archivio della Curia Patriarcale di Venezia
Archivio di Stato di Firenze
Archivio di Stato di Venezia
Biblioteca Civica Correr, Venice
Biblioteca Civica di Padova
British Library (Manuscripts), London
Biblioteca Marciana, Venice (Ulrich Middeldorf Collection)
Library, Randolph Macon College, Ashland,
    Virginia (James Rives Childs Collection)

Secondary sources

Anderson, Fred. *Crucible of War: The Seven Years' War and the Fate of Empire in British North America, 1754–1766*. New York: Knopf, 2000.

Barbier, Edmond Jean François. *Journal historique et anecdotique du règne de Louis XV.* Paris: Renouard, 1847–56 (4 vols.).

Beckford, William. *Dreams, Waking Thoughts and Incidents.* Edited by Robert Gemmett. Rutherford, 1971.

Bernis, François-Joaquin de. *Mémoires du cardinal de Bernis.* Paris: Mercure de France, 2000.

Bignami, Giuseppe. "Costantina dalle Fusine: un incontro," *Intermédiaire des Casanovistes* 13 (1996): 23.

———. *Mademoiselle X.C.V.* Genoa: Pirella, 1985 (an introduction to Giustiniana's work).

Blunt, Anthony, and Croft-Murray Edward. *Venetian Drawings of the XVII & XVIII Centuries in the Collection of Her Majesty the Queen of Windsor Castle.* London: Phaidon Press, 1957.

Brooke, John. *King George III.* London: Constable, 1972.

Brosses, Charles de. *Lettres d'Italie du président de Brosses.* Paris: Mercure de France, 1986.

Brunelli, Bruno. *Un'amica del Casanova.* Naples: Remo Sandron, 1924. In English, *Casanova Loved Her.* New York: Liveright, 1929.

Brusatin, Manlio. "Qualche donna e l'architettura funzionale a Venezia nel XVIII secolo," *Scritti di Amici per Maria Cionini*. Turin: 1977.

———. *Venezia nel Settecento: stato, architettura, territorio*. Turin: Einaudi, 1980.

Capon, Gaston. *Casanova à Paris*. Paris: Schemit, 1913.

Casanova, Giacomo. *Fuga dai Piombi*. Milan: Rizzoli, 1950.

———. *History of My Life* (12 vols.). Translated by Willard Trask. Baltimore: Johns Hopkins University Press, 1997.

Childs, J. Rives. *Casanova*. London: Allen & Unwin, 1961.

Comisso, Giovanni. *Agenti segreti veneziani nel '700*. Milan: Bompiani, 1945.

Craveri, Benedetta. *La civiltà della conversazione*. Milan: Adelphi, 2001.

———. *Madame du Deffand e il suo mondo*. Milan: Adelphi, 1982.

Cucuel, Georges. *La Pouplinière et la musique de chambre au XVIIIème siècle*. Paris: Fishbacher, 1913.

Damerini, Gino. *Settecento veneziano*. Milano: Mondadori, 1939.

Da Ponte, Lorenzo. *Memorie*. Milano: Garzanti, 1976.

Darnton, Robert. *The Business of Enlightenment*. Cambridge: Belknap Press, 1979.

Davis, James C. *The Decline of the Venetian Nobility as a Ruling Class*. Baltimore: Johns Hopkins University Press, 1962.

Denon, Dominique-Vivant. *Lettres à Bettine*. Edited by Piergiorgio Brigliadori et al. Arles: Actes Sud, 1999.

Desprat, Jean-Paul. *Le cardinal de Bernis (1715–1794): la belle ambition*. Paris: Perrin, 2000.

Eglin, John. *Venice Transfigured: The Myth of Venice in British Culture 1660–1797*. New York: Palgrave, 2001.

Einaudi, Luigi. "L'economia pubblica veneziana dal 1736 al 1755." *La Riforma Sociale* 14 (1904).

Fleming, John. *Robert Adam and His Circle*. London: John Murray, 1962.

Freemantle, Anne, ed. *The Wynne Diaries*. Oxford: Oxford University Press, 1935.

Fumaroli, Marc. *L'Age de l'éloquence*. Paris: Champion, 1980.

George, M. D. *London Life in the 18th Century*. London: Penguin, 1966.

Georgelin, Jean. *Venise au siècle des Lumières*. Paris: École des Hautes Etudes de Sciences Sociales, 1978.

Goldoni, Carlo. *Memorie*. Torino: Einaudi, 1967.

———. *Opere*. Milan: Mondadori, 1959.

Gozzi, Carlo. *Memorie inutili (1722–1806)*. Turin: Unione tipografica edtrice torinese, 1923.

Grosley, Pierre-Jean. *Nouveaux mémoires, ou observations sur l'Italie et les italiens*. London: Jean Nourse, 1764.

———. *A Tour to London* (2 vols.). London: Lockyer Davis, 1772.

Gugitz, Gustav. "Eine Geliebte Casanovas." In *Zeitschrift für Bucherfreunde*, 1910, 151–171.

———. *Giacomo Casanova und sein Lebensroman*. Vienna: Strache, 1921.

Haskell, Francis. *Patrons and Painters, Art and Society in Baroque Italy*. New Haven, Conn.: Yale University Press, 1980.

Havelock, Ellis. "An Anglo-Italian friend of Casanova's," *Anglo-Italian Review* 2, no. 12, 206–220.

Henry, Charles. "Jacques Casanova de Seingalt et la critique historique." *Revue Historique* 41 (novembre–décembre 1889), 311–316.

Infelise, Mario, ed. *Carlo Lodoli: Della censura dei libri*. Venice: Marsilio, 2001.

Ingamells, John. *A Dictionary of English and Irish Travellers in Italy 1701–1800*. New Haven, Conn.: Yale University Press, 1997.

Isenberg, Nancy. "Mon cher frère: Eros mascherato nell'epistolario di Giustiniana Wynne a Andrea Memmo (1758–1760)." In *Trame parentali/trame letterarie*, ed. M. Del Sapio. Naples: Liguori, 2000, 251–265.

Lane, Frederic C. *Venice, a Maritime Republic*. Baltimore: Johns Hopkins University Press, 1973.

Lever, Evelyne. *Madame de Pompadour*. Paris: Perrin, 2000.

Marmontel, Jean-François. *Mémoires*. Edited by John Renwick, Clermont-Ferrand, G. de Bussac, 1972.

Mars, Francis L. "Pour le dossier de Miss XCV." *Casanova Gleanings* 5 (1962): 21–29.

———. "Une grande épistolière méconnue: Giustiniana Wynne." In *Problemi di lingua e letteratura italiana del '700*. Wiesbaden: F. Steiner Verlag, 1965. pp. 318–322.

McClellan, G. B. *Venice and Bonaparte*. Princeton: Princeton Univeristy Press, 1931.

Memmo, Andrea. *Elementi dell'architettura Lodoliana*. Rome: Pagliarius, 1786.

———. *Elementi dell'architettura Lodoliana. Edizione corretta e accresciuta dall'autore*, (2 vols.). Zara: 1833–1834.

Mitford, Nancy. *Madame de Pompadour*. London: Hamish Hamilton, 1954.

Molmenti, Pompeo. *Carteggi casanoviani*. Milan: Remo Sandron, 1920.

———. *Epistolari veneziani del secolo XVIII*. Milan: Remo Sandron, 1914.

———. *La storia di Venezia nella vita privata* (3 vols.). Bergamo: Istituto italiano di arti grafiche, 1908.

Monnier, Philippe. *Venice in the Eighteenth Century*. London: Chatto & Windus, 1906.

Montagu, Mary Wortley. *The Complete Letters of Lady Mary Wortley Montagu* (3 vols.). Edited by Robert Halsband. Oxford: Clarendon Press, 1967.

Morris, Jan. *Venice*. London: Faber & Faber, 1960.

Norwich, John Julius. *A History of Venice*. New York: Knopf, 1982.

Ortolani, Giuseppe. *Voci e visioni del Settecento veneziano*. Bologna: Zanichelli, 1926.

Parreaux, André. *Daily Life in England in the Reign of George III*. London: Allen & Unwin, 1969.

Picard, Liza. *Dr. Johnson's London*. London: Phoenix Press, 2000.

Pupillo, Marco. "Contarina Barbarigo: primi appunti sui disegni di architettura e le collezioni d'arte." In *Gentildonne artiste intellettuali al tramonto della Serenissima*. Milan: 1998.

Ravà, Aldo. *Lettere di donne a Casanova*. Milan: Treves, 1912.

Rudé, George. *Hanoverian London, 1714–1808*. London: Secker and Warburg, 1971.

Rykwert, Joseph. *The First Moderns*. Cambridge: MIT Press, 1980.

Samaran, Charles. *Jacques Casanova, vénitien*. Paris: Calmann-Levy, 1914.

Tabacco, Giovanni. *Andrea Tron (1712–1785) e la crisi dell'aristocrazia senatoria*. Trieste: Tip. Smolars, 1957.

Tassini, Giuseppe. *Curiosità veneziane*. Venice: Filippi, 1990.

Torcellan, Gianfranco. "Andrea Memmo." In *Illuministi italiani*, vol. 7, Milan: Ricciardi, 1965.

———. "Contarina Barbarigo." In *Settecento Veneto e altri scritti storici*. Turin: 1969.

———. *Una figura della Venezia settecentesca: Andrea Memmo*. Venice: 1963.

Vivian, Frances. *Il console Smith, mercante e collezionista*. Vicenza: Neri Pozza, 1971.

Walpole, Horace. *The Letters of Horace Walpole* (8 vols.). Edited by Peter Cunningham. London: Richard Bentley, 1857.

———. *Memoirs of the Reign of King George II*. New Haven, Conn.: Yale University Press, 1985.

Watzlawick, Helmut. "Clarification of Dossier Wynne." *Casanova Gleanings* 16 (1973): 31–32.

———. "Note on Giustiniana Wynne's Marriage." *Casanova Gleanings* 16 (1973): 14.

Williamson, Rebecca. "Giustiniana's Garden: An Eighteenth Century Woman's Construction." In *Gendered Landscapes, An Interdisciplinary Exploration of Past Place and Space*. Edited by B. Szczgiel, J. Carubia, and L. Dowler. University Park, Penn State University Press, 2000.

Wolff, Larry. *Venice and the Slavs*. Stanford, Ca.: Stanford University Press, 2001.

Wynne, Giustiniana. *À André Memmo Chevalier de l'Etole d'Or et procurateur de Saint Marc à l'occasion du mariage de sa fille aînée avec Louis Mocenigo*. Venice: Rosa, 1787.

———. *Alticchiero*. Padua: 1787.

———. *Du séjour des comtes du Nord à Venise*. London: 1782.

———. *Il trionfo dei gondolieri*. Venice: Stamperia Graziosi, 1786.

——— with Bartolomeo Benincasa. *Les Morlacques*. Modena: 1788.

———. *Pièces morales et sentimentales*. London: J. Robson, 1785.

Zorzi, Alvise. *La repubblica del leone, storia di Venezia*. Milan: Rusconi, 1979.

ACKNOWLEDGMENTS

This book would not have seen the light if my father, Alvise di Robilant, had not discovered the letters of Andrea Memmo to Giustiniana Wynne. By the time of his death in 1997, he had spent many hours decoding and transcribing the letters and had done considerable research on the main characters of this story. The material he collected, his notes, and, above all, the many conversations we had about his discovery have inspired me throughout the writing of *A Venetian Affair*. It is his book, too, in more ways than I can say.

I first mentioned the story of Andrea and Giustiniana to Michael Carlisle, an old friend from Columbia University, in a long and rather rambling e-mail I sent to him in the winter of 2000. His enthusiastic response was crucial in getting me started on this project. Within a matter of days he became my agent, sold the book proposal, and set me to work. His encouragement and support have been unstinting.

My publisher, Sonny Mehta, took a gamble on a first-time author. I am deeply grateful to him for taking it. From day one it has been a privilege and a pleasure to work with all the people involved in the making of this book at Knopf. Deborah Garrison has been a devoted editor, stepping in nimbly to egg me on or to help me out. Her assistant, Ilana Kurshan, has been an effective and cheerful coordinator of our busy transatlantic correspondence.

I spent a year in Venice with my family to write *A Venetian Affair*. Claudio Saracco let us stay in his lovely little house at Campiello agli Incurabili and turned out to be a delightful and undemanding landlord. Most of the book was written at the Fondazione Querini Stampalia, off Campo Santa Maria in Formosa. I could not have dreamed of finding a more pleasant atmosphere in which to work. My sincerest thanks go to Giorgio Busetto, the indefatigable director of the foundation, and to his wonderful staff.

The first person to ever write extensively about Andrea and Giustiniana was the Venetian historian Bruno Brunelli. His book, *Casanova Loved Her*, published in 1924, was based in large part on Giustiniana's letters to Andrea. A lot of rich material has surfaced since then, apart from the letters discovered by my father, so it was possible for me to write a more complete and possibly more accurate account of their love story. Yet I always felt I was working in Brunelli's shadow, and *A Venetian Affair*, perhaps inevitably, owes much to the lingering appeal of his book.

Rebecca Williamson, of the University of Illinois at Urbana-Champaign, who has written perceptively about Giustiniana, gave me helpful guidance and advice. The architectural historian Susanna Pasquali, of the University of Ferrara, shared with me her knowledge about Andrea's later correspondence. I also benefited from

Acknowledgments

the suggestions of a happy band of *casanovisti:* Helmut Watzlawick, Giuseppe Bignami, and Furio Luccichenti. My greatest thanks go to Nancy Isenberg, of the University of Rome. Nancy has developed quite a passion for Andrea and Giustiniana's story over the years. She has shared her considerable knowledge with me generously and enthusiastically, and has made important contributions to the final shape of my work.

A Venetian Affair has been at the center of my family's life for three years. My young sons Tommaso and Sebastiano have been devoted supporters of the book even as they knew it was taking much of my time away from them. To my wife, Alessandra, I owe the most: for joining me in a project that has meant so much to me, and sharing in the many joys and the occasional miseries that have accompanied the writing of this book.

INDEX

abortion, 185–91, 193

Adam, Robert, 62

alchemy, 189–91

Alps, 118, 119, 136, 137, 140, 146–8, 168, 246, 251

Alticchiero, 276, 278

Alvisetto, 27, 30, 32, 34, 37, 76, 90

America, 151, 157, 234, 239

Amsterdam, 168

Andrea-Giustiniana relationship, 4–11; Andrea's patronizing tone in, 33, 45, 93, 111–12; death of Giustiniana, 277–8; early courtship, 9–10, 25–36, 37–55; end of, 263, 267, 289; first meeting, 9, 25; forbidden by Mrs. Anna, 13–14, 26, 75, 80, 91; Giustiniana in London, 208, 213, 215–38, 240–9; Giustiniana in Paris, 147–80, 244; Giustiniana's return to Italy, 244–63, 265–71; infidelity, 120–2, 186; jealousy, 37–45, 49–54, 103–5, 120–2, 139, 154–5, 158–62, 218–19, 229, 237, 241, 245, 268; lovemaking, 29, 33, 37, 54, 73–4, 97–9, 110–11; marriage negotiations, 78–86, 91–102, 105–12, 115–19; secret language, 6, 28, 95, 98; secret meetings and correspondence, 27–37, 45–55, 60, 63, 66–70, 73–5, 83–4, 90–1, 97–100, 109–15, 136, 270–1; separation and decline, 118–48, 153–6, 208, 219, 229–31, 263; Smith debacle, 58–86, 90, 105, 120, 121; spies, messengers, and informers, 27–34, 37, 67–8, 73, 74–7, 83, 90, 97, 108, 109–10, 136, 138; Wynne Affair, 186, 188, 194–205, 220; Zandiri incidents, 99–100, 123–31, 136

architecture, 17, 21, 137–8, 280, 282; Palladian, 19, 61, 125; Turin, 137–8, 140–1

art, 18–19, 53 and *n.*, 62, 113, 141, 164, 225 and *n.*

Austria, 88, 133, 157, 239, 267–73; Giustiniana in, 272–3

Avogaría di Comun, 91–2, 94

Baglioni family, 96

balls, 8, 41–2

Barbarigo, Caterina (Cattina), 49, 279

Barbarigo, Contarina, 279–80, 284

Beckford, William, 274

Bellini, Giovanni, 18, 62

Benincasa, Count Bartolomeo, 276–7

Bentivoglio family, 84–6

Bernis, Abbé de, 119, 145–6, 150–1, 156–7, 168

bloodletting, 95, 108, 109

Bolzano, 168

Bonzio, Signor, 97, 112, 113, 114, 116–17

Bordoni, Faustina, 16

Brenta Canal, 61, 63, 66, 67, 72, 263, 276

Brescia, 118, 127, 131, 253

Brunelli, Bruno, 5

Brussels, 203–9

burchielli, 61

Bussalova, 137

Bute, Earl of, 212, 235

Bute, Lady, 224

Wynne, Giustiniana, 4–11, 21–4;
ancestry, 22–3; Austrian period,
272–3; birth, 6, 22; birth of her son in
Conflans convent, 192, 196–7, 200;
Casanova and, 23–4, 167–70,
182–205, 275, 277; character, 10, 24,
45; death, 277–8, 291; education, 23;
gambling habit, 274; as hostess, 46,
277; illnesses, 95–6, 108–9, 146, 239,
244–6, 260, 277; independence prized
by, 216–17, 232–3, 237, 247–8, 256,
267, 291; journey across Europe,
118–48, 212, 246, 249–52, 274;
Knyphausen and, 226–38, 240–1, 247,
248, 256, 260; La Pouplinière and,
121–2, 133, 156, 163, 170–205; in
London, 208–49; marriage to Count
Rosenberg, 267–73; men and, 40,
43–5, 102–4, 120–2, 141–3, 158–62,
165–6, 170–208, 226–38, 256, 266–7;
in Milan, 133–6; *Les Morlacques*,
276–7, 286; naturalization papers, 191,
202; in Paris, 23–4, 148–95, 202–5,
220, 244, 250–1; physical appearance,
10, 22, 24, 169, 217, 243, 249;
pregnancy and abortion attempts,
181–95; return to Italy, 244–63,
265–76; Smith's courtship of, 58–86,
121; titles of nobility, 22, 268–70,
272–3; in Turin, 136–46; writing
career, 275–7, 286, 290, 291; Wynne
Affair, 181–205, 220, 244, 250; *see also*
Andrea-Giustiniana relationship
Wynne, Richard, 22, 46, 170 and n.,
275, 277, 278; in England, 209, 220,
244, 246, 273
Wynne, Sir Richard, 22–3, 116, 119, 212,
216; death, 24, 25, 210
Wynne, Tonnina, 22, 46, 71, 94, 113,
141–2, 150; in London, 209, 211, 217,
244
Wynne, William, 22, 46, 170 and n.; in
England, 209, 220, 244, 246, 273
Wynne Affair, 181–205, 220, 244, 250;
Casanova's role in, 182–202, 204;
legal proceedings, 188–9, 193–9, 202,
204

Zandiri, Giacomo, 99–100, 116, 118,
123–31, 136, 138, 146, 156, 205
Zanetti, Tonnin, 113 and n.
Zimmermans, 171, 176
Zuccarelli, Francesco, 62